A. Wheatley   1976   4.99

A. Wheatley   1976   4.99

Family Circle

CAREFREE CROCKERY COOKBOOK

The Family Circle, Inc. New York

Published by The Family Circle, Inc.,
a New York Times Company
First Printing
Copyright © 1976 by The Family
Circle, Inc. This volume includes
a selection of the slow cooker recipes
from "301 Splendid Casseroles".
Published simultaneously in Canada.
Protected under Berne and other
international copyright conventions.
All rights reserved. Title and trade-mark
FAMILY CIRCLE registered
U.S. Patent Office, Canada, Great
Britain, Australia, New Zealand and
other countries. Marca Registrada.
This volume may not be reproduced in
whole or in part in any form without
written permission from the publisher.

ISBN 0-405-09845-6

Library of Congress Catalog
Card Number: 76-19182
Printed in the United States of America

SPECIAL PROJECT STAFF

Executive Editor	**Marie T. Walsh**
Creative Director	**Joseph Taveroni**
Editor	**Carol Botwin**
Art Director	**Carol Ceraldi**

CONTENTS

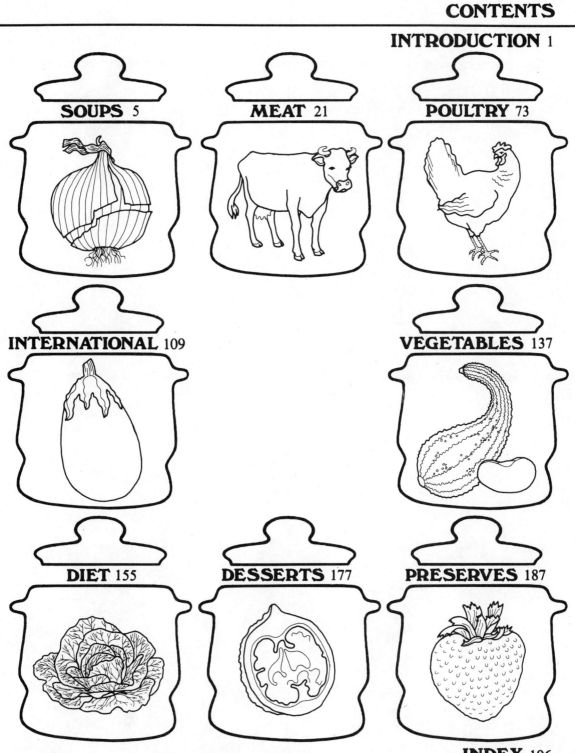

American women have never been busier. More and more of them work each year, more and more of them go back to school, take part-time jobs, involve themselves in politics and community affairs.

For today's busy woman, the electric slow cooker can seem like a blessing. It lets you put ingredients into a pot and walk away, for a whole day, if necessary, and still come home to a well-prepared meal.

The secret, of course, is very low temperature cooking. In electric slow cookers food can simmer for hours on end and still not get too well done. Because these appliances seal in moisture, nothing gets dried out either. And for health conscious cooks, the slow cooker has an extra bonus. Vitamins are preserved in food cooked on low temperatures.

Most electric slow cookers have two low-temperature settings: low, which generally simmers food on 190° to 200° and high, which cooks at 290° to 300°. Some appliances have an extra setting for keeping food warm. These should never be used for cooking. Bacteria in raw food gets safely destroyed at the cooker's normal low setting of 190°, but anything below that—and warming temperatures are below 190°—is dangerous.

Although some people worry about the amount of electricity a slow cooker will use, the actual wattage that these appliances run on is low, and the cost to cook a dish comes to no more than a handful of pennies.

Even if you expect to be away for more than the cooking time designated in a recipe you can still use your slow cooker by plugging it into either the timer receptacle in your electric range, or an appliance timer—both will start your cooker while you're out. To use them, follow manufacturer's instructions.

Be patient the first few times you use your slow cooker. It takes about two hours for the temperature to reach 160°, which isn't even hot enough for simmering, so the food may seem to be just sitting there—but please do not lift the cover at this time, or at any other time unless a recipe tells you to. Each peek costs you cooking time—generally from fifteen to twenty minutes.

Unless a recipe gives you different instructions, the only time a lid should be lifted is for stirring. Most slow cooking doesn't require it, but, in testing, we did find, in special cases, that stirring at the midway point, distributed ingredients more evenly and kept heavier foods from sinking to the bottom. Even

The tiny 2-quart stoneware pot (left) sits on a separate electric base for low-heat cooking or can go into oven as baking dish. Giant 8-quart cooker/fryer (right) has a nonstick cooking surface and can also roast.

A new addition to slow cookery is the removable stoneware bowl. It is designed to go into dishwashers and can go from refrigerator to cooker.

Some recent models of deep fryers serve two purposes. With new low settings they can be used for slow cooking, too.

A glass ceramic casserole that heats on its ceramic cooking surface is another way to cook food the low temperature way.

used for slow cooking

The heat control is the power center of the slow cooker. Some models have separate, removable controls.

Large recipes can be made in a 6-quart roaster / slow cooker with a removable porcelain enamel cooking well.

An all-purpose, 5½-quart capacity pot slow cooks and also deep fries.

An electric frypan (left) can also be used as a slow cooker. Follow directions on page 34. The electric frypan at right has a 2½-quart crockery insert. Low heat setting is 280° to 300°.

Slow Cookers can be used to serve.

This has colonial motif.

for all cookers, see buyer's guide, page 112.

these recipes will survive, however, if you are not around to stir.

For the use, care and cleaning of your electric slow cooker you should carefully read and follow directions in the manufacturer's booklet. But there are some general rules that can guide you:

• Thaw frozen foods before placing them in a slow cooker with a ceramic pot. Sudden changes in temperature can cause damage. So can sharp utensils.

• Before using a slow cooker for the first time wash in sudsy hot water and rinse well. If yours has a nonstick surface then rub the inside of the slow cooker with a little vegetable oil on a paper towel, and allow oil to remain.

• Make sure your electric slow cooker and its cord, or extension cord, are out of the reach of children.

• Use an extension cord only if its electrical rating is equal to or greater than the electrical rating of your appliance. Most brands require heavy duty cords.

• Never touch a slow cooker with wet hands, or place it on a wet surface.

• Never touch the outside of a slow cooker while it's hot. If your appliance has a removable heat control never touch it without a pot holder and do not pull it out of the cooker until it has cooled.

• The liquid ingredients of a recipe should come to no more than one cup. If you have followed a favorite recipe, however, and find yourself with too much liquid at the end, you can remedy the situation by thickening: turn heat control to high (290° to 300°). Combine ¼ cup all-purpose flour and ½ cup cold water in a cup; stir into liquid in slow cooker; cover; cook 15 minutes.

• If you live above a 4000 foot altitude, increase cooking time 1 hour on low (190° to 200°) for every 1000 feet of altitude above 4000 feet.

• Before cleaning your slow cooker, check the manufacturer's manual to see if it can be immersed in water.

• In general, to clean, fill with hot sudsy water and allow to stand for a few minutes to loosen stubborn food particles. Do not use harsh abrasives or scouring pads. Rinse with plenty of hot water and dry completely.

• To remove mineral stains on crockery, fill cooker with hot water and 1 cup white vinegar; cover. Turn heat control to high (290° to 300°) for 2 hours. Then clean the ordinary way, without presoaking.

Happy carefree cooking!

SOUPS

Old-fashioned soups that simmer all day—the kind you may remember from your grandmother's kitchen—are once again possible—even for busy women. Thanks to the slow cooker, you can put up a pot in the morning and forget about it until you return later and find the house filled with the aroma of a comforting broth, or a hearty soup that banishes chills in cold weather and is satisfying enough by itself to be the basis of a family dinner when it's served with chunks of crusty bread.

The fact that a slow cooker seals in moisture makes it especially ideal for making soup.

Slow cookers are terrific, too, for turning leftover carcasses and bones, with the addition of some vegetables, into delicious broths that are also easy on the budget.

You don't have to be limited to made-from-scratch recipes, however. Packaged mixes and canned products can be used as the bases for a variety of delicious soups.

For milk-based recipes that have no other liquid in the ingredients, use one or two cups of water for cooking, then stir in the milk or cream called for at the last moment, and heat again before serving. Milk and cream tend to break down when cooked over extended periods—something to remember in all recipes you use in crockery cooking.

MAYTIME CHICKEN BREAST SOUP

*Cook on 190° to 200° for **6** hours, or on 290° to 300° for **3** hours.*

Makes 6 servings.

You can vary the vegetables in this recipe for a change of pace. Pictured on page 57.

1. Combine chicken breasts, onion, turnip, celery, instant chicken broth, salt, peppercorns and water in a slow cooker.
2. Cook on low (190° to 200°) 6 hours, or on high (290° to 300°) 3 hours.
3. Remove chicken breasts from cooker; strain broth into a large bowl; remove skin from chicken breasts; return broth to cooker; cover.
4. Turn cooker to high (290° to 300°); heat 15 minutes; add potatoes and cook 20 minutes; add carrots, broccoli and yellow squash; cook 20 minutes; add peas and chicken breasts; simmer 10 minutes longer, or until chicken breasts are heated through.
5. Combine cornstarch and cold water in a cup; stir into boiling liquid; cover; cook 15 minutes. Ladle into heated soup bowls.

3 whole chicken breasts, split (about 12 ounces each)
1 large onion, sliced
1 white turnip, pared and diced
2 stalks celery with leaves, chopped
2 envelopes or teaspoons instant chicken broth
2 teaspoons salt
6 peppercorns
8 cups water
6 small boiling potatoes, pared
2 large carrots, pared and sliced
6 stalks broccoli, trimmed
1 small yellow squash, tipped and sliced
1 cup frozen green peas (from a 1½-pound bag), thawed
3 tablespoons cornstarch
½ cup cold water

food safety temperatures

The USDA has set up this chart as a guide to the safest temperatures for holding various foods:

0°	Safest temperature to store frozen foods. Do not store foods above 10°.
32° to 40°	The best temperature for holding foods in refrigerator.
60° to 125°	DANGER ZONE for all perishable foods.
140° to 165°	This is the temperature at which bacteria begin to be destroyed in cooking. Foods can be warmed at 140°, but not cooked.
212°	This is the temperature that a water-bath canner reaches and is safe for most jams, jellies, pickles and high-acid tomatoes.
240°	This is the temperature at which to process all low-acid vegetables, meats and poultry in a home-size pressure canner.

CLASSIC BEEF BROTH

Bake at 450° for 40 minutes.
Cook on 190° to 200° for **10** hours,
or on 290° to 300° for **5** hours.
Makes 12 cups.

Slow cookers are taking the place of the old soup pot which simmered for hours on the back of a wood-burning stove.

1. Put the meat bones, carrots, onions, leek and celery into a roasting pan.
2. Roast in hot oven (450°) 40 minutes, or until bones are well browned.
3. Place browned bones and vegetables in a 5-quart electric slow cooker; add water, parsley, garlic, salt, bay leaf and cloves; cover cooker.
4. Cook on low (190° to 200°) 10 hours, or on high (290° to 300°) 5 hours, or until broth is rich and flavorful; strain broth through cheesecloth into a large bowl.
5. Refrigerate broth, up to 4 days, leaving the fat layer on surface until ready to use; then lift off fat and discard. To freeze broth, pour into recipe-size plastic freezer containers to within ½-inch of top; seal; label and date. Freeze. Plan to use within 3 months.

3 pounds meaty beef bones
1 veal bone, cracked (optional)
3 large carrots, pared and chopped
2 large onions, halved
1 leek, trimmed
2 celery stalks with leaves, chopped
10 cups water
Handful parsley
2 cloves garlic, peeled
1 tablespoon salt
1 bay leaf
3 whole cloves

MINESTRONE

Cook on 190° to 200° for **8** hours,
or on 290° to 300° for **4** hours.
Makes 8 servings.

This version of an Italian favorite includes salami and garden vegetables.

1. Pick over beans and rinse under running water. Combine beans and water in a large saucepan. Bring to boiling; cook 2 minutes; remove from heat; cover; let stand 1 hour. (Or combine beans and water in an electric slow cooker and let stand all night at room temperature.)
2. Combine beans and liquid with salami, celery, tomatoes, cabbage, zucchini, turnip, parsley, salt and basil in slow cooker; cover.
3. Cook on low (190° to 200°) 8 hours, or on high (290° to 300°) 4 hours; stir in cooked macaroni and cook 10 minutes.
4. Ladle into soup bowls; sprinkle with grated Parmesan cheese.

1 cup dried white beans (cannellini), from a 1-pound package
8 cups water
½ pound salami, diced
2 cups chopped celery
1 can (1 pound) tomatoes
4 cups shredded cabbage
2 large zucchini, trimmed and sliced
1 cup cubed pared yellow turnip
¼ cup chopped parsley
1 teaspoon salt
1 teaspoon leaf basil, crumbled
½ cup elbow macaroni, cooked
Grated Parmesan cheese

OLD FARM BEAN SOUP

*Cook on 190° to 200° for **8** hours,
then on 290° to 300° for **4** hours.
Makes 8 servings.*

*Mothers have known for generations that a bubbling
pot of rich bean soup makes hearty family eating
that's easy on the budget.*

1. Pick over beans and rinse under running water.
   Combine beans and water in a large kettle. Bring to
   boiling; cover; cook 10 minutes. Remove from heat;
   let stand 1 hour; pour into an electric slow cooker. (Or
   soak beans in water in slow cooker overnight.)
2. Place beans and liquid in slow cooker; score salt pork,
   almost to rind; push down into beans; stir in onion,
   carrot, sausage links, bay leaf, salt, pepper and leaf
   thyme; cover.
3. Cook on low (190° to 200°) 8 hours; stir beans; turn
   heat control to high (290° to 300°) and cook for 4
   hours; stir beans with a wooden spoon and mash some
   of them against the side of the cooker to thicken soup.
   Taste beans; season with additional salt and pepper, if
   desired.

*1 package (1 pound) dried navy
   or pea beans
6 cups water
¼ pound salt pork
1 large onion, chopped (1 cup)
1 large carrot, pared and
   chopped
4 smokie sausage links, scored
   (from a 12-ounce package)
1 bay leaf
1½ teaspoons salt
½ teaspoon pepper
¼ teaspoon leaf thyme, crumbled*

GARDEN PATCH SOUP

*Cook on 190° to 200° for **5** hours,
or on 290° to 300° for **3** hours.
Makes 6 servings.*

*An easy-to-make soup that's ready to simmer in about
15 minutes.*

1. Combine onion, potatoes, corn, lima beans, chicken
   broth, tomato juice, chicken, salt, pepper, butter or
   margarine and Worcestershire sauce in a slow cooker;
   cover.
2. Cook on low (190° to 200°) 5 hours, or on high (290°
   to 300°) 3 hours. Serve with wedges of process American cheese and crackers for a complete meal.

*1 medium-size onion, chopped
   (½ cup)
2 medium-size potatoes, peeled
   and chopped
1 can (1 pound) whole-kernel
   corn, drained
1 package (10 ounces) frozen
   lima beans, thawed
2 cans (13¾ ounces each)
   chicken broth
1 can (26 ounces) tomato juice
1 cup diced cooked chicken
1½ teaspoons salt
¼ teaspoon pepper
1 tablespoon butter or margarine
1 tablespoon Worcestershire sauce*

ENGLISH GIBLET SOUP

Cook on 190° to 200° for **10** hours, or on 290° to 300° for **5** hours.
Makes 6 servings.

Frugal British cooks have always known how to get the most from a chicken.

1. Sauté chicken giblets in butter or margarine in a large skillet or an electric slow cooker with a browning unit.
2. Stir in flour and cook, stirring constantly, 5 minutes, or until flour browns.
3. Combine chicken giblets with CLASSIC CHICKEN BROTH or instant chicken broth and water, salt, pepper and bay leaf in an electric slow cooker; cover.
4. Cook on low (190° to 200°) 10 hours, or on high (290° to 300°) 5 hours, or until giblets are tender.
5. Stir in rice and celery and cook 15 minutes to heat rice. Serve in heated soup bowls topped with chopped parsley, if you wish.

1 pound chicken giblets
3 tablespoons butter or margarine
½ cup all-purpose flour
8 cups Classic Chicken Broth (recipe on page 12)
OR: 8 envelopes or teaspoons instant chicken broth and 8 cups water
2 teaspoons salt
¼ teaspoon pepper
1 bay leaf
2 cups cooked rice
½ cup chopped celery

LIMA BEAN SOUP

Cook on 190° to 200° for **10** hours, or on 290° to 300° for **5** hours.
Makes 6 servings.

An old-time favorite that still delights families.

1. Wash beans and pick over; combine with water in a kettle. Heat to boiling; cook 2 minutes; cover. Remove from heat; let stand 1 hour.
2. Combine soaked beans and liquid, ham bone, onion, salt and pepper in slow cooker; cover.
3. Cook on low (190° to 200°) 10 hours, or on high (290° to 300°) 5 hours, or until beans are tender.
4. Remove ham bone and cool until easy to handle. Strip off meat, removing any fat; dice meat; return to slow cooker.
5. Stir in 1 to 2 cups milk, depending on how thick you like soup. Turn heat control to high (290° to 300°); heat 15 minutes.
6. Ladle into soup bowls; sprinkle with chopped parsley and serve with French bread, if you wish.

1 package (1 pound) dried large lima beans
5 cups water
1 meaty bone from baked ham
1 medium-size onion, diced (½ cup)
1 teaspoon salt
¼ teaspoon pepper
1 to 2 cups milk

DANISH OXTAIL SOUP

Bake at 450° for 45 minutes.
Cook on 190° to 200° for **8** hours.
or on 290° to 300° for **4** hours.
Makes 6 servings.

Laugh at rainy days when you have this bubbling soup waiting at home in your slow cooker.

1. Spread oxtails in a single layer in shallow roasting pan. Roast in very hot oven (450°) 45 minutes, or until nicely browned. Drain off fat, reserving 2 tablespoons in pan.
2. Sauté onion, carrots, parsnip and turnip in reserved fat in a large skillet or an electric slow cooker with a browning unit, 10 minutes, or until soft. Add browned oxtails. Drizzle brandy over; ignite carefully with a lighted match.
3. Place oxtail mixture in slow cooker; add water, salt, pepper, savory and bay leaf; cover slow cooker.
4. Cook on low (190° to 200°) 8 hours, or on high (290° to 300°) 4 hours, or until oxtails are tender.
5. Ladle into soup bowls; place half an EGG MIMOSA in each, sprinkle with parsley. Serve with crusty French bread.

EGGS MIMOSA—Cut 3 hard-cooked eggs in half lengthwise. Carefully remove yolks, keeping whites whole. Press yolks through a sieve; spoon back into whites.

3 pounds oxtails, cut up
1 large onion, chopped (1 cup)
2 large carrots, pared and sliced
1 large parsnip, pared and sliced
1 white turnip, pared and sliced
2 tablespoons brandy
6 cups water
1 tablespoon salt
½ teaspoon pepper
½ teaspoon leaf savory, crumbled
1 bay leaf
Eggs Mimosa (recipe follows)
Chopped parsley

slow cooker bonus

Dumplings can be made successfully in your slow cooker if you follow these directions:
- Use a recipe that has at least 1 teaspoon baking powder to each cup of sifted all-purpose flour.
- The slow cooker should be at least ¾ full and the level of the liquid should not be above the level of the food. If the liquid is above the food, remove excess liquid from cooker with a bulb baster before dropping dumpling batter onto food. (Excess liquid can prevent dumplings from cooking completely.)
- Dumplings can either be cooked for 30 minutes on high (290° to 300°) with the cooker covered, or cooked on high (290° to 300°) 15 minutes uncovered, then 15 minutes covered.

HUNGARIAN GOULASH SOUP

*Cook on 190° to 200° for **8** hours, or on 290° to 300° for **4** hours.*
Makes 8 servings.

This dish, sometimes called "Gulyas", tastes best if you use Hungarian paprika as seasoning.

1. Melt shortening in a large skillet or a 5-quart electric slow cooker with a browning unit. Add beef cubes and stir over high heat for 5 minutes.
2. Add paprika and mix well. Stir in tomato purée. Pour into a 5-quart slow cooker; stir in CLASSIC BEEF BROTH or instant beef broth and water, potatoes, onions, celery, carrot, caraway seeds, salt and pepper; cover.
3. Cook on low (190° to 200°) 8 hours, or on high (290° to 300°) 4 hours. Taste and add additional salt and pepper, if you wish. Serve in heated soup bowls with pumpernickel bread and pickled beets.

2 tablespoons vegetable shortening
1½ pounds lean beef, cubed
1 tablespoon paprika
¼ cup tomato purée
6 cups Classic Beef Broth (recipe on page 7)
  OR: 6 envelopes or teaspoons instant beef broth and 6 cups water
2 large potatoes, pared and diced
2 large onions, chopped (2 cups)
1 cup chopped celery
1 large carrot, pared and chopped
1 teaspoon caraway seeds, crushed
1 teaspoon salt
¼ teaspoon pepper

BONUS BEEF SOUP

*Cook on 190° to 200° for **10** hours, or on 290° to 300° for **5** hours.*
Makes 6 servings.

Never let beef bones go to waste. Pack in plastic bags and freeze until you have enough to make this delicious soup.

1. Combine beef bones, water, tomatoes, carrots, turnip, onion, celery, bay leaf, salt, thyme and pepper in an electric slow cooker; cover.
2. Cook on low (190° to 200°) 10 hours, or on high (290° to 300°) 5 hours.
3. Turn heat control to high (290° to 300°); stir in cooked macaroni and spinach; cook 10 minutes; taste and season with salt and pepper. Serve with rye bread and a Waldorf salad.

4 to 6 beef bones
8 cups water
1 can (1 pound) tomatoes
2 medium-size carrots, pared and chopped
1 white turnip, pared and chopped
1 large onion, chopped (1 cup)
1 cup chopped celery
1 bay leaf
2½ teaspoons salt
1 teaspoon leaf thyme, crumbled
¼ teaspoon pepper
1 cup elbow macaroni, cooked
1 cup chopped raw spinach

CLASSIC CHICKEN BROTH

Cook on 190° to 200° for **10** *hours, or on 290° to 300° for* **5** *hours.*
Makes 12 cups.

You see it called for in gourmet recipes. Now let your slow cooker do the work while you're away—or even asleep.

1. Combine chicken with giblets, but not livers, in a 5-quart electric slow cooker. Add carrots, parsnip, onion, celery, and parsley; pour water over; sprinkle with salt and peppercorns; cover.
2. Cook on low (190° to 200°) 10 hours, or on high (290° to 300°) 5 hours, or until chicken is tender; remove chicken and vegetables from broth.
3. Strain broth through cheesecloth into a large bowl. (There should be about 12 cups.) Cool chicken until cool enough to handle; remove and discard skin and bones. Save chicken meat for use in casseroles or cold salads.
4. Refrigerate broth, up to 4 days, leaving the fat layer on surface until ready to use; then lift off and discard. To freeze broth, pour into recipe-size plastic freezer containers to within ½-inch of top; seal; label and date. Freeze. Plan to use within 3 months.

1 stewing chicken (about 5 pounds)
2 medium-size carrots, pared
1 large white parsnip, pared
1 large onion, chopped (1 cup)
2 stalks celery with leaves, chopped
Handful parsley
10 cups water
2 tablespoons salt
12 peppercorns

COMPANY SOUP

Cook on 190° to 200° for **5** *hours, or on 290° to 300° for* **3** *hours.*
Makes 6 servings.

Garnish this tasty soup with bacon, green onions and cucumbers.

1. Combine chicken broth, wine, chicken, peas, water chestnuts, olives, salt, pepper and tarragon in an electric slow cooker; cover.
2. Cook on low (190° to 200°) 5 hours, or on high (290° to 300°) 3 hours.
3. Ladle into soup bowls and pass tiny bowls of bacon, green onions and cucumber to sprinkle on top.

3 cans (13¾ ounces each) chicken broth
¼ cup dry white wine
1½ cups chopped cooked chicken
1 package (10 ounces) frozen green peas, thawed
1 can (5 ounces) water chestnuts, sliced
⅓ cup sliced ripe olives
1½ teaspoons salt
⅛ teaspoon pepper
1 teaspoon leaf tarragon, crumbled
Chopped cooked bacon
Sliced green onions
Cucumber slices

SCANDINAVIAN SUPPER SOUP

In the land of the Midnight Sun, families appreciate steaming bowls of thick pea soup. Your family will, too.

1. Pick over peas and rinse under running water; place peas in an electric slow cooker; pour in boiling water; cover. Let stand 1 hour.
2. Score salt pork and push down into peas; add carrots, leek, onion, salt, thyme, pepper and frankfurters; cover.
3. Cook on low (190° to 200°) 10 hours, stirring after 5 hours, if possible, or on high (290° to 300°) 5 hours, stirring after 3 hours, if possible.
4. Ladle soup into soup bowls; sprinkle with chopped parsley.

1 package (1 pound) dried yellow split peas
6 cups boiling water
½ pound lean salt pork
3 large carrots, pared and sliced
1 large leek, trimmed and sliced
1 large onion, chopped (1 cup)
1 teaspoon salt
1 teaspoon leaf thyme, crumbled
¼ teaspoon pepper
1 pound frankfurters, scored
Chopped parsley

PETITE MARMITE HENRY IV

Marmite is French for stock pot. Henry IV was the French king who promised a chicken in every pot.

1. Place chicken, beef, chicken wings, and beef bones in a 5-quart electric slow cooker; add water, carrots, leeks, celery, turnip, onion and salt. Tie parsley, garlic, peppercorns and bay leaf in cheesecloth; add to cooker; cover.
2. Cook on low (190° to 200°) 10 hours, or on high (290° to 300°) 5 hours, or until chicken is tender. Remove chicken and beef. Let cool enough to handle, then slice or cut in julienne pieces; reserve.
3. Strain broth through cheesecloth into a heated soup tureen; add meat and freshly cooked carrot and turnip slices, if you wish. Taste and season with additional salt and pepper.

1 stewing chicken (about 5 pounds)
1 pound boneless chuck
½ pound chicken wings
1 pound beef bones
12 cups cold water
2 large carrots, pared and sliced
3 leeks, trimmed and sliced
2 stalks celery, chopped
1 white turnip, pared and diced
1 large onion stuck with 6 cloves
1 tablespoon salt
Handful parsley
2 cloves garlic, peeled
5 peppercorns
1 bay leaf

POTAGE PARMENTIER

This potato soup is named in honor of Antoine Parmentier who worked to make potatoes popular among the French.

1. Sauté leeks and onion in butter or margarine in a large skillet or 5-quart electric slow cooker with a browning unit until soft.
2. Combine with potatoes, CLASSIC CHICKEN BROTH or instant chicken broth and water, salt, bay leaf and pepper in a 5-quart slow cooker; cover.
3. Cook on low (190° to 200°) 8 hours, or on high (290° to 300°) 4 hours. Stir in cream; taste and add additional salt and pepper, if desired. Heat 15 minutes before serving.

HOSTESS TIP: This is the origin of VICHYSSOISE. To make VICHYSSOISE: Cool soup slightly; then process, a few cups at a time, in an electric blender container until smooth. Pour into a glass bowl and chill thoroughly. Serve in chilled bowls with a sprinkling of chopped chives.

4 leeks, trimmed and sliced
1 large onion, chopped (1 cup)
¼ cup (½ stick) butter or margarine
4 large potatoes, pared and diced
6 cups Classic Chicken Broth (recipe on page 12)
OR: 6 envelopes or teaspoons instant chicken broth and 6 cups water
1 teaspoon salt
1 bay leaf
¼ teaspoon white pepper
2 cups light cream

OLD-FASHIONED LENTIL SOUP

Ham bone plus the last meaty pickings from it go into this thick hearty soup.

1. Combine ham bone, water, lentils, carrots, onion, salt, sugar, pepper and bay leaf in an electric slow cooker; cover.
2. Cook on low (190° to 200°) 10 hours, or on high (290° to 300°) 5 hours.
3. Take out ham bone; strip off bits of meat and add to soup. Remove bay leaf.
4. Ladle soup into heated serving bowls.

1 ham bone (from baked ham)
6 cups water
1 ¼ cups dried lentils (from a 1-pound package)
4 medium-size carrots, pared and sliced
1 large onion, chopped (1 cup)
2 teaspoons salt
1 teaspoon sugar
¼ teaspoon pepper
1 bay leaf

BORSCHT

A Russian favorite that is classically served with a dollop of sour cream.

1. Sauté cabbage, onions, celery, beets and carrots in butter or margarine in a large skillet or a 5-quart slow cooker with a browning unit.
2. Combine vegetables with chicken wings, cubed beef, water, tomato paste, salt and pepper in a 5-quart slow cooker; cover cooker.
3. Cook on low (190° to 200°) 8 hours, or on high (290° to 300°) 4 hours, or until soup is rich and flavorful. Taste and season with additional salt and pepper, if you wish.
4. Serve in heated soup bowls and top each serving with sour cream.

2 cups shredded cabbage
2 large onions, chopped (2 cups)
1 cup chopped celery
4 large beets, pared and shredded
2 large carrots, pared and
    shredded
3 tablespoons butter or margarine
2 pounds chicken wings
1 pound boneless chuck, cubed
10 cups water
1 can (6 ounces) tomato paste
2 teaspoons salt
¼ teaspoon pepper
    Dairy sour cream

MEAT BALL CHOWDER

Tiny balls of mint-seasoned beef and pork cook in a rich onion broth.

1. Mix ground beef and pork with egg, mint leaves, salt and pepper in a bowl; shape into tiny balls.
2. Pour boiling water into an electric slow cooker; stir in onion soup mix, meat balls, stewed tomatoes and kidney beans with liquid; cover.
3. Cook on low (190° to 200°) 8 hours, or on high (290° to 300°) 4 hours; stir parsley into hot soup.
4. Ladle into soup bowls; serve with chowder crackers, if you wish.

¾ pound ground chuck
¾ pound ground pork
1 egg
2 teaspoons dried mint leaves,
    crumbled
1½ teaspoons salt
¼ teaspoon pepper
4 cups boiling water
1 envelope (2 to a package) onion
    soup mix
1 can (1 pound) stewed tomatoes
1 can (1 pound) red kidney beans
¼ cup chopped parsley

POT AU FEU

Serve this very French soup in deep bowls with toasted French bread and a big salad. Great meal!

1. Trim excess fat from beef; cut into 3 or 4 pieces. Place in electric slow cooker with marrow bone and water.
2. Add carrots, onions, potatoes, turnips, celery, parsnip, parsley and salt; cover slow cooker.
3. Cook on low (190° to 200°) 8 hours, or on high (290° to 300°) 4 hours, or until beef and vegetables are very tender. Remove beef and marrow bone from slow cooker; disconnect cooker; drop a few ice cubes into broth. (If your slow cooker is crockery, you might prefer to pour broth into a large metal bowl before adding ice cubes to avoid damage due to temperature change.)
4. Cut beef into small pieces; skim fat from top of broth; return beef and broth (if removed from cooker) to cooker; taste and season with salt and pepper.
5. Turn heat control to high (290° to 300°); cover; heat 30 minutes or until soup is steamy-hot. Ladle into heated deep bowls and serve at once.

Suggested Variations: Try substituting leeks for the onion in this recipe; peeled tomatoes add a new touch; green beans and peas give a springtime flavor to the soup. Note: If you are in a hurry at dinner time, reheat soup in a metal saucepan on top of the range. Soup also freezes well.

1 bottom round roast (about 3 pounds)
1 marrow bone, cracked
4 cups cold water
4 large carrots, pared and sliced
4 medium-size onions, peeled and sliced
3 potatoes, pared and diced
3 white turnips, pared and diced
2 cups sliced celery
1 small parsnip, pared and diced
¼ cup chopped parsley
2 teaspoons salt

quick soup tips

- Try slipping a strip of orange and/or lemon rind into a soup, stews or pot roasts, or into a saucepan of vegetables as they cook. Rinds can add exquisite flavor at no extra expense. The easiest way to peel an orange or lemon so that you get the colored part of the rind only, not the bitter white part, is with a swivel-bladed vegetable peeler.
- Stir canned seafood—shrimps, crab, lobster or tuna—into canned condensed vegetable soup and seasoned stewed tomatoes for a fast gumbo.
- For an instant tomato bouillon, heat 2½ cans canned tomato juice and 1 can condensed beef broth with 1 teaspoon crumbled leaf basil just to boiling; serve hot with a garnish of popcorn.

PHILADELPHIA PEPPER POT

Cook on 190° to 200° for **8** hours, or on 290° to 300° for **4** hours.
Makes 8 servings.

A tripe soup that is said to go back to the time of George Washington.

1. Brown salt pork in a large skillet or an electric slow cooker with a browning unit; remove and reserve.
2. Sauté leeks, onion and green peppers in pan drippings until soft; stir in flour and cook 2 minutes.
3. Combine mixture with salt pork and tripe in an electric slow cooker. Add potatoes, tomatoes, CLASSIC BEEF BROTH or instant beef broth and water, salt, pepper, bay leaf and thyme; cover.
4. Cook on low (190° to 200°) 8 hours, or on high (290° to 300°) 4 hours, or until broth is rich and flavorful. Taste and season with salt and pepper. Serve with refrigerated flaky biscuits and a hearty Burgundy, if you wish.

½ cup diced salt pork
3 leeks, trimmed and chopped
1 medium-size onion, chopped (½ cup)
3 green peppers, halved, seeded and chopped
1 cup chopped celery
1 tablespoon all-purpose flour
1 cup diced parboiled tripe
2 medium-size potatoes, pared and diced
3 small tomatoes, peeled and chopped
8 cups Classic Beef Broth (recipe page 7)
  OR: 8 envelopes or teaspoons instant beef broth and 8 cups water
1 tablespoon salt
½ teaspoon freshly ground pepper
1 bay leaf
¼ teaspoon leaf thyme, crumbled

SCOTCH LAMB BROTH

Cook on 190° to 200° for **10** hours, or on 290° to 300° for **5** hours.
Makes 8 servings.

The last of a leg of lamb can be substituted for the lamb combination.

1. Trim excess fat from lamb. Place in an electric slow cooker with leeks, celery, carrots, onion, water, salt and pepper. Stir in pearl barley; cover.
2. Cook on low (190° to 200°) 10 hours, or on high (290° to 300°) 5 hours, or until meat is tender and barley is cooked. Stir in cream just before serving.

2 pounds lamb shoulder combination
2 leeks, trimmed and sliced
2 cups chopped celery
2 large carrots, pared and chopped
1 medium-size onion, chopped
8 cups water
2 teaspoons salt
½ teaspoon pepper
½ cup pearl barley
1 cup light cream

TURKEY BROTH

A great way to get extra mileage from your holiday birds.

1. Break turkey carcass into pieces small enough to fit into your slow cooker; add onion, carrot, celery tops, salt, pepper, monosodium glutamate, enough water to cover. Cover slow cooker.
2. Cook on low (190° to 200°) 8 hours, or on high (290° to 300°) 4 hours. Cool.
3. When cool enough to handle, lift out turkey carcass, remove any bits of meat and chop coarsely. Strain broth; add meat, cool, then skim fat from top. Reheat and serve immediately or store in freezer for use later.

1 turkey carcass
1 large onion, sliced
1 large carrot, sliced
¼ cup celery tops
1 tablespoon salt
¼ teaspoon pepper
  Water
¼ teaspoon monosodium glutamate

OLD-FASHIONED BEEF AND VEGETABLE SOUP

This hearty soup, chock-full of vegetables and meat, is a meal in itself.

1. Combine BASIC BEEF BROTH in slow cooker with potatoes, carrots, celery, onions, tomatoes, salt and pepper.
2. Cook on low (190° to 200°) 8 hours, or on high (290° to 300°) 4 hours.
3. Stir in cabbage, corn and meat; turn heat control to high (290° to 300°) and cook 15 minutes longer or just until all vegetables are crisply tender. Sprinkle with parsley.
4. Ladle into soup bowls. Serve with chunks of crusty bread.

6 cups Basic Beef Broth (recipe page 7)
2 large potatoes, peeled and diced (2 cups)
2 large carrots, pared and sliced
1 cup sliced celery
2 small onions, peeled and quartered
1 can (1 pound) whole tomatoes
2 teaspoons salt
⅛ teaspoon pepper
½ head green cabbage, shredded (2 cups)
1 cup frozen corn (from a plastic bag), thawed
3 cups diced cooked beef
1 tablespoon chopped parsley

MULLIGATAWNY SOUP

Cook on 190° to 200° for **4** hours,
or on 290° to 300° for **2** hours.
Makes 6 servings.

A classic soup with origins in India, is richly flavored with exotic curry.

1. Sauté onion until soft in butter or margarine in skillet or electric slow cooker with browning unit; stir in apple, curry powder and salt; sauté 5 minutes longer, or until apple is soft; add flour.
2. Combine onion mixture, carrots, celery, CLASSIC CHICKEN BROTH and chicken in slow cooker. Cover.
3. Cook on low (190° to 200°) 4 hours, or on high (290° to 300°) 2 hours. Stir in lemon juice.
4. Ladle into soup plates or bowls; pass hot cooked rice and chopped parsley and lemon slices, if you wish, for each to add his own garnish. Good with crusty French bread.

1 large onion, chopped (1 cup)
¼ cup (½ stick) butter or margarine
1 medium-size apple, pared,
*   quartered, cored and chopped*
5 teaspoons curry powder
1 teaspoon salt
¼ cup all-purpose flour
3 medium-size carrots, pared and
*   sliced*
2 stalks of celery, sliced
6 cups Classic Chicken Broth
*   recipe page 12)*
3 cups cooked diced chicken
1 tablespoon lemon juice
2 cups hot cooked rice
¼ cup chopped parsley
6 lemon slices (optional)

BASIC VEGETABLE SOUP

Cook on 190° to 200° for **6** hours,
or on 290° to 300° for **3** hours.
Makes 6 servings.

You don't have to be a vegetarian to love this tasty broth. Excellent between meals for dieters.

1. Combine water, celery, onion, cabbage, carrot, peppercorns, salt, bay leaf and monosodium glutamate in slow cooker; cover.
2. Cook on low (190° to 200°) 6 hours, or on high (290° to 300°) 3 hours; strain. Serve as vegetable bouillon, or as a base for making other soups.

4 cups water
2 cups chopped celery stalks and
*   leaves*
1 large onion, chopped (1 cup)
½ cup chopped cabbage
1 carrot, diced
6 peppercorns
1½ teaspoons salt
1 bay leaf
¼ teaspoon monosodium
*   glutamate*
2½ cups tomato juice

WINTER'S BEST SOUP

Cook on 190° to 200° for **10** hours,
or on 290° to 300° for **5** hours
Makes 6 servings.

If this is waiting in your slow cooker you don't have to be afraid of the coldest days.

1. Remove marrow from marrow bones to make MARROW BALLS.
2. Combine bones and water, tomatoes, carrots, turnips, onion, celery, cloves, bay leaf, thyme, salt, sugar, pepper, lima beans and green beans in slow cooker; cover.
3. Cook on low (190° to 200°) 10 hours, or on high (290° to 300°) 5 hours.
4. Remove bones, skim off fat; add macaroni, turn heat control to high (290° to 300°); add spinach and MARROW BALLS; cover; cook 15 minutes.

3 three-inch beef marrow bones
1 beef knuckle bone, cracked
10 cups water
1 can (about 1 pound) tomatoes
3 medium-size carrots, pared and diced
2 small white turnips, pared and diced
1 medium-size onion, chopped (½ cup)
1 cup diced celery
6 whole cloves
1 bay leaf
1 teaspoon leaf thyme, crumbled
2 teaspoons salt
1 teaspoon sugar
¼ teaspoon pepper
1 cup dried lima beans (from a 1-pound package)
½ pound green beans, tipped and cut
1 cup shell macaroni, cooked
2 cups chopped raw spinach
Marrow Balls (recipe follows)

MARROW BALLS —
Combine mashed beef marrow, bread crumbs, egg, parsley, salt and pepper in small bowl; form lightly into 24 balls.

Marrow Balls
½ cup mashed beef marrow (from beef marrow bones)
1 cup soft bread crumbs
1 egg, beaten
1 tablespoon minced parsley
½ teaspoon salt
⅛ teaspoon pepper

leftovers for soup

- Meat, fish and poultry bones, left after cooking, can be used as the foundation of soups, sauces and stews.
- Add vegetables and fruit parings to the pot, too—you'll be surprised at the flavor they impart.

20

MEAT

Tasty stews, pot roasts and meat loaves are often eliminated in favor of quick-cooking steaks and chops by women who work outside the home. Today, meat dishes that take more time to cook can be part of every woman's daily menus if they are prepared the slow cooker way.

Budgets can be stretched, too, because cheaper, tougher cuts of meat become miraculously tender and tasty when they are cooked slowly.

Before cooking meat, carefully trim away all excess fat. Too much fat can raise the temperature in an electric slow cooker and this, in turn, will cause your dish to get too well done.

Some appliances come with browning units which you will see referred to in some recipes. Browning meat is not essential in slow cooking, but it does help develop a richer flavor in the food and remove some of the fat, especially in pork, lamb or sausage.

When you brown meat in a slow cooker remember to turn the temperature control knob back to the proper setting for the rest of the cooking time.

If you brown by the conventional method, in a skillet, you may find it helpful to do this the night before.

Some slow cookers have heat coils on the bottom. If your model does, and you are cooking a mixed meat and vegetable dish, it is best to place some of the vegetables at the bottom of the slow cooker, then place the meat on top. The vegetables will keep the meat from sticking.

BEEF À LA MODE

Red wine helps to tenderize a less-tender cut of beef and make a superb gravy, too. Shown on page 64.

1. Place meat in a large glass or ceramic bowl; pour mixture of Burgundy, sliced onion, garlic, bay leaves, thyme, salt and pepper over. Cover; store in refrigerator overnight, turning meat several times to marinate on all sides.
2. When ready to cook, remove meat from marinade and pat dry with paper towels; brown in hot oil in a large skillet or an electric slow cooker with a browning unit.
3. Place beef in slow cooker with marinade, broth and vegetables; cover.
4. Cook on low (190° to 200°) for 10 hours, or on high (290° to 300°) for 6 hours. Remove from cooker and keep warm; remove bay leaves from cooking liquid.
5. Pour liquid, half at a time, into an electric blender container; add flour, half at a time; cover container; whirl at high speed 1 minute. (Or press liquid through a sieve with a wooden spoon into a bowl; cool slightly; stir in flour until well-blended.) Pour liquid into a large saucepan; bring to boiling. Cook, stirring constantly, until sauce thickens and bubbles 3 minutes.
6. Place beef and part of the sauce in a heated casserole; surround with BUTTER BRAISED VEGETABLES; spoon remaining sauce over meat, just before serving.

1 round or boneless chuck roast (about 4 pounds)
2 cups red Burgundy wine
1 large onion, sliced
2 cloves garlic, minced
2 bay leaves
1 teaspoon leaf thyme, crumbled
2 teaspoons salt
½ teaspoon freshly ground pepper
2 tablespoons olive oil or vegetable oil
1 can condensed beef broth
⅓ cup all-purpose flour
Butter Braised Vegetables (recipe follows)

BUTTER BRAISED VEGETABLES — *Makes 10 servings.*

1. Sauté whole green beans in butter or margarine in a large skillet until a bright green; remove; brown white onions and carrots in the same skillet. Combine instant chicken broth and hot water in a cup; pour into skillet; cover.
2. Simmer 25 minutes; return green beans to skillet; simmer 10 minutes longer, or until vegetables are tender.

Butter Braised Vegetables
1 pound green beans, tipped
1 pound small white onions, peeled
1 pound carrots, pared and cut into 5-inch pieces
¼ cup (½ stick) butter or margarine
1 envelope or teaspoon instant chicken broth
½ cup water

22

STUFFED POT ROAST

Cook on 190° to 200° for **10** hours, or on 290° to 300° for **5** hours. Makes 2 meals of 6 servings each.

Pepperoni adds an exotic new flavor to pot roast in a recipe that is generous enough for leftovers.

1. Stand roast on end and cut a small hole through center with a sharp thin-blade knife; stuff hole with pepperoni, twisting and pushing as you work. (Do not remove strings from roast.)
2. Brown roast in a large skillet or an electric slow cooker with a browning unit. Drain off all fat. Stir in bouillon, vinegar and red pepper seasoning.
3. Cook on low (190° to 200°) 10 hours, or on high (290° to 300°) for 5 hours, or until meat is tender; place on heated serving platter and keep warm.
4. Turn heat control to high (290° to 300°). Combine ¼ cup all-purpose flour and ½ cup cold water in a cup; stir into liquid in slow cooker; cover; cook 15 minutes.
5. Carve roast into ¼-inch slices and serve with gravy.

1 eye round beef roast (about 4 pounds)
1 package (5 ounces) whole pepperoni
1 can condensed beef bouillon
1 cup cider vinegar
Several drops bottled red pepper seasoning
¼ cup all-purpose flour
½ cup water
1 tablespoon brown sugar

MEMPHIS PORK SUPPER

Cook on 190° to 200° for **8** hours, or on 290° to 300° for **4** hours. Makes 8 servings.

Pork, apples, onion and sweet potatoes make this Southern-style main dish.

1. Pare and quarter sweet potatoes.
2. Trim all fat from pork; brown, a few pieces at a time, in a little of the trimmed fat in a large skillet or an electric slow cooker with a browning unit; remove with a slotted spoon and reserve.
3. Arrange potatoes around edge of an electric slow cooker; place half of meat in middle. Top with layer each of half of the onion slices and apple rings; sprinkle with half the brown sugar. Repeat to make a second layer of meat and onion; overlap remaining apple rings around edge; sprinkle remaining brown sugar over. Combine apple juice, salt, marjoram and pepper in a 2-cup measure; pour over apple rings; cover.
4. Cook on low (190° to 200°) 8 hours, or on high (290° to 300°) 4 hours, or until pork is tender. Sprinkle with chopped parsley, just before serving.

8 medium-size sweet potatoes (about 3 pounds)
3 pounds boneless pork shoulder, cubed
3 medium-size onions, sliced
4 medium-size tart red apples, cored and sliced into rings
2 tablespoons brown sugar
2 cups apple juice
2 teaspoons salt
1 teaspoon leaf marjoram, crumbled
¼ teaspoon pepper
Chopped parsley

23

VERMONT CORNED BEEF

Cook on 190° to 200° for **10** hours, or on 290° to 300° for **5** hours.
Makes 8 servings.

Our favorite way with corned beef, but it must be the "mild cure" corned beef, otherwise the dish is too salty. Pictured on page 63.

1. Wash corned beef in cold running water. Place in an electric slow cooker; top with sugar, orange slices, mixed pickling spices and bay leaf.
2. Arrange carrots, onions and turnips around meat in slow cooker; pour wine and water over; cover.
3. Cook on low (190° to 200°) 10 hours, or on high (290° to 300°) 5 hours, or until meat is tender when pierced with a two-tined fork.
4. Slice meat and place on a heated serving platter and arrange boiled potatoes, chopped turnip greens and lima beans around it.

1 *"mild cure" corned beef brisket (about 4 pounds)*
¼ *cup firmly packed brown sugar*
1 *California orange, sliced*
1 *tablespoon mixed pickling spices*
1 *bay leaf*
2 *large carrots, pared and sliced*
2 *large onions, peeled and quartered*
3 *small white turnips, pared and quartered*
1 *cup dry white wine*
½ *cup water*

SLUMGULLION ON A BUN

Cook on 190° to 200° for **8** hours, or on 290° to 300° for **4** hours.
Makes 6 servings.

Sort of a "Sloppy Joe." Everyone can spoon up his serving when he gets home.

1. Shape ground beef into a large patty in a large skillet or an electric slow cooker with a browning unit. Brown 5 minutes on each side, then break up into chunks; push to one side.
2. Add onion and garlic; sauté just until soft. Stir in spaghetti sauce mix and tomato juice, then celery and corn.
3. Spoon mixture into cooker; cover.
4. Cook on low (190° to 200°) 8 hours, stirring after 4 hours if possible, or on high (290° to 300°) 4 hours, stirring after 2 hours, if possible. Add stuffed olives and serve over toasted buns.

1½ *pounds ground chuck*
1 *large onion, chopped (1 cup)*
1 *clove garlic, minced*
1 *envelope (1½ ounces) spaghetti sauce mix*
2 *cups tomato juice*
1 *cup chopped celery*
1 *can (12 or 16 ounces) whole-kernel corn*
¼ *cup sliced stuffed olives*
6 *split hamburger buns, toasted*

KUN KOKI POT ROAST

Cook on 190° to 200° for **10** hours,
or on 290° to 300° for **6** hours.
Makes 8 servings.

Plan ahead when serving this savory beef dish, as meat seasons in a special soy marinade overnight before cooking.

1. Toast sesame seeds in a small skillet over low heat, shaking pan often, just until golden-brown.
2. Combine seeds with water, soy sauce, molasses, vinegar, green onions, garlic powder and cayenne in a 2-cup measure. Trim excess fat from beef; place in a large glass bowl; pour marinade over; cover. Refrigerate, turning meat several times to season evenly, overnight, in marinade.
3. When ready to cook, remove meat from the marinade, then pat dry with paper towels. Brown pot roast in a large skillet or an electric slow cooker with a browning unit. Place meat in slow cooker; pour marinade over; cover.
4. Cook on low (190° to 200°) 10 hours, or on high (290° to 300°) 6 hours, or until beef is tender when pierced with a two-tined fork. Remove beef to a heated platter to keep warm.
5. Turn heat control to high (290° to 300°). Combine cornstarch with ¼ cup cold water in a cup; stir into liquid in slow cooker until well-blended. Cover; simmer 15 minutes.
6. Carve meat into ¼-inch-thick slices; serve with gravy.
Suggested Variation: Pork is equally delicious in this recipe. Use a fresh picnic shoulder (about 5 pounds).

2 tablespoons sesame seeds
1 cup water
¼ cup soy sauce
2 tablespoons light molasses
2 tablespoons wine vinegar or
    cider vinegar
2 green onions, sliced
1 teaspoon garlic powder
⅛ teaspoon cayenne pepper
1 boneless shoulder or chuck pot
    roast (about 4 pounds)
2 tablespoons cornstarch

know your vinegars

- *Cider Vinegar:* The best all-round vinegar, this is made from apple juice and is medium-tart in flavor.
- *White Vinegar:* This crystal-clear, sharply acid vinegar, distilled from barley malt, corn or rye, is the one to use in pickling because it will not discolor the pickles.
- *Wine Vinegar:* Both red wine and white wine vinegars are available. They have a delicate wine bouquet, are best used for dressing green salads or making sauces.
- *Herb Vinegars:* The most familiar is tarragon vinegar. But in gourmet sections of your supermarket you may also see such specialties as dill, garlic or shallot vinegar.

YANKEE BEEF PLATTER

Cook on 190° to 200° for **10** hours, or on 290° to 300° for **6** hours.
Makes 8 servings.

Pot roast on special? Try slow cooking it and notice how much less shrinkage you'll have.

1. Trim excess fat from beef; pierce meat all over with a fork; place in a large glass or earthenware bowl.
2. Sprinkle with onion, salt, pepper and cloves. Add bay leaf and wine to bowl. Refrigerate, turning meat several times, overnight to marinate.
3. When ready to cook meat, remove from marinade; pat dry with paper towels. Brown in a large skillet or an electric slow cooker with a browning unit.
4. Place beef in slow cooker; stir in marinade, plus celery, garlic and onion soup; cover.
5. Cook on low (190° to 200°) 10 hours, or on high (290° to 300°) 6 hours, or until beef is tender when pierced with a two-tined fork. Remove beef to a heated platter and keep warm.
6. Turn heat control to high (290° to 300°). Combine flour and ¼ cup cold water in a cup; stir into liquid in slow cooker until well-blended; cover; simmer 15 minutes.
7. Carve part of the roast into ¼-inch-thick slices. Arrange slices with rest of roast and BRAISED LEEKS on a large serving platter. Add parsley potatoes and steamed whole carrots, if you wish. Serve gravy separately to spoon over all.

1 boneless rolled chuck roast
   (about 4 pounds)
1 tablespoon minced dried onion
2 teaspoons salt
½ teaspoon freshly ground pepper
⅛ teaspoon ground cloves
1 bay leaf
1 cup dry red wine
1 cup thinly sliced celery
2 cloves garlic, sliced
1 can condensed onion soup
2 tablespoons all-purpose flour
   Braised Leeks (recipe follows)

BRAISED LEEKS—Trim roots and about half of the green tops from 1 bunch leeks; split each leek lengthwise; wash well. Arrange pieces, cut-side down, in a large skillet. Add just enough water to cover; bring to boiling; cover. Simmer 5 minutes; drain; return to pan. Add 3 tablespoons butter or margarine and sprinkle with ½ teaspoon each salt and celery salt. Cook slowly, 5 minutes longer, or until leeks are tender.

Suggested Variation: Green onions can be substituted for the leeks; use 2 bunches sliced in 3-inch pieces and cook a total of 6 minutes.

BEEF AND SPANISH RICE

This is the perfect recipe for a 2½-quart slow cooker.

1. Sauté bacon until crisp in a large skillet; remove and drain on paper towels; reserve for garnish.
2. Mix ground beef lightly with egg, bread crumbs, and 1 teaspoon of the salt until well-blended; shape into 16 balls.
3. Brown in drippings in same pan.
4. Stir onion, celery, green pepper and chili powder into pan; sauté just until vegetables are soft.
5. Stir in rice, tomatoes, water and remaining salt; bring to boiling, stirring lightly to blend well.
6. Place mixture in a 2½-quart electric slow cooker; cover.
7. Cook on low (190° to 200°) 8 hours, or on high (290° to 300°) 4 hours, stirring, if possible, halfway through cooking, or until rice is tender and liquid is almost absorbed. Top with cooked bacon. Serve with an avocado and grapefruit section salad, if you wish.

4 slices bacon, diced
1 pound ground chuck
1 egg
½ cup soft white bread crumbs (1 slice)
2 teaspoons salt
1 large onion, chopped (1 cup)
½ cup chopped celery
1 large green pepper, halved, seeded and chopped
1 to 3 teaspoons chili powder
1 cup uncooked rice
1 can (1 pound) tomatoes
1 cup water

DENVER LAMB STEW

Lamb lovers will enjoy this hearty dish for a cold winter's dinner.

1. Trim excess fat from lamb; rub lamb on all sides with garlic; place in an electric slow cooker.
2. Add green beans, onions, potatoes, tomatoes, salt and marjoram; cover.
3. Cook on low (190° to 200°) 8 hours, or on high (290° to 300°) 4 hours, or until meat is tender. Serve with chunks of crusty French bread.
   Suggested Variations: Omit tomatoes and add 2 cups dry red wine. Acorn squash slices and zucchini sticks can be substituted for the potatoes and green beans in this stew.

2 pounds boneless lamb shoulder, cubed
1 clove garlic, peeled and halved
1 pound green beans, tipped and cut into 1-inch pieces
12 small white onions, peeled
6 small potatoes, pared
1 can (1 pound) tomatoes
1 teaspoon salt
1 teaspoon leaf marjoram, crumbled

RAGOÛT OF LAMB

Cook on 190° to 200° for **7** *hours,*
or on 290° to 300° for **4** *hours.*
Makes 6 servings.

When you add quick-cooking tapioca to your slow cooker recipe at the beginning, you have a thickened gravy or sauce at the end with no additional work.

1. Trim excess fat from lamb; shake in a plastic bag with flour, 1 teaspoon of the salt and ¼ teaspoon of the pepper.
2. Heat butter or margarine and oil in a large skillet or an electric slow cooker with a browning unit; brown lamb, a few pieces at a time, in hot fat.
3. Combine browned lamb, chicken broth, wine, carrots, onions, tomatoes, garlic, parsley, tapioca, bay leaf, caraway seeds and remaining 1 teaspoon salt and ¼ teaspoon pepper in slow cooker; cover.
4. Cook on low (190° to 200°) for 7 hours, or on high (290° to 300°) for 4 hours, or until lamb is tender. Taste and season with additional salt and pepper, if you wish. Serve with mashed potatoes and a crisp salad with a mint-lemon dressing, if you wish.

2 pounds lean boneless lamb, cubed
¼ cup all-purpose flour
2 teaspoons salt
½ teaspoon pepper
2 tablespoons butter or margarine
2 tablespoons olive oil or vegetable oil
1 can condensed chicken broth
¼ cup dry white wine
4 large carrots, pared and cut into sticks
4 medium-size onions, peeled and quartered
3 tomatoes, peeled and chopped
1 clove garlic, minced
2 tablespoons chopped parsley
1 tablespoon quick-cooking tapioca
1 bay leaf
½ teaspoon caraway seeds, crushed

guide to wines

Wine in cooking adds the gourmet touch. Everyday stew becomes ragoût, and pot roast turns into Beef à la Mode. Wine rounds out the flavors, tenderizes tougher cuts of meat and gives distinction to your cooking. Here are a few tips for successful cooking with wines:

• Dry sherry and Madeira go well in shellfish and creamed dishes.
• Dry white wines are for poultry and veal casseroles.
• Hearty red wines are best for beef, game and some fish, chicken and duck dishes.
• Dry vermouth can be used in place of white wine, and stores for months.
• Use the same wines you drink for cooking.
• Pour a few drops of olive oil over the surface of a dry wine you plan to use just for cooking, if you must keep it for more than a few days. This prevents the air from destroying the wine.

BEEF JARDINIÈRE

Cook on 190° to 200° for **10** hours,
or on 290° to 300° for **5** hours.
Makes 4 servings.

Jardinière means gardener's style—or presented with a bouquet of vegetables.

1. Trim excess fat from beef; brown beef quickly in a few melted trimmings in a large skillet or an electric slow cooker with a browning unit.
2. Place meat in slow cooker with tomatoes, salt, bay leaf, thyme and pepper; cover cooker.
3. Cook on low (190° to 200°) for 10 hours, or on high (290° to 300°) 5 hours.
4. Turn heat control to high (290° to 300°); add carrots and celery; cover. Cook 20 minutes longer, or until vegetables are crisply tender. Serve with a light red wine and crusty French bread.

1½ pound beef chuck, cubed
1 can (1 pound) tomatoes
1 teaspoon salt
1 bay leaf
½ teaspoon leaf thyme, crumbled
¼ teaspoon pepper
4 carrots, pared and cut into
    3-inch lengths
4 celery stalks, cut into 3-inch
    lengths

HOPPING JOHN

Cook on 190° to 200° for **8** hours,
or on 290° to 300° for **4** hours.
Makes 8 servings.

Some say this dish was named for a famous waiter in a fashionable Charleston, South Carolina hotel.

1. Sauté bacon until crisp in a large skillet or an electric slow cooker with a browning unit; remove with a slotted spoon and drain on paper towels.
2. Shape meatloaf mixture into a patty in same pan; brown 5 minutes on each side, then break up into chunks; push to one side. Add onion to pan and sauté just until soft. Stir in cooked bacon, celery, blackeyed peas, salt, basil, thyme, bay leaf, red-pepper seasoning, instant beef broth, and water. Bring to boiling.
3. Combine ground beef mixture, uncooked rice and tomato juice in an electric slow cooker; cover.
4. Cook on low (190° to 200°) 8 hours, or on high (290° to 300°) 4 hours, stirring, if possible, halfway through cooking, or until rice is tender. Serve with crisp cucumber and onion slices, if you wish.

2 slices bacon, diced
1 pound ground meatloaf mixture
1 medium-size onion, chopped
    (½ cup)
1 cup chopped celery
2 packages (10 ounces each)
    frozen blackeyed peas, partly
    thawed
1 teaspoon salt
1 teaspoon leaf basil, crumbled
½ teaspoon leaf thyme, crumbled
1 bay leaf
    Few drops bottled red-pepper
    seasoning
1 envelope or teaspoon instant
    beef broth
½ cup water
½ cup uncooked rice
2 cups tomato juice

NEW STYLE SAUERBRATEN STEW

Cook on 190° to 200° for **8** hours, then on 290° to 300° for **1½** hours.
Makes 8 servings.

If you like your stew on the spicy side, simmer the spice bag in the cooker. Otherwise, discard after marinating.

1. Combine meat marinade and vinegar in a small saucepan; tie cloves, peppercorns, allspice, bay leaf and celery seeds in cheesecloth and add to saucepan. Bring to boiling; let cool.
2. Trim excess fat from meat; pierce all over with a two-tined fork. Place in a glass or earthenware bowl. Pour marinade over and let stand 20 minutes, basting several times with marinade.
3. Remove meat from marinade; reserve marinade. Cube meat and roll in a mixture of flour and sugar on wax paper.
4. Brown meat in vegetable shortening in a large skillet or an electric slow cooker with a browning unit; remove and reserve. Sauté onions and carrots until soft in pan drippings; stir in wine.
5. Combine meat with onions and carrots in slow cooker; add reserved marinade and spice bag, if you wish; cover cooker.
6. Cook on low (190° to 200°) 8 hours; turn heat control to high (290° to 300°); stir in gingersnap crumbs.
7. Cook 1 hour longer, stirring several times. Drop GINGER DUMPLINGS onto surface; cover; cook 30 minutes longer, or until dumplings are light and fluffy. Serve at once.

1 envelope (about 1 ounce) instant meat marinade
⅔ cup white vinegar
6 whole cloves
6 peppercorns
6 whole allspice
1 bay leaf
½ teaspoon celery seeds
1 cross rib beef pot roast (about 3 pounds)
½ cup all-purpose flour
2 tablespoons sugar
3 tablespoons vegetable shortening
6 small yellow onions, peeled and halved
4 large carrots, pared and sliced
½ cup dry red wine
⅓ cup crushed gingersnaps
Ginger Dumplings (recipe follows)

GINGER DUMPLINGS—Sift 1½ cups sifted all-purpose flour, 2 teaspoons baking powder and ½ teaspoon salt into a medium-size bowl. Stir in ¼ cup crushed gingersnap crumbs. Blend in 1 tablespoon vegetable shortening with a fork until crumbly. Stir in ¾ cup milk, just until mixture is moist. Drop onto hot food in slow cooker. Cook on high (290° to 300°) 30 minutes, or until puffy and light. (No peeking, or the dumplings won't puff up.)

HARVEST PORK CHOPS

Cook on 190° to 200° for **8** hours,
or on 290° to 300° for **4** hours.
Makes 6 servings.

Pork chops are extra moist and juicy when made the slow-cooking way.

1. Combine unthawed fruit juice, soy sauce, ginger, salt and marjoram in 2-cup measure; let stand.
2. Trim excess fat from chops; brown chops well in remaining fat in a large skillet or an electric slow cooker with a browning unit; remove and reserve. Drain all fat from pan. Stir in fruit juice mixture; bring to boiling, stirring up all the cooked-on bits in bottom of pan.
3. Wash and slice squash into 1-inch thick rings; remove seeds; halve rings.
4. Arrange browned chops and squash rings in slow cooker; pour fruit juice mixture over; cover.
5. Cook on low (190° to 200°) 8 hours, or on high (290° to 300°) 4 hours, or until pork is tender.
6. Put pickled red peppers into slow cooker 5 minutes before serving. Serve with frozen Italian vegetables in cream sauce.

1 can (6 ounces) frozen
    concentrate for pineapple-
    orange juice
3 tablespoons soy sauce
2 teaspoons ground ginger
1 teaspoon salt
½ teaspoon leaf marjoram,
    crumbled
6 loin, rib or shoulder pork chops,
    cut ¾-inch thick
2 acorn squashes
3 pickled sweet red peppers,
    halved

MUSHROOM STEAK

Cook on 190° to 200° for **8** hours,
or on 290° to 300° for **4** hours.
Makes 8 servings.

Try finding a more popular food combination—and so quick to fix.

1. Trim excess fat from roast; combine dry soup mix and onion on a sheet of aluminum foil or wax paper. Roll roast in mixture to coat well.
2. Place coated roast in an electric slow cooker; pour wine or water over; cover.
3. Cook on low (190° to 200°) 8 hours, turning after 4 hours, if possible, or on high (290° to 300°) 4 hours, turning after 2 hours, if possible, or until meat is tender. Serve with mashed potatoes and buttered green beans, if you wish.

1 chuck roast, cut 1½-inches thick
    (about 3 pounds)
1 envelope (2 to a package)
    mushroom soup mix
1 tablespoon minced dried onion
1 cup dry red wine or water

NAVARIN PRINTANIER

A savory lamb stew that's abundant with spring vegetables.

1. Heat oil in a large skillet or an electric slow cooker with a browning unit; brown lamb, a few pieces at a time. Remove pieces, as they brown.
2. Pour off all but 1 tablespoon fat; add shallots or onion and garlic; sauté, stirring often, 5 minutes, or until golden-brown. Return lamb to pan. Sprinkle flour over meat; cook over moderate heat, stirring and tossing meat with wooden spoon until evenly coated, about 5 minutes. (This browns the flour slightly.) Stir in beef broth and tomatoes; bring to boiling, stirring constantly to loosen browned bits. Stir in salt and thyme. Place lamb mixture in slow cooker; cover.
3. Cook on low (190° to 200°) 6 hours, or on high (290° to 300°) 4 hours.
4. One hour before serving, heat butter or margarine in a skillet; add onions, turnips, carrots and potatoes. Sauté, stirring 10 minutes, or until vegetables are browned and glazed. Add water; cover; simmer 30 minutes, or until crisply tender.
5. Add glazed vegetables and peas to lamb, pushing them down under liquid; cover; simmer for 20 minutes longer, or until lamb and vegetables are tender. Sprinkle with parsley.

3 tablespoons olive oil or vegetable oil
2 pounds lean boneless lamb, cubed
3 tablespoons finely chopped shallots
* OR: 1 small onion, chopped (¼ cup)*
1 clove garlic, minced
3 tablespoons all-purpose flour
1 can condensed beef broth
2 large tomatoes, peeled and chopped
2 teaspoons salt
1 teaspoon leaf thyme, crumbled
2 tablespoons butter or margarine
12 small white onions, peeled
4 small white turnips, pared and quartered
4 large carrots, pared and cut into 2-inch lengths
12 small new potatoes, peeled
1 cup frozen peas (from a 1½-pound bag), thawed
2 tablespoons chopped parsley
¼ cup water

saving on meat

- Substitute ground pork for ground lamb. It is often cheaper.
- If you want fresh pork, try the shoulder instead of leg (fresh ham) or loin. The shoulder may cost so much less that you can buy an extra pound or two for the same price.
- When buying ham, consider all cuts and prices, then choose what best fits your purse and purpose. Whole or half smoked hams usually cost the same price per pound. And though a butt portion may cost a few cents more than a shank end, it's a better choice because it contains more meat.

RIBS AND LENTIL STEW

Cook on 290° to 300° for **2** hours,
then on 190° to 200° for **8** hours.
Makes 6 servings.

*Seasoned just right for most tastes, you can add more
thyme if your family prefers more pungent food.*

1. Trim away as much fat as possible from short ribs.
   Place in an electric slow cooker; combine water, wine,
   salt, bay leaf, thyme and celery seeds in a 4-cup
   measure; pour over ribs.
2. Stir in onion, garlic, lentils and tapioca; cover.
3. Cook on high (290° to 300°) 2 hours; turn heat control
   to low (190° to 200°) and cook 8 hours longer, or until
   lentils are tender. Unplug slow cooker; remove cover;
   let fat rise to surface and skim off. Stir in hot cooked
   pasta and top with chopped parsley, if you wish.

3 pounds short ribs, cut-up
2 cups water
1 cup dry red wine
1 teaspoon salt
1 bay leaf
¼ teaspoon leaf thyme, crumbled
¼ teaspoon celery seeds, crushed
1 large onion, chopped (1 cup)
1 clove garlic, minced
*1 cup dried lentils (from a
     1-pound package)*
*1 tablespoon quick-cooking
     tapioca*
*1 cup small shells or elbow
     macaroni, cooked*

LANCASHIRE HOT POT

Cook on 190° to 200° for **8** hours,
or on 290° to 300° for **4** hours.
Makes 8 servings.

*Lancashire, a county in northwestern England, is the
home of hot-pot cooking. This is one of their best.*

1. Trim excess fat from beef. Halve kidneys; cut out
   tubes and white membrane, then cut kidneys into
   ½-inch cubes. Shake meats, part at a time, with flour
   in a plastic bag to coat well.
2. Dissolve instant beef broth in boiling water in a 2-cup
   measure; stir in Worcestershire sauce.
3. Layer vegetables and meats into an electric slow
   cooker this way: Half of each of potatoes, onions and
   meats, sprinkling each layer lightly with salt and
   pepper. Repeat with remaining vegetables, meats, salt
   and pepper.
4. Pour broth mixture over; dot with butter or margarine; cover.
5. Cook on low (190° to 200°) 8 hours, or on high (290°
   to 300°) 4 hours, or until meats are tender. A baked
   apple cobbler with pour cream makes a good dessert.

*1½ pounds boneless beef chuck,
     cubed*
2 veal kidneys
¼ cup all-purpose flour
*2 envelopes or teaspoons instant
     beef broth*
2 cups boiling water
*1 tablespoon Worcestershire
     sauce*
*6 medium-size potatoes, pared
     and thinly sliced*
3 large onions, sliced
2 teaspoons salt
¼ teaspoon pepper
*2 tablespoons butter or
     margarine*

ELECTRIC FRYPAN VEAL AND DILL

Cook on "simmer" for **8** *hours.*
Makes 6 servings.

You can use your electric frypan instead of a slow cooker if you follow the cooking directions below.

1. Find "simmer" on your electric frypan by pouring 2 cups cold water into frypan and turn heat control to about 200°. (If there is no marking for 200°, try some place between the lowest setting on the control and the first temperature marking.) Allow water to heat until tiny pin-point bubbles begin to form on the bottom of the frypan. This is the simmer point. If water begins to boil, then lower temperature control, just a little. You want the pin-point bubbles, but not the rolling boil. Pour out water, and mark the simmer spot on heat control with red paint or nail polish.

2. Place veal, potatoes, onions, zucchini, water, instant chicken broth, salt and dillweed in electric frypan; stir to blend well. (Don't worry that the water level is so low; the steam will baste the food.) Cover with frypan dome, being sure that the vents are closed.

3. Turn heat control to "simmer" and cook 8 hours, or until veal and vegetables are tender.

4. Turn heat control to 250° and add mushrooms; cook 5 minutes. Combine flour and cold water in a cup; stir into liquid in frypan; cover; cook 15 minutes.

COOK'S TIP: Recipes that have been tested on a higher setting (250°) of the electric frypan cook much more quickly than on the setting (290° to 300°) of the slow cooker. So it is wisest to follow only the "simmer" setting on the electric frypan for the low setting of the slow cooker recipes in this section.

1½ pounds boneless veal shoulder, cubed
6 medium-size boiling potatoes, pared and quartered
12 small white onions, peeled
6 small zucchini, cut into 1-inch pieces
1½ cups water
2 envelopes or teaspoons instant chicken broth
2 teaspoons salt
1 teaspoon dillweed
½ pound mushrooms, quartered OR: 1 can (3 or 4 ounces) sliced mushrooms
¼ cup all-purpose flour
½ cup cold water

the frypan crockery insert

This is the special crockery insert that comes with an electric frypan. As it is made of crockery, it should be treated with the same care as other crockery slow cookers. A few other points should be noted:
• Set the frypan heat control to 280° to 300°. Follow cooking times for low (190° to 200°) directions in these recipes. (Do not set the frypan heat control below 280°, or the internal temperature of the food will not reach the 180° necessary for cooking raw food safely.)
• Use pot holders when removing the crockery insert from frypan before serving and place on a heat-proof pad before setting on table.

ELDORADO LAMB PILAF

Cook on 190° to 200° for **8** hours, or on 290° to 300° for **4** hours.
Makes 6 servings.

Try lamb made with bulgur wheat and rice, Conquistador-style.

1. Brown lamb in an 8-cup flame-proof casserole or a large skillet; break into chunks; remove with a slotted spoon; reserve. Pour off all but 3 tablespoons of the pan drippings.
2. Sauté onion and garlic in drippings until soft; stir in curry powder and rosemary; cook 2 minutes; add instant chicken broth, salt and water. Bring to boiling; stir in bulgur wheat and rice. Spoon mixture into slow cooker; cover.
3. Cook on low (190° to 200°) 8 hours, stirring after 4 hours, if possible, or on high (290° to 300°) 4 hours, stirring after 3 hours, if possible, or until liquid is absorbed and rice is tender. Sprinkle with chopped mint or parsley, just before serving.

1 pound ground lamb
1 large onion, chopped (1 cup)
1 clove garlic, minced
1 teaspoon curry powder
1 teaspoon leaf rosemary, crumbled
2 envelopes or teaspoons instant chicken broth
2 teaspoons salt
4 cups water
1 cup bulgur wheat (from a 1-pound package)
¾ cup uncooked long-grain rice
Chopped fresh mint or parsley

BURGER BURGOO

Cook on 190° to 200° for **8** hours, or on 290° to 300° for **4** hours.
Makes 6 servings.

Meat and rice simmer in an herbed tomato sauce. Easy, yet delicious.

1. Shape ground beef into large patty; brown in a large skillet or an electric slow cooker with a browning unit 5 minutes on each side, then break up into chunks. Push to one side.
2. Add onion, celery and garlic; sauté 5 minutes, or until soft.
3. Stir in sugar, basil, salt, pepper, bay leaf, vegetable juice and rice; bring to boiling; remove from heat.
4. Place mixture in slow cooker; cover.
5. Cook on low (190° to 200°) 8 hours, or on high (290° to 300°) 4 hours, or until liquid is absorbed and rice is very tender.

2 pounds ground beef
1 large onion, chopped (1 cup)
1 cup sliced celery
1 clove garlic, minced
1 tablespoon sugar
1 tablespoon leaf basil, crumbled
2 teaspoons salt
⅛ teaspoon pepper
1 bay leaf
1 can (46 ounces) mixed vegetable juice
1 cup uncooked rice

STUFFED BEEF ROLL

*Cook on 190° to 200° for **10** hours,*
*or on 290° to 300° for **5** hours.*
Makes 6 servings.

With its herb stuffing, each slice looks like a giant pin-wheel.

1. Ask your meatman to split flank steak, butterfly fashion. Or you can do it yourself with a sharp long-blade knife. Work slowly, cutting with a sawing motion, as evenly as possible.
2. Sauté ¼ cup onion in butter or margarine just until soft in medium-size saucepan. Stir in bread stuffing, parsley, Parmesan cheese, garlic salt and water; toss with fork until moist and well-mixed.
3. Lay steak flat on counter top; spread stuffing over steak to within 1 inch of edges. Starting at one end, roll up, jelly-roll style; fasten with 2 or 3 wooden picks. Fold up ends of roll to hold in stuffing; fasten with more wooden picks.
4. Rub roll well with flour; brown in vegetable oil in heavy kettle or electric slow cooker with a browning unit.
5. Stir in saved 1¼ cups onion; sauté just until soft. Stir in spaghetti-sauce mix, tomatoes, and mushrooms and liquid; combine beef and sauce in slow cooker; cover.
6. Cook on low (190° to 200°) 10 hours or on high (290° to 300°) 5 hours.
7. Remove roll to carving board; take out wooden picks. Carve meat in ½-inch-thick slices. Serve sauce with meat roll.

1 flank steak (1½ to 2 pounds)
3 medium-size onions, chopped (1½ cups)
¼ cup (½ stick) butter or margarine
2 cups ready-mix bread stuffing (half an 8-ounce package)
¼ cup chopped parsley
2 tablespoons grated Parmesan cheese
½ teaspoon garlic salt
½ cup water
¼ cup all-purpose flour
¼ cup vegetable oil
1 envelope (1½ ounces) spaghetti-sauce mix
1 can (about 2 pounds) Italian tomatoes
1 can (3 or 4 ounces) mushroom stems and pieces

freezer tips

- Keep freezer door closed tightly—if freezer is fully stocked, the contents will stay frozen for at least two days; if it is half-full, the food will stay frozen for about one day.
- For periods longer than a day or two, buy dry ice—25 pounds for each cubic foot of freezer space—and place large chunks (with gloved hands) on top of the food. If the freezer is fully stocked, the dry ice will keep the food frozen three to four days; in a half-filled freezer, the dry ice will keep the food frozen up to two to three days.
- If uncooked foods have thawed, cook, then safely refreeze. Any cooked foods should be heated and eaten.

EL RANCHO ROAST

Cook on 190° to 200° for **10** hours,
or on 290° to 300° for **6** hours.
Makes 8 servings.

Ripe olives and cinnamon give this roast its tantalizing flavor.

1. Trim excess fat from beef; brown meat in a large skillet or an electric slow cooker with a browning unit.
2. Place beef in slow cooker. Combine tomato paste, olives, water, lemon juice, sugar, salt, cinnamon and pepper in a small bowl; pour over meat; cover.
3. Cook on low (190° to 200°) 10 hours, or on high (290° to 300°) 6 hours, or until beef is tender when pierced with a two-tined fork. Remove beef to a heated platter and keep warm.
4. Turn heat control to high (290° to 300°). Combine flour and ⅓ cup cold water in a cup; stir into liquid until well-blended; cover; simmer 15 minutes. Slice meat; serve with gravy.

Suggested Variations: Use a boned and rolled lamb shoulder or shank-half of a leg of lamb for the beef. Serve with saffron rice, if you wish.

1 round, rump, sirloin tip or
    boneless chuck roast (about 4
    pounds)
1 can (6 ounces) tomato paste
1 cup sliced pitted ripe olives
¼ cup water
2 tablespoons lemon juice
1 tablespoon sugar
2 teaspoons salt
1 teaspoon ground cinnamon
½ teaspoon pepper
3 tablespoons all-purpose flour

PARTY RAGOÛT

Cook on 190° to 200° for **10** hours,
or on 290° to 300° for **5** hours.
Makes 8 servings.

No need to brown the meats for this party-size lamb and veal dish.

1. Combine meats with potatoes, onion, lettuce, salt, pepper and rosemary in a 5-quart slow cooker.
2. Dissolve instant chicken broth in hot water in 4-cup measure; pour over meats and vegetables; cover.
3. Cook on low (190° to 200°) 10 hours, or on high (290° to 300°) 5 hours; remove meats and vegetables with a slotted spoon to the center of a heated serving platter; arrange cooked peas and squash in piles; keep warm while making sauce.
4. Strain juices in slow cooker into a large saucepan; bring to boiling. Combine cornstarch and ¾ cup water in a cup; stir in bubbling liquid; cook, stirring constantly, until mixture thickens and bubbles 1 minute; spoon over platter.

2 pounds lean boneless lamb
    shoulder, cubed
18 small new potatoes, pared
1 Bermuda onion, sliced thin
4 cups shredded lettuce
1 tablespoon salt
¼ teaspoon pepper
1 teaspoon leaf rosemary, crumbled
3 envelopes instant chicken broth
4 cups hot water
3 cups frozen peas, cooked (from
    a 1½-pound bag)
4 medium-size yellow squash,
    tipped, sliced and cooked
⅓ cup cornstarch
¾ cup water

LAREDO BARBECUED POT ROAST

Cook on 190° to 200° for **10** hours, or on 290° to 300° for **6** hours.
Makes 8 servings.

Try the rich flavor of barbecued beef, Texas-style, with a crown of Cornmeal Dumplings.

1. Trim excess fat from beef; brown in a large skillet or an electric slow cooker with a browning unit; remove and reserve. Sauté onion and garlic until soft in pan drippings.
2. Place pot roast in slow cooker with onion and garlic. Combine tomato sauce, brown sugar, vinegar, mustard, Worcestershire sauce, salt, Italian herbs and pepper in a small bowl; pour over beef; cover.
3. Cook on low (190° to 200°) 10 hours, or on high (290° to 300°) 6 hours, or until beef is tender when pierced with a two-tined fork. Remove beef to a heated platter and keep warm.
4. Turn heat control to high (290° to 300°) while making dumplings.
5. Drop CORNMEAL DUMPLINGS into cooker by tablespoons; cover. Cook without peeking 30 minutes. Carve beef into thin slices and serve with sauce and dumplings from slow cooker.

CORNMEAL DUMPLINGS—Combine ⅔ cup milk and 2 tablespoons vegetable oil in a medium-size bowl. Sift ¾ cup sifted all-purpose flour, ½ cup yellow cornmeal, 2 teaspoons baking powder and 1 teaspoon salt over. Stir just until mixture is moist. (Dough will be soft.) Drop onto hot food in slow cooker. Cook on high (290° to 300°) 30 minutes, or until puffy light. (No peeking, or the dumplings won't puff up.)

1 cross rib beef pot roast, (about 3 pounds)
1 large onion, chopped (1 cup)
1 clove garlic, minced
1 can (8 ounces) tomato sauce
¼ cup firmly packed brown sugar
3 tablespoons cider vinegar
1 tablespoon prepared mustard
1 tablespoon Worcestershire sauce
2 teaspoons salt
1 teaspoon mixed Italian herbs, crumbled
¼ teaspoon pepper
Cornmeal Dumplings (recipe follows)

guides for cooking with herbs

- Keep herbs and spices in alphabetical order on the spice shelf and you will always be able to find them quickly.
- Use a new herb by itself the first few times you cook with it. Then you will learn how pungent it is, and how it blends with other foods.
- Give herbs time to season foods. If the cooking time is short, let the herb soak in part of the cooking liquid while preparing other ingredients.
- To determine the strength of an herb, crush a bit of it in the palm of your hand and sniff its aroma.

LIVER RAGOÛT

Cook on 190° to 200° for **8** hours, or on 290° to 300° for **4** hours. Makes 6 servings.

Here's an unusually good way to prepare beef liver. Economical, too.

1. Brown the whole piece of liver slowly in oil in a large skillet or an electric slow cooker with a browning unit; remove and reserve. Stir in water and seasoning mix; bring to boiling.
2. Place liver with carrots and onions in slow cooker; pour hot liquid over; cover.
3. Cook on low (190° to 200°) 8 hours, or on high (290° to 300°) 4 hours, or until liver is tender when pierced with a two-tined fork.
4. Remove liver to a serving platter; arrange vegetables in mounds around edge; sprinkle with chopped parsley. Serve gravy separately.

1½ pounds unsliced beef liver
2 tablespoons vegetable oil
1½ cups water
1 envelope (about 1½ ounces) beef-stew seasoning mix
1 bag (1 pound) frozen whole carrots
1 can (1 pound) small boiled onions, drained
Chopped parsley

LOUISIANA HOT POT

Cook on 190° to 200° for **8** hours, or on 290° to 300° for **4** hours. Makes 8 servings.

One pot cooking takes on a Southern flavor with ham and sweet potatoes in a mild curry broth.

1. Trim excess fat from ham. Shake cubes, part at a time, with flour in a plastic bag to coat well.
2. Mix salt, curry powder and pepper in a cup until well-blended.
3. Layer vegetables and meat into an electric slow cooker this way: Half each of sweet potatoes, onions, ham, peas and olives, sprinkling each layer lightly with seasoning mixture. Repeat with remaining vegetables, ham and seasoning.
4. Pour boiling water over; dot with butter or margarine; cover.
5. Cook on low (190° to 200°) 8 hours, or on high (290° to 300°) 4 hours, or until meat and vegetables are tender.

1 can (2 pounds) ham, cubed
¼ cup all-purpose flour
2 teaspoons salt
1 teaspoon curry powder
¼ teaspoon pepper
6 medium-size sweet potatoes, pared and cut into ¼-inch thick slices
2 medium-size onions, sliced
1 package (10 ounces) frozen green peas, thawed
¼ cup sliced stuffed olives
2 cups boiling water
2 tablespoons butter or margarine

Cook on 190° to 200°
for **10** to **12** hours.
Makes 6 servings.

CHOLENT

This is a traditional Sabbath dish in Jewish house-holds.

1. Pick over lima beans; rinse under running cold water; place in a glass bowl; cover with cold water; cover bowl with plastic wrap; let soak overnight at room temperature; drain.
2. Trim excess fat from brisket; brown in oil in a large skillet or an electric slow cooker with a browning unit; remove and reserve. Sauté onion and garlic until soft in pan drippings.
3. Arrange brisket, onions and garlic in slow cooker; add drained lima beans, barley or kasha, marrow bone, salt, pepper and bay leaf; add water just to cover surface of food; cover.
4. Cook on low (190° to 200°) 10 to 12 hours, or until brisket is tender; taste and season with salt and pepper if you wish.

Suggested Variations: Orthodox Jewish housewives couldn't turn the stove on or off on the Sabbath, so many of them prepared dishes to cook in a pre-heated oven overnight. Seasonings vary with the country. Many cooks use paprika, ginger, allspice berries, or a little brown sugar. A split calve's foot is often substituted for the marrow bone. A rich dumpling (Kreaidel) is often cooked with the CHOLENT.

1 cup dried lima beans (from a 1-pound package)
Water
1 beef brisket (about 3 pounds)
2 tablespoons vegetable oil
2 large onions, sliced
1 clove garlic, minced (optional)
1 cup barley or kasha
1 marrow bone
2 teaspoons salt
¼ teaspoon pepper
1 bay leaf

hamburger tips

• Meat balls will be even size if you pat meat into a rectangle about an inch thick, then divide it: first in half, then quarters, eighths, and sixteenths, depending on what size ball you want.

• When buying ground meat for hamburgers, meatballs or for meat loaves, buy the lean ground round. It's more expensive than regular hamburger, true, but it has only 612 calories per pound versus 1600 (regular hamburger is about 30 percent fat). To break that down into ¼-pound servings, lean ground round runs about 150 calories per portion; regular hamburger, 400.

PRESCOTT BEEF BURGOO

Cook on 190° to 200° for **8** hours, or on 290° to 300° for **4** hours.
Makes 8 servings.

Ground beef, rice and vegetables bubble away all day in this Arizona-style dish.

1. Shape meat into a large patty in a large skillet or an electric slow cooker with a browning unit; brown 5 minutes on each side, then break up into chunks. Push to one side.
2. Add onion and garlic; sauté 5 minutes, or until soft. Stir in chili powder and cook 2 minutes. Add salt, pepper and tomato juice; bring to boiling.
3. Layer ⅓ each of the cabbage, rice, green beans and meat mixture into slow cooker; repeat to make 2 more layers of each; cover cooker.
4. Cook on low (190° to 200°) 8 hours, or on high (290° to 300°) 4 hours, or until vegetables are tender. Serve with chunks of corn bread and a crisp green salad.

2 pounds ground beef
1 large onion, chopped (1 cup)
1 clove garlic, minced
1 to 3 tablespoons chili powder
1 tablespoon salt
¼ teaspoon pepper
1 can (46 ounces) tomato juice
4 cups shredded cabbage
1 cup uncooked rice
½ pound green beans, tipped and cut up

DODGE CITY SHORT RIBS

Cook on 190° to 200° for **10** hours, or on 290° to 300° for **5** hours.
Makes 6 servings.

Hefty chunks of beef simmer in a pungent sauce with lots of vegetables.

1. Trim excess fat from short ribs; brown, a few at a time, in their own fat in large skillet or an electric slow cooker with a browning unit; remove and reserve. Stir onions into pan drippings; sauté until golden. Add tomatoes, cloves, bay leaf, mustard and salt.
2. Place short ribs with tomato mixture in slow cooker; add turnip, potatoes and peas; cover.
3. Cook on low (190° to 200°) 10 hours, or on high (290° to 300°) 5 hours, or until short ribs are tender. Unplug slow cooker; remove cover; let fat rise to surface and skim off. Serve ribs with chunks of sour dough bread and canned pears topped with chocolate sauce.

3 pounds short ribs, cut-up
1 large onion, chopped (1 cup)
1 can (1 pound, 4 ounces) tomatoes
3 whole cloves
1 bay leaf
1 teaspoon dry mustard
1 teaspoon salt
1 small yellow turnip, pared and cubed
3 large potatoes, pared and quartered
1 package (10 ounces) frozen peas, thawed

41

CATTLEMAN'S BEEF AND BEANS

*Cook on 290° to 300° for **2** hours, then on 190° to 200° for **8** hours.*
Makes 8 servings.

Since the days of the cowboys in the Golden West, kettles of beef and richly flavored beans have been he-man food.

1. Rinse beans under running water; place in a large kettle with water; bring to boiling; cover kettle; lower heat; cook 15 minutes; let stand 1 hour.
2. Trim all excess fat from beef; brown meat on all sides in remaining fat in a large skillet or an electric slow cooker with a browning unit.
3. Place meat in the bottom of slow cooker; add beans and liquid, onion, molasses, salt, ginger, mustard, pepper and bay leaf. Add more water, if needed, to cover meat and beans; cover.
4. Cook on high (290° to 300°) 2 hours; stir beans, adding more liquid, if needed, to keep beans and meat covered.
5. Turn heat control to low (190° to 200°) and cook for 8 hours, or until beans are very tender and liquid is absorbed. Taste and season with a spoonful of hot prepared mustard, if you wish.
6. Remove meat to a carving board and cut into slices; spoon beans around beef on a platter; serve with crusty bread.

1 package (1 pound) dried pinto, small lima or pea beans
6 cups water
1 boneless beef brisket or round roast (about 3 pounds)
1 large onion, chopped (1 cup)
⅓ cup dark molasses
2 teaspoons salt
½ teaspoon ground ginger
½ teaspoon dry mustard
¼ teaspoon pepper
1 bay leaf

some meat-stretching secrets

Nothing stretches the food budget more effectively than making a little meat go a long way. Here are some sure-fire ways to do it:
• Put potatoes, pasta, legumes and whole grains to good use. They're budget priced, nutritious and pair happily with most cuts of meat.
• Scrutinize your favorite main dish recipes. Can you reduce the quantity of meat in them? *Slightly?* Chances are you can, cutting costs but not the quality.
• Substitute meat drippings, rendered chicken fat for the more expensive butter and margarine. They've excellent flavor (*except* for lamb and mutton drippings, which are both strong-flavored and difficult to digest).
• Bolster meat-stretched recipes with sensational salads or vegetables. And accompany with husky peasant breads.

BURGUNDY MEAT LOAF

Cook on 290° to 300° for **1** hour, then on 190° to 200° for **4** hours.
Makes 6 servings.

Try our trick with foil for the easy removal of any meat loaf from your deep slow cooker.

1. Combine meatloaf mixture, onion, eggs, bread crumbs, parsley, wine, basil, salt and pepper in a large bowl; mix.
2. Crisscross 3 bacon slices on a 12-inch square of aluminum foil; shape meatloaf mixture into a 6-inch round on top of bacon. Top with remaining bacon slices, halved, and bay leaf. Lift foil with loaf into an electric slow cooker; cover.
3. Cook on high (290° to 300°) 1 hour; turn heat control to low (190° to 200°); cook 4 hours longer, or until meatloaf is well-done.
4. Remove loaf from slow cooker by lifting the foil "ears" as easy-lift handles, tilting fat back into slow cooker. Discard bacon and bay leaf.
5. Serve on heated platter and spoon part of the heated tomato sauce over. Great with buttered noodles and Frenched green beans, if you wish. Beef broth or tomato juice may be substituted for the Burgundy.

2 pounds ground meatloaf
 mixture
1 small onion, chopped (¼ cup)
2 eggs
1 cup soft white bread crumbs
 (2 slices)
½ cup chopped parsley
½ cup dry red Burgundy wine
1 tablespoon finely chopped
 fresh basil
 OR: 1 teaspoon leaf basil,
 crumbled
1½ teaspoons salt
¼ teaspoon freshly ground
 pepper
5 slices bacon
1 bay leaf
1 can (8 ounces) tomato sauce
 with mushrooms, heated

ONION PORK SAUTÉ

Cook on 190° to 200° **6** hours, or on 290° to 300° **3** hours.
Makes 6 servings.

An easy recipe for lazy days.

1. Brown chops in a large skillet or electric slow cooker with a browning unit. Arrange, overlapping in slow cooker; top each with a slice of onion. Dissolve instant beef broth in hot water in a 1-cup measure; pour over the chops; cover.
2. Cook on low (190° to 200°) 6 hours, or on high (290° to 300°) 3 hours, or until chops are tender. Remove with onions and keep hot. Sprinkle onions with paprika, if you wish.
3. Stir evaporated milk into drippings in slow cooker. Turn heat control to high (290° to 300°). Heat, stirring several times for 15 minutes: Serve in separate bowl to spoon over the chops.

6 rib pork chops, cut ½-inch thick
1 large onion, cut in 6 slices
1 envelope or teaspoon instant
 beef broth
½ cup hot water
½ cup evaporated milk

COUNTRY LAMB DINNER

Meaty shanks, five vegetables, and zippy gravy make this inviting platter meal.

1. Brown lamb shanks in a kettle or electric slow cooker with a browning unit. Push to one side. Stir garlic into drippings and sauté until soft.
2. Stir in water, salt, and oregano. Combine with lamb shanks in slow cooker with potatoes, onions. Cover cooker.
3. Cook on low (190° to 200°) 8 hours, or on high (290° to 300°) 4 hours.
4. Lift lamb shanks and vegetables from cooker with a slotted spoon and arrange with cabbage and beets on a heated large serving platter; sprinkle potatoes with paprika, if you wish. Keep hot while making gravy.

HORSERADISH GRAVY— Makes about 1¾ cups.
Strain broth from slow cooker into a 2-cup measure; add water, if needed, to make 1½ cups. Melt 2 table-spoons butter or margarine in a small saucepan; stir in 2 tablespoons flour, 1 teaspoon dillweed, and ½ tea-spoon salt; cook, stirring constantly, just until bubbly. Stir in 1½ cups broth; continue cooking and stirring until gravy thickens and boils 3 minutes. Stir in 1 tablespoon prepared horseradish and a few drops bottled gravy coloring to darken, if you wish.

4 lamb shanks, (about 3 pounds)
1 clove garlic, minced
4 cups water
2 teaspoons salt
1 teaspoon leaf oregano, crumbled
4 medium-size potatoes, pared
8 small onions, peeled
6 medium-size carrots, pared and
    quartered lengthwise
1 small head cabbage, cored,
    quartered, cooked
1 can (1 pound) sliced beets, heated
    Horseradish Gravy (recipe
    follows)

how to store ground meat

- To use the same day or the next: Tear off a corner of the transparent covering to expose the meat to the air, or remove wrapper entirely and rewrap meat loosely in wax paper or foil. Store in the meat-keeper or coldest part of your refrigerator.
- To freeze ground meat for patties: Shape meat lightly into patties, preferably plain, as seasoning flavors tend to build during freezing. Wrap patties in freezer paper, foil, transparent wrap or bags and seal tightly. For single servings, wrap each patty separately. For family servings, stack three, four, or more patties with double-thick wax paper or foil between, then wrap and seal. Come cooking time, patties are easy to separate.

BEEF BARBECUE

Cook on 190° to 200° for **8** hours,
or on 290° to 300° for **4** hours.
Makes 12 servings.

Use the 5-quart slow cooker to make this party-size recipe.

1. Mix ground beef and sausage meat in a bowl; shape into 2 large patties. Brown, 1 at a time, 5 minutes on each side in a large kettle or 5-quart electric slow cooker with a browning unit. Remove and reserve.
2. Pour off all but 2 tablespoonfuls of the drippings. Add onions and garlic; sauté just until soft. Stir in celery and green pepper; continue cooking just until celery is soft, then stir in chili powder; cook 2 minutes longer.
3. Combine meat, broken into chunks, and sautéed vegetables in a 5-quart slow cooker. Stir in catsup, brown sugar, mustard, salt, paprika, pepper, water, vinegar and Worcestershire sauce; stir until well-blended; cover.
4. Cook on low (190° to 200°) 8 hours, stirring after 4 hours, if possible, or on high (290° to 300°) 4 hours, stirring after 2 hours, if possible. Spoon over your choice of hot corn bread squares, rice, toast or tamales, if you wish.

3 pounds ground chuck
1 pound bulk sausage meat
2 large onions, chopped (2 cups)
1 clove garlic, minced
2 cups chopped celery
1 small green pepper, halved, seeded and chopped
2 to 4 teaspoons chili powder
1 bottle (14 ounces) catsup
2 tablespoons brown sugar
1 tablespoon dry mustard
1 tablespoon salt
2 teaspoons paprika
½ teaspoon pepper
3½ cups water
¼ cup cider vinegar
2 tablespoons Worcestershire sauce

SAUCY MEATBALLS

Cook on 190° to 200° for **8** hours,
or on 290° to 300° for **4** hours.
Makes 8 servings.

Everyone loves meatballs and these are extra moist and flavorful.

1. Mix ground beef and sausage meat lightly with applesauce, bread crumbs, prunes, salt and pepper until well-blended; shape into 24 balls.
2. Place in an electric slow cooker; blend soup and water in a 2-cup measure; pour over meatballs; cover.
3. Cook on low (190° to 200°) 8 hours, or on high (290° to 300°) 4 hours. Serve with thin spaghetti and a crisp salad.

1½ pounds ground chuck
½ pound bulk sausage meat
1 jar (8 ounces) junior applesauce (baby-pack)
1 cup soft whole-wheat bread crumbs (2 slices)
8 prunes, pitted and chopped
1 teaspoon salt
¼ teaspoon pepper
1 can condensed tomato soup
¼ cup water

LAMB SHANKS AND VEGETABLES

*Cook on 190° to 200° for **8** hours, or on 290° to 300° for **4** hours.*
Makes 4 servings.

Dried rosemary leaves give lamb an especially lovely flavor and slow cooking develops that flavor.

1. Trim excess fat from lamb shanks. Shake in a plastic bag with flour, 1 teaspoon of the salt and pepper.
2. Brown in oil on all sides in a large skillet or an electric slow cooker with a browning unit.
3. Place lamb shanks in slow cooker; arrange onions and carrots around meat; add chicken broth, wine or water, garlic, rosemary, thyme and celery powder; cover cooker.
4. Cook on low (190° to 200°) 8 hours, or on high (290° to 300°) 4 hours, or until lamb shanks are tender when pierced with a two-tined fork. Remove shanks and vegetables to a heated serving platter and keep warm.
5. Turn heat control to high (290° to 300°). Pour liquid from cooker into a 2-cup measure; let fat rise to the top; skim off; return liquid to cooker. Combine 2 tablespoons flour and ¼ cup cold water in a cup; stir into liquid until well-blended; flavor with a few drops bottled gravy coloring; cover; cook 15 minutes. Spoon over shanks and serve with wheat pilaf, if you wish.

4 lamb shanks (about 3 pounds)
¼ cup all-purpose flour
2 teaspoons salt
¼ teaspoon pepper
3 tablespoons vegetable oil
4 medium-size onions, peeled and halved
4 large carrots, pared and cut in 1-inch pieces
½ cup chicken broth
½ cup dry white wine or water
1 clove garlic, minced
½ teaspoon leaf rosemary, crumbled
¼ teaspoon leaf thyme, crumbled
⅛ teaspoon celery powder

for crockery cookers

Here's a kitchen formula for removing stains that may build up on the surface of a crockery slow cooker:

1 cup water
½ cup chlorine bleach
2 tablespoons baking soda

Pour mixture into slow cooker and wipe well over stained area. Cover cooker. Set heat control to high (290° to 300°) for 2 hours. Wash to sudsy hot water, rinse well and wipe with a towel.

SANTA CLARA PORK POT

Cook on 190° to 200° for **10** hours, or on 290° to 300° for **5** hours.
Makes 6 servings.

Dried apricots and prunes cook along with the pork in this hearty dish.

1. Trim excess fat from pork; brown on all sides in a large skillet or an electric slow cooker with a browning unit; sprinkle with salt, ginger, pepper and mustard to coat well.
2. Meanwhile, remove the thin, bright-colored rind from the orange and lemon with a sharp knife; reserve. Squeeze juice from orange and lemon into a 1-cup measure; add water to fruit juices to make 1 cup liquid.
3. Place pork in slow cooker with rinds and juices and corn syrup; add onions and cover cooker.
4. Cook on low (190° to 200°) 10 hours, or on high (290° to 300°) 5 hours; add apricots and prunes.
5. Turn heat control to high (290° to 300°). Simmer 15 minutes. Combine cornstarch and ¼ cup cold water in a cup; stir into liquid in slow cooker until well-blended. Cover; cook 15 minutes longer. Serve with boiled potatoes and cold beer, if you wish.

1 rib-end pork loin (about 3 pounds)
2 teaspoons salt
½ teaspoon ground ginger
¼ teaspoon pepper
¼ teaspoon dry mustard
1 large orange
1 lemon
Water
2 tablespoons dark corn syrup
1 pound small white onions, peeled
1 cup dried apricots
1 cup dried pitted prunes
2 tablespoons cornstarch

SPICY LAMB

Cook on 190° to 200° for **8** hours, or on 290° to 300° for **4** hours.
Makes 6 servings.

An unusual combination of flavors makes this an interesting, hearty dish.

1. Cut meat into 2-inch strips. Sauté in butter or margarine until brown in a large skillet or electric slow cooker with a browning unit; remove and reserve.
2. Sauté the onion and garlic in the remaining fat until soft. Stir in the flour, water, beef broth, cinnamon, ginger, cardamom, raisins, salt and pepper.
3. Combine lamb and sauce in a slow cooker; add squash and lemon juice; cover.
4. Cook on low (190° to 200°) 8 hours, or on high (290° to 300°) 4 hours.

2 pounds lean boneless lamb
3 tablespoons butter or margarine
1 large onion, sliced
2 cloves of garlic, minced
2 tablespoons all-purpose flour
1½ cups water
2 envelopes instant beef broth
½ teaspoon ground cinnamon
½ teaspoon ground ginger
½ teaspoon ground cardamom
⅔ cup golden raisins
1 teaspoon salt
⅛ teaspoon pepper
3 small yellow squashes, cubed
¼ cup lemon juice

NANTUCKET PORK PLATTER

Smoked pork boneless butt or cottage roll simmers with winter vegetables for a new twist on New England Boiled Dinner.

1. Place meat, potatoes, Brussel sprouts, carrots, onion, cloves and bay leaf in an electric slow cooker; pour water over; cover.
2. Cook on low (190° to 200°) 10 hours, or on high (290° to 300°) 5 hours, or until meat and vegetables are tender when pierced with a two-tined fork.
3. Lift meat from broth, saving 1 cup of the broth; place meat on a heated serving platter. Arrange vegetables around edge; keep hot while making sauce. An apple cobbler with pour cream would make a perfect ending to this Yankee meal.

RAISIN SAUCE— Makes 1½ cups. Combine 3 tablespoons brown sugar, 1 tablespoon cornstarch, ⅛ teaspoon cinnamon, and ⅛ teaspoon ground allspice in a small saucepan; stir in the 1 cup saved broth, 1 tablespoon bottled lemon juice and ¼ cup raisins. Cook, stirring constantly, until sauce thickens and bubbles 1 minute; stir in 1 tablespoon butter or margarine until melted. Serve hot in heated gravy boat.

1 smoked boneless shoulder butt or cottage roll (about 2 pounds)
4 large boiling potatoes, pared and quartered
1 pound Brussel sprouts, washed and trimmed
OR: 1 package (10 ounces) frozen Brussel sprouts, thawed
6 medium-size carrots, pared and cut into 2-inch pieces
1 large onion, chopped (1 cup)
6 whole cloves
1 bay leaf
3 cups water
Raisin Sauce (recipe follows)

be a better shopper

- Learn to read labels. There are appreciable price differences between foods of identical quality in your supermarket. Compare ingredients in various packages. Experiment. Only after you have taken the time to compare ingredients, flavor and cost can you decide on the best buy in an informed way.
- Figure your meat costs on the price per cooked serving rather than the price per pound. To do this, simply divide the cost of the meat purchase by the number of cooked portions you'll get from the piece.

CASSOULET

Cook on 190° to 200° for **10** hours,
or on 290° to 300° for **5** hours.
Makes 6 servings.

*A classic lamb and dried bean dish from the Langue-
doc region of France.*

1. Pick over beans and rinse. Cover lima beans with
   water in a large kettle; bring to boiling; cover; cook 2
   minutes. Remove from heat; let stand 1 hour.
2. While beans cook, brown lamb in oil in an electric
   slow cooker with a browning unit, or a large skillet.
   Push to one side of pan and sauté onion and garlic
   lightly; stir in tomatoes and molasses; cover; simmer
   15 minutes.
3. Combine beans and liquid with lamb mixture in kettle;
   add salt, grated carrot and bacon (do not cut slices);
   cover; cook 1 hour, or until skins of beans burst when
   you blow on a few in a spoon; place in cooker; cover.
4. Cook on low (190° to 200°) 10 hours, or on high (290°
   to 300°) 5 hours, or until beans are tender. Serve with
   a platter of cold marinated vegetables and a fresh fruit
   dessert for a truly French meal.

1 package (1 pound) large dried
  lima beans
4 cups water
1 pound lean boneless lamb
  shoulder, cubed
2 tablespoons vegetable oil
1 large onion, chopped (1 cup)
1 clove garlic, minced
1 can (1 pound) tomatoes
¼ cup light molasses
2 teaspoons salt
1 cup grated raw carrot
4 slices bacon, diced

SACRAMENTO BEEF POT

Cook on 190° to 200° for **10** hours,
or on 290° to 300° for **5** hours.
Makes 8 servings.

Red wine gives beef a hearty flavor.

1. Trim all excess fat from meat. Brown beef in its own
   fat in a large skillet or an electric slow cooker with a
   browning unit; remove and set aside. Drain all but 2
   tablespoons fat from skillet. Sauté onion until soft in
   fat.
2. Place meat, sautéed onion, potatoes, zucchini, red
   pepper rings, wine or broth, salt, pepper and bay leaf
   in slow cooker; cover.
3. Cook on low (190° to 200°) 10 hours, or on high (290°
   to 300°) 5 hours, or until meat is tender when pierced
   with a two-tined fork. Place meat and vegetables on
   heated platter and keep warm.
4. Turn heat control to high (290° to 300°). Combine
   flour and water in a cup; pour into liquid in slow
   cooker; cover. Cook 15 minutes; pass sauce separately
   in heated gravy boat.

1 beef blade or round-bone chuck
  roast (about 4 pounds)
1 medium-size onion, sliced
6 medium-size potatoes, pared
  and halved
6 small zucchini, sliced
1 red pepper, sliced in rings
1 cup dry red wine or beef broth
2 teaspoons salt
¼ teaspoon pepper
1 bay leaf
3 tablespoons all-purpose flour
⅓ cup cold water

GLAZED STUFFED LAMB LOAF

*Cook on 290° to 300° for **1** hour, then on 190° to 200° for **4** hours.*
Makes 8 servings.

Buttery apricot stuffing swirls through a tender lamb loaf. Pungent mint jelly adds the sparkling glaze.

1. Sauté onion in butter or margarine until soft in a large skillet; stir in apricots, instant chicken broth, 1 teaspoon of the marjoram and water; heat to boiling.
2. Remove skillet from heat; stir in bread cubes until well blended; allow to cool while making meat mixture.
3. Combine lamb, egg, salt, remaining 1 teaspoon marjoram and pepper in a large bowl. Mix lightly until well blended.
4. Crisscross 3 bacon slices on a 12-inch square of aluminum foil; shape meat mixture into two 6-inch rounds. Spread onion mixture between the meat rounds, as filling. Top stuffed meat rounds with remaining bacon slices, halved. Lift foil with loaf into electric slow cooker; cover.
5. Cook on high (290° to 300°) 1 hour; turn heat control to low (190° to 200°); cook 4 hours longer, or until meatloaf is well done.
6. Melt jelly in a small saucepan; brush over meat roll. Cook 10 minutes longer, or until well glazed.
7. Remove loaf from slow cooker by lifting the foil "ears" as handles, tilting fat back into slow cooker. Discard bacon. Garnish with canned apricots and fresh mint, if you wish.

1 medium-size onion, chopped (½ cup)
¼ cup (½ stick) butter or margarine
½ cup chopped dried apricots
1 envelope or teaspoon instant chicken broth
2 teaspoons leaf marjoram, crumbled
¾ cup water
4 cups cubed soft white bread (8 slices)
2 pounds ground lean lamb
1 egg
1 teaspoon salt
¼ teaspoon pepper
5 slices bacon
¼ cup mint jelly

odds and ends for meat savers

- If tongue is a favorite at your house, you'll save by buying fresh tongue instead of smoked.
- Save on bacon by using ends and pieces, cuts or slab bacon instead of fancy-quality sliced bacon. Buy perfect slices only for "show."
- Buy bologna by the chunk and slice it yourself. You may save as much as 10¢ a pound.
- Take a good look at canned meats. Every ounce is edible, so cost per serving is significantly less than for home-cooked counterparts.

SOUTHAMPTON VEAL ROLL

Cook on 190° to 200° for **8** *hours,*
or on 290° to 300° for **4** *hours.*
Makes 8 servings.

An elegant choice when veal is on special at the market.

1. Trim excess fat from veal; rub well with mixture of flour, mustard, brown sugar, salt, poultry seasoning and pepper to coat evenly.
2. Brown meat slowly in oil in a large skillet or an electric slow cooker with a browning unit.
3. Place veal in slow cooker with onion, celery, parsley and wine or water; cover.
4. Cook on low (190° to 200°) 8 hours, or on high (290° to 300°) 4 hours, or until veal is tender when pierced with a two-tined fork; place on heated serving platter and keep warm.
5. Turn heat control to high (290° to 300°). Combine ¼ cup all-purpose flour and ½ cup cold water in a cup; stir into liquid in slow cooker; cover; cook 15 minutes. Stir in horseradish and serve in heated gravy boat. Serve veal with asparagus spears and potato balls.

1 rolled boned veal shoulder,
(about 3 to 4 pounds)
2 tablespoons all-purpose flour
1 tablespoon dry mustard
1 tablespoon brown sugar
2 teaspoons salt
1 teaspoon poultry seasoning
⅛ teaspoon pepper
2 tablespoons vegetable oil
1 large onion, chopped (1 cup)
¼ cup chopped celery
2 tablespoons chopped parsley
½ cup dry white wine or water
2 teaspoons prepared horseradish

BEEF AND SQUASH

Cook on 190° to 200° for **10** *hours,*
or on 290° to 300° for **5** *hours.*
Makes 8 servings.

An early American recipe combines vegetables and meat in a hearty main course.

1. Trim all fat from beef. Shake cubes, a few at a time, with flour in a paper bag to coat well.
2. Combine tomato juice, bouillon cubes and sugar in a small saucepan; heat, crushing cubes to dissolve, just to boiling.
3. Combine parsley, garlic, salt, pepper and nutmeg in a cup.
4. Layer vegetables and meat into a slow cooker this way: Half of each of potatoes, onions and beef, sprinkling each layer lightly with seasoning mixture. Repeat with remaining potatoes, onions, beef and seasoning mixture.
5. Cut each squash half into 6 slices; pare; arrange on top. Pour hot tomato-juice mixture over; dot with butter or margarine; cover.
6. Cook on low (190° to 200°) 10 hours, or on high (290° to 300°) 5 hours.

2 pounds beef chuck, cut in 1-inch
cubes
¼ cup all-purpose flour
1 cup tomato juice
2 beef bouillon cubes
1 tablespoon brown sugar
¼ cup finely chopped parsley
2 cloves of garlic, minced
1 tablespoon salt
¼ teaspoon pepper
¼ teaspoon ground nutmeg
4 medium-size potatoes, pared
and sliced thin (4 cups)
8 small onions, peeled and
quartered
1 acorn squash, split and seeded
2 tablespoons butter or margarine

BEEF BURGUNDY

This recipe takes a little time, but the resulting dish will make your reputation as a cook.

1. Cut bacon into 1-inch pieces; place in a saucepan; cover with water. Bring to boiling; lower heat and simmer 10 minutes. Dry bacon on paper towels. Fry bacon until crisp in a large skillet or an electric slow cooker with a browning unit. Remove bacon and reserve; pour off all but 2 tablespoons of the bacon fat into a cup.

2. Brown beef, a few pieces at a time, in fat; remove and reserve; Sauté onion, carrot, celery and garlic in pan drippings, adding more bacon fat, if needed; stir in salt, thyme, bay leaf and pepper.

3. Place beef in cooker with vegetable mixture; add wine; cover cooker.

4. Cook on low (190° to 200°) 8 hours, or on high (290° to 300°) 4 hours; remove bay leaf. Remove beef from liquid with slotted spoon; keep warm in a heated casserole.

5. Pour liquid, half at a time, into an electric blender container; add flour, half at a time; cover container; whirl at high speed 1 minute. (Or press liquid through a sieve with a wooden spoon into a bowl; cool slightly; stir in flour until well-blended.) Pour liquid into a large saucepan; bring to boiling. Cook, stirring constantly, until sauce thickens and bubbles 3 minutes longer.

6. One hour before serving, wipe mushrooms with damp paper towel; flute mushrooms by marking the center of each cap with a small, sharp paring knife. Starting there, make a curved cut, about ⅛-inch deep, to edge. Repeat around to make 8 even cuts. Now make a second cut just behind each line, angling knife so you can lift out a narrow strip; set mushrooms aside. Cut leeks into 5-inch pieces and halve; wash well to remove all sand; pare and cut carrots into 5-inch pieces.

7. Sauté mushrooms in butter or margarine in a large skillet; remove; sauté leeks lightly in skillet; remove; add carrots and sauté 5 minutes; add instant chicken broth and water to skillet; cover and simmer 15 minutes, or until carrots are almost tender; push to one

½ pound thickly sliced bacon
2 pounds lean boneless beef chuck, cubed
1 large onion, chopped (1 cup)
1 cup finely chopped carrot
1 cup finely chopped celery
2 cloves garlic, minced
2 teaspoons salt
1 teaspoon leaf thyme, crumbled
1 bay leaf
¼ teaspoon pepper
2 cups dry red wine
¼ cup all-purpose flour
1 pound mushrooms
1 bunch leeks
1 bunch carrots
¼ cup (½ stick) butter or margarine
1 envelope or teaspoon instant chicken broth
½ cup water

side. Return mushrooms and leeks to skillet. Cover; simmer 10 minutes, or until vegetables are tender.

8. Surround beef with vegetables; sprinkle beef with cooked bacon. Pour vegetable liquid in skillet into sauce, pour over beef and vegetables.

HOSTESS TIP: The finished dish can be held in a very slow oven (275°) for 1 hour before serving. Beef can be cooked and sauce made the day before. Cool, then cover and refrigerate. One hour before serving, place casserole in oven. Set oven control on moderate (350°) and bake 1 hour, or until bubbly-hot, while preparing vegetables.

ARIZONA MEAT AND BEANS

Cook on 190° to 200° for **10** *hours, or on 290° to 300° for* **6** *hours. Makes 8 servings.*

Use whatever cut of beef is on special. This is a delicious bean dish, simple and economical.

1. Pick over beans and rinse well. Combine beans and water in a large kettle. Bring to boiling; cover; cook 2 minutes. Remove from heat; let stand 1 hour; pour into an electric slow cooker. (Or soak beans in water in cooker overnight at room temperature.)

2. Brown salt pork in a large skillet; remove with a slotted spoon to cooker; sauté onion, garlic and green pepper in pan drippings; remove with slotted spoon to cooker. Brown beef, a few pieces at a time in pan drippings; remove to cooker with slotted spoon; stir in salt, oregano, red pepper, cumin and tomato sauce. (Add more water, if necessary, to bring liquid level above beans.) Cover.

3. Cook on low (190° to 200°) 10 hours, or on high (290° to 300°) 6 hours, or until beans are tender.

1 package (1 pound) dried navy, pinto or cranberry beans
6 cups water
¼ pound salt pork, diced
1 large onion, chopped (1 cup)
1 clove garlic, minced
1 large green pepper, halved, seeded and chopped
1½ pounds boneless chuck, cubed
1½ teaspoons salt
½ teaspoon leaf oregano, crumbled
¼ teaspoon crushed red pepper
¼ teaspoon ground cumin
1 can (8 ounces) tomato sauce

HERB STUFFED VEAL SHOULDER

Cook on 190° to 200° for **8** hours, or on 290° to 300° for **4** hours.

Makes 6 servings.

This makes an elegant dinner to have waiting for you after a busy day.

1. Untie veal; spread flat; sprinkle with ½ teaspoon of the salt and ⅛ teaspoon of the pepper.
2. Cook bacon until crisp in a small skillet; drain bacon on paper towels; reserve. Pour off drippings; return 1 tablespoon drippings to skillet. Add ¼ cup of the chopped onion; cook just until soft.
3. To make herb stuffing: Combine bread crumbs, parsley, pimiento, and tarragon in a medium-size bowl; toss lightly to mix; stir in reserved bacon and cooked onion.
4. Sprinkle stuffing mixture over veal; roll up tightly and re-tie. Brown veal on all sides in butter or margarine in a kettle or electric slow cooker with a browning unit; stir in celery, remaining onion, 1 cup water, and remaining salt and pepper; heat to boiling. Combine veal and sauce in slow cooker; cover.
5. Cook on low (190° to 200°) 8 hours, or on high (290° to 300°) 4 hours or until meat is tender. Remove meat to heated platter.
6. Strain veal stock from cooker into a 2-cup measure; add water, if necessary, to make 2 cups liquid.
7. Return liquid to slow cooker. Blend flour with ½ cup water until smooth; stir into liquid in slow cooker; cover. Turn heat control to high (290° to 300°); cook 15 minutes. Serve veal with gravy and cooked white beans.

1 shoulder of veal, boned and
   rolled in one piece, (about
   3 pounds)
1 teaspoon salt
¼ teaspoon pepper
2 slices bacon, diced
¾ cup chopped onion
1 cup fresh bread crumbs
   (about 2 slices)
¼ cup chopped parsley
¼ cup chopped pimiento
½ teaspoon leaf tarragon,
   crumbled
2 tablespoons butter or margarine
½ cup chopped celery
Water
¼ cup all-purpose flour
Cooked white kidney beans
   (cannellini)

new ways to save

• Consider cooking for two or more meals when you prepare a dish that requires long cooking, like stuffed cabbage, stew or even soups. You'll save on fuel, electricity and your precious time as well.

• Snack foods are costly, so change your children's snack habits. Offer them cottage cheese mixed with diced fruit, or a slice of American cheese with crackers, or fresh fruit. Your budget and their nutrition will benefit.

COLONIAL HOT POT

Cook on 190° to 200° for **8** hours, or on 290° to 300° for **4** hours.
Makes 8 servings.

The Indians introduced the first settlers to the wonders of squash. Since then, thrifty homemakers have added it to their hearty one pot meals.

1. Trim all excess fat from beef. Shake cubes, part at a time, with flour in a plastic bag to coat well.
2. Combine tomato juice and instant beef broth in a small saucepan; heat just to boiling; remove from heat.
3. Combine parsley, garlic, salt and pepper in a cup.
4. Layer vegetables and meat into an electric slow cooker this way: Half of each of potatoes, onions and beef, sprinkling each layer lightly with seasoning mixture. Repeat with remaining potatoes, onions, beef and seasoning.
5. Cut each squash half into 6 slices; pare; arrange on top. Pour hot tomato juice mixture over; dot with butter or margarine; cover.
6. Cook on low (190° to 200°) 8 hours, or on high (290° to 300°) 4 hours, or until meat and vegetables are tender.

2 pounds boneless chuck, cubed
¼ cup all-purpose flour
2 cups tomato juice
2 envelopes or teaspoons instant beef broth
¼ cup finely chopped parsley
2 cloves garlic, minced
1 tablespoon salt
¼ teaspoon pepper
4 medium-size potatoes, pared and thinly sliced
8 small yellow onions, peeled and quartered
1 acorn squash, split and seeded
2 tablespoons butter or margarine

PORK AND SWEET POTATOES

Cook on 190° to 200° for **6** hours, or on 290° to 300° for **3** hours.
Makes 6 servings.

A tasty dish that has its origins in southern country cooking.

1. Trim any excess fat from chops with sharp knife.
2. Heat large skillet or electric slow cooker with browning unit; rub with piece of cut-off fat; brown chops on both sides in pan; save.
3. Spread undrained sauerkraut in bottom of slow cooker; sprinkle with dry mustard and water.
4. Arrange sweet-potato slices around edge; place browned chops in center; sprinkle with salt and pepper.
5. Combine apricot jam and ginger; spread over sweet potatoes; cover cooker.
6. Cook on low (190° to 200°) 6 hours, or on high (290° to 300°) 3 hours, or until chops and potatoes are tender when tested with a fork.

6 loin, rib, or shoulder pork chops, cut ½-inch thick
2 cans (1 pound each) sauerkraut
⅛ teaspoon dry mustard
¼ cup water
6 medium-size sweet potatoes, pared and sliced lengthwise
½ teaspoon salt
⅛ teaspoon pepper
½ cup apricot jam
¼ teaspoon ginger

55

LAMB BURGUNDY

The French way of making lamb with wine is a special treat for family or friends.

1. Cut bacon into 1-inch pieces; place in a saucepan; cover with water. Bring to boiling; lower heat and simmer 10 minutes. Dry bacon on paper towels. Fry bacon until crisp in a large skillet or an electric slow cooker with a browning unit. Remove bacon and reserve; pour off all but 2 tablespoons of the bacon fat into a cup.
2. Brown lamb, a few pieces at a time in fat; remove and reserve. Sauté onion, carrot, celery and garlic in pan drippings, add more bacon fat, if needed; stir in salt, rosemary, bay leaf and pepper.
3. Place lamb in cooker with vegetable mixture; add wine; cover cooker.
4. Cook on low (190° to 200°) 8 hours; or on high (290° to 300°) 4 hours; remove bay leaf. Remove lamb from liquid with a slotted spoon; keep warm in a heated casserole.
5. Pour liquid, half at a time, with half of the flour into an electric blender container; whirl at high speed 1 minute. (Or press liquid through a sieve with a wooden spoon into a bowl; cool slightly; stir in flour until well blended.) Pour liquid into a large saucepan; bring to boiling. Cook, stirring constantly, until sauce thickens and bubbles 3 minutes longer.
6. Sauté green onions in butter or margarine in a large skillet two minutes; push to one side; add wax beans and asparagus in separate piles; add canned mushrooms; add instant chicken broth and water; cover; simmer 15 minutes, or until vegetables are tender.
7. Surround lamb with vegetables; sprinkle lamb with cooked bacon. Pour vegetable liquid into sauce, pour over lamb and vegetables.

½ pound thickly sliced bacon
2 pounds lamb shoulder, cubed
1 large onion, chopped (1 cup)
1 cup finely chopped carrots
1 cup finely chopped celery
2 cloves garlic, minced
2 teaspoons salt
1 teaspoon leaf rosemary, crumbled
1 bay leaf
¼ teaspoon pepper
2 cups dry red wine
¼ cup all-purpose flour
2 bunches green onions
2 tablespoons butter or margarine
1 can (6 ounces) sliced mushrooms
1 package (10 ounce) frozen wax beans
1 package (10 ounce) frozen asparagus spears
1 pound canned, sliced mushrooms
1 envelope or teaspoon instant chicken broth
½ cup water

time-savers for meat shoppers

Shop for a week's supply of meat at once. Trim all the meat before storing, then take care of the trimmings in one sweep—simmer them into soup or stock, or if they're nice and lean, grind for patties, meatballs or timbales.

A chunk of chicken
and tender vegetables turn
Maytime Chicken Breast Soup
into a meal in itself. Recipe
is on page 6.

Aromatic bitters and a lemon-butter glaze give a distinctive West Indian flavor to Caribbean Roast Chicken. Recipe on page 76.

to defrost frozen birds:

Take the bird out of the freezer a day or two ahead and put it in the refrigerator. Don't unwrap it, because the skin tends to dry and toughen when exposed to air. To defrost poultry faster, place it (still wrapped) under cold running water.

An old-fashioned favorite
can be made the new
slow cooker way. Our
recipe for Brunswick Stew
(page 86) blends chicken
with fresh corn and okra.

storage tip

Leave packaged corn in its wrapper
and chill in your vegetable
crisper. Husks still on? Bundle
ears—husks and all—into
a damp towel, then place in
the refrigerator until cooking time.
Whenever possible, cook
the corn the same day you buy it.

tips for frozen-food shoppers

Buy in quantity. Frozen vegetables
such as peas, corn, potatoes,
green beans and mixed vegetables,
packed in 1½- and 2-pound
plastic bags, are bargains, regardless
of the size of your family. Just
open the bag, take out what you need,
reclose and pop back into the freezer.

keeping color in

To help red cabbage keep its bright red color during cooking, add 1 to 2 tablespoons of lemon juice or of cider vinegar or a few slices of fresh apple.

A bouquet of buttered
braised vegetables surrounds
Beef à la Mode, a pot roast
simmered in wine that is
part of classic French
cuisine. Recipe on page 22.

WINE BRAISED OXTAILS

Cook on 290° to 300° for **2** hours,
then on 190° to 200° for **8** hours.
Makes 6 servings.

Great when the gravy is spooned over mountains of mashed potatoes.

1. Shake oxtails, a few pieces at a time, in a mixture of flour, salt and pepper in a plastic bag to coat well.
2. Brown in shortening in a large skillet or an electric slow cooker with a browning unit; remove and reserve.
3. Sauté onions, turnips, carrots, leek and parsley in pan drippings 5 minutes; season with allspice and thyme.
4. Combine oxtails and vegetables in slow cooker; pour beef broth and wine over; add bay leaf; cover.
5. Cook on high (290° to 300°) 2 hours. Turn heat control to low (190° to 200°) and cook for 8 hours, or until oxtails are so tender that meat falls from bones.
6. Unplug slow cooker and let mixture cool 5 minutes for fat to rise to the surface; skim off fat. Serve oxtails with a big bowl of mashed potatoes and a coleslaw and apple salad, if you wish.

3½ pounds oxtails, cut up
⅓ cup all-purpose flour
2 teaspoons salt
¼ teaspoon pepper
3 tablespoons vegetable shortening
12 small white onions, peeled
2 small white turnips, pared and cubed
2 large carrots, pared and sliced
1 large leek, washed and sliced
¼ cup chopped parsley
4 whole allspice
¼ teaspoon leaf thyme, crumbled
1 can condensed beef broth
1 cup dry red wine
1 bay leaf

COOK'S TIP: This recipe can be started the night before and slow cook while you sleep. In the morning, place in a refrigerator container and cover. Refrigerate until evening. Remove fat layer from oxtails and then heat in a large saucepan or place in an 8-cup casserole and bake in moderate oven (350°) for 1 hour, 15 minutes, until bubbly-hot.

entertaining with wine

Here is a guide to how many servings various bottles of wine will give you:
• A fifth bottle (the approximate amount of most bottles) of dry wine should give you about six servings.
• A bottle of sweet dessert wine should give you about eight servings, since people will drink less of it.
• Half a gallon of wine gives about 32 to 40 servings.
• How much wine to serve depends on the occasion and the people you are entertaining. You can figure, generally, on one bottle for every three guests.

SPICY GLAZED PORK CHOPS WITH APRICOTS

*Cook on 190° to 200° for **6** hours, or on 290° to 300° for **3** hours.*
Makes 6 servings.

Syrup from apricots gives chops and fruit a shiny coat and tart-sweet flavor.

1. Drain syrup from apricots into medium-size saucepan; stir in steak sauce, salt and cloves. Heat to boiling; cook, uncovered, 15 minutes, or until syrup thickens slightly.
2. Brush chops on both sides with half of syrup; arrange in slow cooker; top with apricots, pour remaining syrup over; cover cooker.
3. Cook on low (190° to 200°) 6 hours, or on high (290° to 300°) 3 hours, or until chops are tender.

1 can (1 pound, 14 ounces) whole apricots
1 tablespoon bottled steak sauce
1 teaspoon salt
¼ teaspoon ground cloves
6 rib or loin pork chops, cut ½-inch thick

CHILI BEEF STEW

*Cook on 190° to 200° for **8** hours, or on 290° to 300° for **4** hours.*
Makes 8 servings.

Chili puts punch in this thrifty, rib-sticking beef and bean stew.

1. Trim away as much fat as possible from short ribs. Heat heavy kettle or electric slow cooker with a browning unit; melt enough fat trimmings to make 2 tablespoons drippings. Brown short ribs well on all sides; remove. Drain off all but 2 tablespoons fat.
2. Sauté onion, green pepper and garlic in same pan. Stir in chili powder; cook, stirring constantly for about 2 minutes. Add tomatoes and green chili peppers. Dissolve instant beef broth in boiling water; stir into tomato mixture; add salt. Combine ribs and tomato mixture in slow cooker; cover. Bring to boiling; lower heat; cover.
3. Cook on low (190° to 200°) 8 hours, or on high (290° to 300°) 4 hours.
4. Remove meat to serving bowl; keep warm. Carefully remove the bones and skim fat from sauce in slow cooker. Turn heat control to high (290° to 300°). Combine ¼ cup all-purpose flour and ½ cup cold water in a cup; stir into liquid in slow cooker; cover; cook 15 minutes. Add kidney beans and corn; heat about 5 minutes. Spoon over meat in serving bowl.

4 pounds short ribs
1 large onion, chopped (1 cup)
1 green pepper, halved, seeded and diced
2 cloves garlic, chopped
2 tablespoons chili powder
1 can (1 pound) tomatoes
1 can (4 ounces) green chili peppers, drained and chopped
1 envelope or teaspoon instant beef broth
1 cup boiling water
1 teaspoon salt
¼ cup all-purpose flour
½ cup water
2 cans (about 1 pound each) kidney beans, drained
1 can (12 or 16 ounces) whole-kernel corn, drained

66

POT ROAST ORIENTAL

*Cook on 190° to 200° for **10** hours,
or on 290° to 300° for **5** hours.
Makes 10 servings.*

Western pot roast goes Oriental with seasonings of soy, sherry and ginger.

1. Season the meat with garlic salt and pepper.
2. Heat the oil in a heavy nonstick pan or electric slow cooker with a browning unit; brown meat on all sides.
3. Combine meat, ginger, soy sauce, sherry and water in slow cooker with onion; cover cooker.
4. Cook on low (190° to 200°) 10 hours, or on high (290° to 300°) 5 hours, or until tender.
5. Remove meat to serving platter; keep warm. Turn heat control to high (290° to 300°); simmer sauce, uncovered, to thicken slightly. Serve sauce with meat.

*1 boneless well-trimmed chuck
   arm roast (about 3 ½ pounds)
2 teaspoons garlic salt
¼ teaspoon pepper
1 tablespoon vegetable oil
1 teaspoon ground ginger
⅓ cup soy sauce
1 cup dry sherry
½ cup water
1 medium-size onion, sliced*

BEER BRAISED LOIN OF PORK

*Cook on 190° to 200° for **10** hours,
or on 290° to 300° for **5** hours.
Makes 8 servings.*

Tender, juicy pork simmers long and lazily in dark beer for a rich, tasty dish.

1. Brown pork loin well on all sides in kettle or 5-quart electric cooker with browning unit; remove from pan.
2. Drain all but 3 tablespoons drippings from pan. Sauté onions and carrots until soft in pork drippings. Stir in beer, salt, pepper, bay leaf and whole cloves. Return pork to slow cooker; cover.
3. Cook on low (190° to 200°) 10 hours, or on high (290° to 300°) 5 hours or until pork is tender when pierced with a 2-tined fork. Place pork on platter and keep warm.
4. Pour cooking liquid from slow cooker into a large bowl. Skim off fat; remove bay leaf. Place liquid and solids in container of electric blender; cover and whirl at low speed until smooth (or press through a sieve). Pour sauce into saucepan. Bring to boiling, stirring often. Stir in a little gravy coloring, if you wish. Spoon the sauce generously over the pork after it has been sliced.

*1 pork loin roast (about 5 pounds)
3 large onions, chopped (3 cups)
1 pound carrots, pared and diced
1 bottle or can (12 ounces)
   dark beer
2 teaspoons salt
¼ teaspoon pepper
1 bay leaf
5 whole cloves*

Cook on 190° to 200° for **6** hours,
or on 290° to 300° for **3** hours.

Makes 6 servings.

BELGIAN BEEF BALLS

Beer turns meat balls into an unusual, sophisticated dish.

1. Mix ground beef with bread crumbs and ½ cup of the beef broth in a large bowl; shape into 12 large balls.
2. Sprinkle ⅓ cup of the flour onto wax paper; roll meat balls in flour to coat.
3. Sauté meat balls in vegetable oil until richly browned in a large skillet or electric slow cooker with a browning unit and remove. Pour off all drippings, then measure 2 tablespoonfuls and return to pan.
4. Stir in onion; sauté until soft. Stir in remaining beef broth, beer, thyme, garlic salt, and pepper; heat to boiling.
5. Blend remaining flour and water to a paste in a cup; stir into liquid in pan. Combine meat balls and sauce in slow cooker; cover.
6. Cook on low (190° to 200°) 6 hours or on high (290° to 300°) 3 hours.
7. Spoon meat balls and gravy onto a heated deep serving platter; sprinkle with parsley. Serve with cooked noodles or boiled potatoes.

1 ½ pounds ground beef
½ cup soft bread crumbs (1 slice)
2 cans condensed beef broth
½ cup all-purpose flour
2 tablespoons vegetable oil
1 large onion, peeled and sliced
1 can (12 ounces) beer
½ teaspoon leaf thyme, crumbled
½ teaspoon garlic salt
¼ teaspoon pepper
¼ cup water
1 tablespoon chopped parsley

make your freezer work for you

In these days of high utility bills, it is a benefit to your budget to follow these rules for successful home freezing:

• Never freeze more than one 4-serving dish for each cubic foot of freezer space at one time.

• Cool hot foods to room temperature before placing in freezer to prevent the freezer from warming up.

• Package foods carefully for the freezer. Use plastic containers with tight-fitting lids and allow about ½-inch of headroom for food to expand.

• Fast-freeze slow cooker dishes by placing them on the coldest part of the freezer.

• Stack packages of frozen foods after making a record of the food, servings and date for future menu planning.

• Plan to use home-frozen dishes within 2 to 3 months when held at 0°F.

• Keep home frozen food moving, store the newest to the back and push the older ones to the front.

• Never thaw a frozen dish at room temperature. This is the perfect way to encourage the growth of those bacteria that cause food poisoning. Either place the frozen dish in the oven and bake or thaw in refrigerator and then bake.

VEAL À LA MODE

A favorite French one-dish dinner—veal and vegetables simmered in a savory broth.

1. Brown veal in shortening in a Dutch oven or electric slow cooker with browning unit.
2. Sprinkle with salad-dressing mix; stir in wine. Heat to boiling.
3. Place in slow cooker with onions, potatoes, carrots and parsnips; cover.
4. Cook on low (190° to 200°) 8 hours, or on high (290° to 300°) 4 hours, or till meat and vegetables are tender. Remove meat to a cutting board; keep warm while making gravy.
5. Drain liquid from mushrooms into a cup; add mushrooms to other vegetables.
6. Turn heat control to high (290° to 300°). Combine ¼ cup all purpose flour with ½ cup mushroom liquid in cup; add water if more liquid is needed; stir into liquid in slow cooker; cover; cook 15 minutes. Serve in a heated gravy boat with veal.

1 rolled, boned veal shoulder roast (4 pounds)
2 tablespoons vegetable shortening
1 envelope onion-flavor salad-dressing mix
1 cup dry white wine
16 small white onions, peeled
2 medium-size potatoes, pared and cubed (2 cups)
2 large carrots, pared and sliced (2 cups)
2 medium-size parsnips, pared and sliced (2 cups)
1 can (6 ounces) sliced mushrooms
¼ cup all-purpose flour

BEEF NAPOLI

Stuff an eye-round roast with pepperoni and slow cook, for a special pot-roast treat.

1. Stand roast on end and cut a small hole through center with a sharp, thin-blade knife; stuff hole with pepperoni, twisting and pushing in as you work. (Do not remove strings from roast.)
2. Brown roast in a large skillet or slow cooker with a browning unit; drain off all fat. Stir in bouillon, vinegar; cover.
3. Cook on low (190° to 200°) 10 hours, or high (290° to 300°) 5 hours. Remove to a serving platter and keep warm while making gravy.
4. Turn heat control to high (290° to 300°). Combine ¼ cup all-purpose flour and ½ cup cold water in a cup; stir into liquid in slow cooker; add sugar; cook 15 minutes. Serve in heated gravy boat, with roast carved into ¼-inch slices.

1 eye-round roast (about 4 pounds)
1 package (5 ounces) whole pepperoni
1 can condensed beef bouillion
½ cup cider vinegar
Several drops bottled red-pepper seasoning
¼ cup all-purpose flour
½ cup water
1 tablespoon brown sugar

CITRUS MEAT BALLS

Cook on 190° to 200° for **8** hours,
or on 290° to 300° for **4** hours.
Makes 6 servings.

Lime adds zest to a dish that originated in the Caribbean.

1. Mix ground beef lightly with lime rind. Shape with tablespoon into 35 small balls.
2. Sauté bacon until crisp in a large skillet or electric slow cooker with a browning unit; remove.
3. Brown meat balls, half at a time, in bacon drippings; remove with a slotted spoon; reserve.
4. Drain all but 2 tablespoons of the drippings from skillet, then sauté onions just until soft.
5. Stir beef broth, water, salt, cayenne, and bay leaf into drippings in pan. Place meat balls with sauce in slow cooker; add potatoes and green pepper; cover.
6. Cook on low (190° to 200°) 8 hours, or on high (290° to 300°) 4 hours. Place on heated platter.
7. Turn heat control to high (290° to 300°). Combine ¼ cup all-purpose flour and ½ cup cold water in a cup; stir into liquid in slow cooker; cover; cook 15 minutes.
8. Add olives and tomatoes and heat 5 minutes.
9. Pour over meatballs and serve.

1½ pounds ground beef
1 teaspoon grated lime rind
6 slices bacon, diced
1 large onion, chopped (1 cup)
1 can condensed beef broth
1 cup water
1½ teaspoons salt
⅛ teaspoon cayenne pepper
1 bay leaf
6 medium-size potatoes, peeled and quartered
2 large green peppers, halved, seeded, and chopped
2 large ripe tomatoes, peeled and quartered
¼ cup ripe olives, sliced
¼ cup all-purpose flour
½ cup water

a chef's tricks for browning

- Choose a large heavy skillet, if you haven't a slow cooker with a browning unit.
- Wipe meat on paper towels beforehand. If using seasoned flour, coat just before cooking.
- Heat fat or oil in pan until almost smoking. Add just enough of the meat to cover the bottom of the pan, leaving a little space around each piece.
- Brown one side until beads of blood show around the bone or on the upper surface, then turn with tongs; repeat until evenly brown on all sides.
- Remove meat with tongs to a bowl or the lid of the cooker while browning remaining pieces; then add browned meat and any juices to cooker.
- For an extra meaty flavor, pour all fat from pan and add a little water, wine or broth; heat and stir to get all the cooked-on juices from the bottom of pan; add to the liquid in cooker.

PARISIAN VEAL

Cook on 190° to 200° for **8** hours,
or on 290° to 300° for **4** hours.
Makes 8 servings.

Vegetables season the meat as it cooks, then thicken the gravy.

1. Brown veal slowly in vegetable oil in a Dutch oven or electric slow cooker with browning unit; remove and reserve.
2. Stir celery, onion, and carrot into drippings in pan; sauté until soft.
3. Stir in water, instant beef broth, marjoram, garlic powder, salt, and pepper; heat to boiling. Place meat in cooker with sauce; cover.
4. Cook on low (190° to 200°) 8 hours, or on high (290° to 300°) 4 hours, or until veal is tender.
5. Place meat on a serving platter; keep hot while fixing gravy.
6. Let liquid in pan stand about a minute, or until fat rises to top, then skim off. Strain liquid into a bowl, pressing vegetables through sieve; return to cooker. Turn heat control to high (290° to 300°). Combine ¼ cup all-purpose flour and ½ cup cold water in a cup; stir into liquid in slow cooker; cook 15 minutes.
7. Slice meat; serve hot with gravy.

1 rolled boned veal shoulder, weighing about 4 pounds
¼ cup vegetable oil
1 cup chopped celery
1 medium-size onion, chopped (½ cup)
½ cup chopped pared carrot
1 cup water
1 envelope or teaspoon instant beef broth
1 teaspoon leaf marjoram, crumbled
½ teaspoon garlic powder
½ teaspoon salt
¼ teaspoon pepper
¼ cup all-purpose flour
½ cup water

LAMB STEW WITH MINT DUMPLINGS

Cook on 190° to 200° for **8** hours,
or on 290° to 300° for **4** hours.
Makes 6 servings.

Tender lamb, colorful vegetables and mint-seasoned dumplings make a perfect main dish for a spring dinner.

1. Trim excess fat from lamb; place in an electric slow cooker; pour boiling water over. Top with celery leaves, salt and peppers; stir in onions, carrots and celery; cover cooker.
2. Cook on low (190° to 200°) 8 hours, or on high (290° to 300°) 4 hours, or until lamb is tender.
3. Turn heat control to high (290° to 300°) while making dumplings.
4. Combine biscuit mix and mint in small bowl; stir in milk just until dumpling mixture is moistened.
5. Drop by tablespoons on top of steaming stew; cover. Cook, without peeking, 30 minutes longer.

2 pounds boneless lamb shoulder, cubed
2 cups boiling water
Handful celery leaves, chopped
2 teaspoons salt
¼ teaspoon pepper
18 small white onions, peeled
6 large carrots, pared and cut into 1-inch lengths
1 cup sliced celery
2 cups biscuit mix
1 tablespoon chopped fresh mint
¾ cup milk

POT ROAST PACIFICA

Meat, fragrant with orange juice and herbs, is a West Coast specialty.

1. Brush beef all over with lemon juice; let stand about 5 minutes.
2. Cook bacon with onion and garlic until bacon is crisp in a large skillet or electric slow cooker with a browning unit; remove and reserve.
3. Brown beef in bacon drippings in pan over medium heat. Combine beef with bacon mixture, orange juice, tomato, sugar, salt, thyme, nutmeg, pepper and bay leaf in slow cooker; cover.
4. Cook on low (190° to 200°) 10 hours, or on high (290° to 300°) 5 hours, or until meat is very tender. Remove to a heated serving platter; keep hot while making gravy:
5. Pour liquid into a 4-cup measure; let stand about 1 minute, or until fat rises to top. Skim off fat; remove bay leaf. Add water, if necessary, to liquid to make 3 cups; return to slow cooker. Turn heat control to high (290° to 300°). Combine 3 tablespoons cornstarch and ¼ cup cold water in a cup; stir into liquid in slow cooker; cover; cook 15 minutes.
6. Carve meat into ¼-inch slices; serve with gravy.

1 blade-bone chuck roast
   (about 4 pounds)
2 tablespoons lemon juice
6 slices bacon, diced
1 medium-size onion, chopped
   (½ cup)
1 clove garlic, minced
1½ cups orange juice
1 large ripe tomato, peeled
   and diced (1 cup)
1 tablespoon sugar
3 teaspoons salt
1 teaspoon leaf thyme, crumbled
½ teaspoon ground nutmeg
¼ teaspoon pepper
1 bay leaf
3 tablespoons cornstarch
¼ cup water

facts about veal

• Substitute veal for beef. Veal is lean and luscious and the lowest-calorie meat of all. A 4-ounce veal cutlet, for example, runs just 186 calories. A comparable beef rib steak, a whopping 455 (and still more if it's "prime ribs"). Pork and lamb are less calorie-laden than beef, but more so than veal: a 4-ounce lamb or pork chop has from 338 to 383 calories.

• If you're trying to save both cash and calories, turn to the less costly cuts of veal. Cubes of veal cut from the shoulder simmer into glorious ragouts and stews, are reasonably priced and weigh in at only 785 calories per pound, as compared with 1,166 for a similar cut of beef.

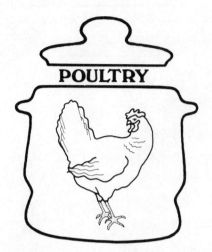

POULTRY

Remember when "a chicken in every pot" was a politician's promise? Now there is a different kind of promise attached to chickens and pots—slow cooker pots, that is. It's the promise of the deep down kind of flavor that only long hours of gentle cooking can provide. And it applies to all other kinds of poultry as well.

You may be tempted to try a favorite chicken recipe in a slow cooker that is not included in this book. Here are some general guidelines for adapting conventional recipes:

• Uncooked poultry (or meat) combinations will require 8 to 10 hours of cooking time on low (190° to 200°) or 4 to 5 hours on high (290° to 300°).

• One hour of simmering on a range, or baking at 350° in the oven is equal to 8 to 10 hours on low, or 4 to 5 hours on a high setting in a slow cooker.

• Reduce the liquid in your recipe to about 1 cup since the slow cooker method saves all the food's natural juices.

• Use canned soups or broths, wine or water as the liquid in your slow cooker.

• Don't add dairy products, such as milk, sour cream, or cream until the final 30 minutes of cooking time.

• Frozen vegetables and frozen fish should be thawed slightly and added only during the last hour of cooking, since they require so little cooking.

how to bone a bird

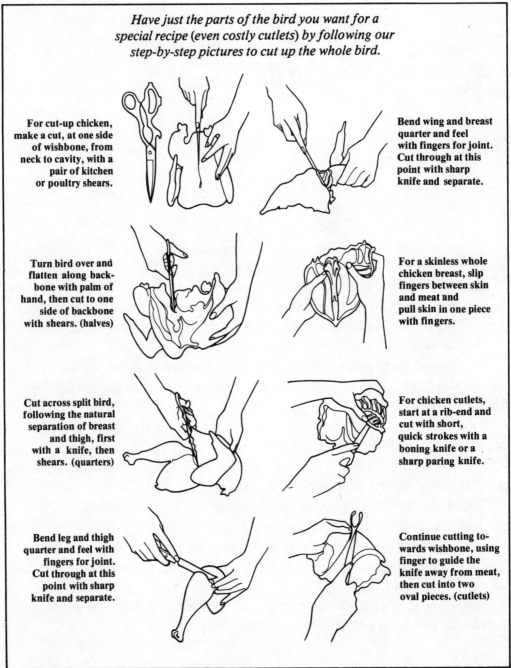

Have just the parts of the bird you want for a special recipe (even costly cutlets) by following our step-by-step pictures to cut up the whole bird.

For cut-up chicken, make a cut, at one side of wishbone, from neck to cavity, with a pair of kitchen or poultry shears.

Bend wing and breast quarter and feel with fingers for joint. Cut through at this point with sharp knife and separate.

Turn bird over and flatten along back-bone with palm of hand, then cut to one side of backbone with shears. (halves)

For a skinless whole chicken breast, slip fingers between skin and meat and pull skin in one piece with fingers.

Cut across split bird, following the natural separation of breast and thigh, first with a knife, then shears. (quarters)

For chicken cutlets, start at a rib-end and cut with short, quick strokes with a boning knife or a sharp paring knife.

Bend leg and thigh quarter and feel with fingers for joint. Cut through at this point with sharp knife and separate.

Continue cutting to-wards wishbone, using finger to guide the knife away from meat, then cut into two oval pieces. (cutlets)

DINDONNEAU AU VIN

Cook on 190° to 200° for **9** hours,
then on 290° to 300° for **3** hours.
Makes 8 servings.

Dindonneau is French for a young turkey. In this recipe it is simmered in wine and herbs. Pictured on page 130-131.

1. Cut bacon into 1-inch pieces; place in a small saucepan; cover with water. Bring to boiling; lower heat and simmer 10 minutes. Dry bacon on paper towels. Fry bacon until crisp in an electric slow cooker with a browning unit or a large kettle. Remove bacon.
2. Shake turkey pieces with flour, salt and pepper in a plastic bag to coat well. Brown turkey, a few pieces at a time, in kettle; remove and reserve.
3. Brown onions in pan drippings until golden; stir in garlic and cook 2 minutes; stir in red wine and bring to boiling, scraping browned bits from bottom of kettle.
4. Place turkey and bacon in slow cooker; tie a "bouquet garni" of parsley, celery leaves, bay leaf and thyme in cheesecloth; push down into liquid in slow cooker; cover.
5. Cook on low (190° to 200°) 9 hours. Then on high (290° to 300°) 3 hours. Remove "bouquet garni."
6. Thirty minutes before serving, wipe mushrooms with a damp towel. Sauté in butter or margarine in a large skillet until soft; remove and keep warm. Add carrots to skillet and saute 3 minutes; pour chicken broth over; cover skillet; simmer 10 minutes; push carrots to one side; add green beans; cover skillet; simmer 15 minutes longer, or until vegetables are crisply-tender.
7. Spread cooked noodles on the bottom of a heated large platter; spoon turkey pieces and onions from slow cooker over noodles; arrange mushrooms, carrots and green beans on platter.

½ pound thickly sliced bacon
1 frozen turkey, thawed and cut up (about 6 pounds)
⅓ cup all-purpose flour
2 teaspoons salt
½ teaspoon freshly ground pepper
1 pound small white onions, peeled
2 cloves garlic, minced
3 cups dry red wine
2 sprigs parsley
2 sprigs celery leaves
1 bay leaf, broken
1½ teaspoons leaf thyme
½ pound mushrooms, quartered
3 tablespoons butter or margarine
16 baby carrots (from a 1-pound bag)
1 pound green beans, tipped
½ cup chicken broth
1 package (1 pound) noodles, cooked and drained

for quicker clean-ups

To remove rust build-up on a cast iron skillet wash it in sudsy water; scrub with a steel wool pad, then rub with vegetable oil. Place on a cooky sheet in a warm oven, turn off oven and keep in overnight. In the morning, rub off the excess oil. Repeat as needed.

CARIBBEAN ROAST CHICKEN

Cook on 190° to 200° for **10** *hours, or on 290° to 300° for* **6** *hours.*
Makes 6 servings.

Aromatic bitters and lemon juice add the flavors of the French West Indies to economical whole chicken. Pictured on pages 58-59.

1. Stuff chicken neck and body cavities lightly with SAVORY STUFFING. Skewer neck to body; push tail inside bird and secure body cavity closed; tie legs together and draw string up and under wings and knot.
2. Brown chicken on all sides in butter in large skillet or electric slow cooker with browning unit.
3. Place chicken in slow cooker; add water, lemon juice and bitters; cover.
4. Cook on low (190° to 200°) 10 hours, or on high (290° to 300°) 6 hours. Arrange on a heated serving platter with LEMON SWIRL CUPS and fresh spinach leaves.

SAVORY STUFFING— *Makes 2½ cups.*
1. Sauté celery leaves and onion in butter or margarine in medium-size saucepan. Add water; bring mixture to boiling.
2. Stir in bread stuffing; toss with fork just until moistened.

LEMON SWIRL CUPS— Makes 2 cups. Hold a lemon vertically and make a one-half-inch lengthwise cut through the center with a sharp paring knife; make the second cut at a 45° angle to the first cut, starting at the base of the first cut. Continue this zig-zag cutting around center of lemon until cuts meet. Pull apart to make cups.

COOK'S TIP: If lemon does not separate easily after going around the first time, repeat, this time making the same cuts, but pushing knife deeper into fruit.

1 roasting chicken (about 4 pounds)
Savory Stuffing (recipe follows)
¼ cup (½ stick) butter or margarine, melted
½ cup water
2 tablespoons lemon juice
1 teaspoon aromatic bitters
Lemon Swirl Cups (recipe follows)
Fresh spinach leaves

Savory Stuffing
½ cup chopped celery leaves
2 tablespoons chopped onion
¼ cup (½ stick) butter or margarine
½ cup water
2 cups prepared bread stuffing mix (½ of an 8-ounce package)

to freeze fresh chicken

Remove the store wrapping, discard the backing board or tray and rinse the chicken in cold water. Pat dry with paper towels, then wrap in plastic wrap, heavy-duty foil or freezer paper and place in your freezer. Label each package, noting which parts are included, and how many; date. It will keep up to 6 months.

76

POACHED CHICKEN

Cook on 190° to 200° for **8** hours, or on 290° to 300° for **4** hours.
Makes 4 servings.

When chickens are on special, poach one or two and keep on hand for salads, sandwiches or casseroles.

1. Place chicken in an electric slow cooker with giblets, but not liver. Add onion, carrot, celery, leek, wine, water, lemon slices, salt, pepper, bay leaf and allspice; cover.
2. Cook on low (190° to 200°) 8 hours, or on high (290° to 300°) 4 hours, or until chicken is tender when pierced with a two-tined fork; remove chicken from broth and let cool.
3. Strain broth through cheesecloth into a bowl; chill and use within 3 days or soften 1 envelope unflavored gelatin in ¼ cup cold water; stir into hot broth until dissolved; pour into a 2-cup mold or 8x8x2-inch pan; chill until firm. Serve as a chicken aspic, if you wish.
4. Slip skin from cooled chicken and pull meat from bones in large pieces. Refrigerate and use within 3 days or pack in plastic freezer containers; seal; label and date. Freeze; use within 3 months.

1 broiler-fryer (about 3 pounds)
1 small onion studded with 4 whole cloves
1 medium-size carrot, pared and diced
1 stalk celery with leaves, chopped
1 leek, trimmed and sliced (optional)
½ cup dry white wine
½ cup water
2 slices lemon
1 teaspoon salt
¼ teaspoon white pepper
1 bay leaf
3 whole allspice

OLD COUNTRY CHICKEN IN THE POT

Cook on 190° to 200° for **8** hours, or on 290° to 300° for **4** hours.
Makes 6 servings.

This is the kind of soup mother brought you when you were sick in bed.

1. Layer chicken, potatoes, carrots, turnips, celery and leek or onion in an electric slow cooker, sprinkling salt between layers; add water.
2. Tie parsley, peppercorns and bay leaf in a piece of cheesecloth. Push under liquid; cover.
3. Cook on low (190° to 200°) 8 hours, or on high (290° to 300°) 4 hours, or until chicken is tender. Ladle into soup bowl.

1 broiler-fryer, cut-up (about 3 pounds)
1 pound small new potatoes, washed
4 large carrots, pared and diced
2 white turnips, pared and diced
2 stalks celery with leaves, chopped
1 leek, trimmed and sliced
*   OR: 1 large onion, chopped (1 cup)*
1 tablespoon salt
6 cups water
*   Handful parsley*
6 peppercorns
1 bay leaf

ARUBA CHICKEN SANCOCHO

*Cook on 190° to 200° for **8** hours, or on 290° to 300° for **4** hours.*
Makes 8 servings.

Caribbean fruit is paired with chicken and pork in this lively dinner-in-a-dish.

1. Sauté onion until golden in oil in a heavy kettle or an electric slow cooker with a browning unit, about 5 minutes. Remove and reserve.
2. Brown chicken, half at a time, in same pan, adding more oil if needed. Place chicken and onion in slow cooker. Add smoked pork and wine.
3. Stir in water, tomato sauce, coconut, and salt. Tie pepper, cloves, bay leaf and thyme in cheesecloth; add to slow cooker; pare sweet potatoes and cut into ½-inch slices. Add to slow cooker, pushing them down into liquid.
4. Cook on low (190° to 200°) 8 hours, or on high (290° to 300°) 4 hours, or until meats and potatoes are tender. Taste and add more salt if needed. (Salt content in pork varies.)
5. Stir bananas and green onions into stew. Cover and simmer 5 to 10 minutes longer. Arrange stew in serving dish. Garnish with additional coconut and green onion, if you wish.

Suggested Variation: You can use 2 cups cubed cooked ham or bologna or 2 cups thickly sliced frankfurters for smoked pork.

1 Spanish onion, sliced
2 tablespoons olive oil or vegetable oil
1 broiler-fryer, cut-up (about 3 pounds)
1 pound smoked pork butt, cut into 1-inch cubes
2 tablespoons sherry cooking wine
2 cups water
1 can (8 ounces) tomato sauce
¼ cup flaked coconut
1½ teaspoons salt
½ teaspoon crushed red pepper
4 whole cloves
1 bay leaf
¼ teaspoon leaf thyme
2 pounds sweet potatoes
2 bananas, peeled and sliced ¾-inch thick
¼ cup sliced green onion

poultry tips

- A marinade is a flavorful liquid that contains an acid, such as lemon juice, vinegar or wine in which poultry pieces soak before cooking. It both tenderizes and adds flavor to the birds.
- Many recipes suggest marinating overnight for best results. Marinades are also used to flavor the birds while cooking.
- If you don't have a roasting pan or dish large enough for marinating a bird or roast, use a jumbo plastic bag. Place bird, or meat and marinade in bag, seal tightly and chill. Remember to turn the bag several times so meat seasons evenly.

CHILI CHICKEN

Cook on 290° to 300° for **2** hours, then on 190° to 200° for **6** hours. Makes 4 servings.

Serve this chili in deep soup bowls, but add forks as well as spoons. A salad of shredded lettuce and toasted corn chips are the perfect accompaniment.

1. Shake chicken pieces in a mixture of flour, 1½ teaspoons of the salt and pepper in a plastic bag to coat evenly.
2. Brown chicken pieces in shortening in a large skillet or an electric slow cooker with a browning unit; remove and reserve. Pour off all but 2 tablespoons of the pan drippings. Sauté onion, garlic and green pepper in drippings until soft.
3. Place chicken pieces and onion mixture in slow cooker. Combine tomatoes, chicken broth, olives, cornmeal, tomato paste, chili powder, remaining 1 teaspoon salt and sugar in a medium size bowl, pour over chicken; cover.
4. Cook on high (290° to 300°) for 2 hours. Stir at this point. Turn heat control to low (190° to 200°) and cook 6 hours longer, or until chicken is tender.

1 broiler-fryer, cut-up (about 3 pounds)
¼ cup all-purpose flour
2½ teaspoons salt
¼ teaspoon pepper
¼ cup vegetable shortening
1 large onion, chopped (1 cup)
1 clove garlic, minced
1 green pepper, halved, seeded and chopped
1 can (1 pound) tomatoes
1 can condensed chicken broth
1 cup chopped ripe olives
½ cup yellow cornmeal
¼ cup tomato paste
1 to 3 tablespoons chili powder
1 teaspoon sugar

CORIANDER CHICKEN

Cook on 190° to 200° for **8** hours, or on 290° to 300° for **4** hours. Makes 6 servings.

Coriander is an herb that is used extensively in North African cooking for a spicy yet fresh flavor.

1. Roll chicken breasts in a mixture of melted butter or margarine, grated onion, coriander and salt in a pie plate to coat well.
2. Place in a 2½-quart electric slow cooker; pour chicken broth and lemon juice over; cover.
3. Cook on low (190° to 200°) 8 hours, or on high (290° to 300°) 4 hours, or until chicken is tender. Stir yogurt and flour together until well-blended in a small bowl. Stir into chicken, just before serving. Serve with rice pilaf and top with sliced green onions, if you wish.

3 whole chicken breasts, split (about 12 ounces each)
¼ cup (½ stick) butter or margarine, melted
1 small onion, grated
1 tablespoon ground coriander
1½ teaspoons salt
½ cup chicken broth
1 tablespoon lemon juice
1 container (8 ounces) plain yogurt
2 tablespoons all-purpose flour

79

MOROCCAN COUSCOUS

Cook on 190° to 200° for **12** hours, or on 290° to 300° for **6** hours.
Makes 16 servings.

Couscous is both the name of the semolina grain and the finished dish. Perfect for a party dish. Photo on page 134.

1. Place turkey and chopped onions, with butter or margarine and oil in the bottom of a 5-quart electric slow cooker. Add salt, pepper, turmeric, cayenne, saffron and cinnamon; cover cooker.
2. Cook on low (190° to 200°) 12 hours, or on high (290° to 300°) 6 hours.
3. Half an hour before serving, add tomatoes, carrots, zucchini, turnips, squash, and chick peas and simmer until tender. Stir in raisins.
4. Cook couscous, following label directions; place on heated serving platter. Spoon turkey and vegetables over couscous and serve.

1 turkey, cut up (about 8 pounds)
6 large onions, (6 cups) chopped
¼ cup (½ stick) butter or margarine
¼ cup olive oil or vegetable oil
1 tablespoon salt
1 teaspoon black pepper
½ teaspoon ground turmeric
¼ teaspoon cayenne pepper (optional)
1 teaspoon saffron threads, crushed
1 three-inch piece stick cinnamon
3 cups water
5 large tomatoes, peeled, seeded and chopped (5 cups)
6 carrots, pared and cut in 1½-inch pieces, cooked and drained
1 pound zucchini, cut in 1½-inch lengths, cooked and drained
3 or 4 white turnips, cut in quarters (optional), cooked and drained
1 large or 2 small acorn squash, peeled, seeded and cut in 1½-to 2-inch chunks, cooked and drained
1 can (1 pound, 13 ounces) chick peas, rinsed
1 cup seedless raisins
2 pounds couscous (coarse semolina)

roquefort or blue cheese?

Both taste somewhat alike, but differ in price because Roquefort is made from sheep's milk and comes from France, while blue cheese is made from cow's milk and is produced widely in our own country.

POT-ROASTED CHICKEN

Cook on 190° to 200° for **10** hours, or on 290° to 300° for **5** hours.
Makes 6 servings.

Beef broth and thyme are the flavor secrets to this French-style chicken dish.

1. Brown chicken on all sides in butter or margarine and thyme until golden in a large skillet or an electric slow cooker with a browning unit.
2. Combine browned chicken and beef broth in slow cooker; cover.
3. Cook on low (190° to 200°) 10 hours, or on high (290° to 300°) 5 hours, or until chicken is tender when pierced with a two-tined fork. Remove chicken to a heated platter and keep warm.
4. Turn heat control to high (290° to 300°). Combine flour and evaporated milk in a cup; stir into liquid in slow cooker until well-blended. Cover; cook 15 minutes. Taste and season with salt and pepper, if you wish. Serve sauce separately in heated gravy boat.

1 stewing chicken (about 5 pounds)
3 tablespoons butter or margarine
2 teaspoons leaf thyme, crumbled
1 can condensed beef broth
3 tablespoons all-purpose flour
1 small can evaporated milk

MISSISSIPPI CHICKEN DINNER

Cook on 190° to 200° for **8** hours, or on 290° to 300° for **4** hours.
Makes 8 servings.

Lima beans and green beans bubble along in the slow cooker with ripe olives and slices of tomato—so good, yet easy to prepare.

1. Shake chicken pieces with a mixture of flour, salt and basil in a plastic bag to coat evenly.
2. Brown slowly in vegetable oil in a large skillet; remove and reserve. Sauté garlic in pan drippings until soft.
3. Stir in lima beans, green beans and ripe olives until well-blended.
4. Layer half the tomato slices, all of bean mixture and chicken in an electric slow cooker; top with remaining tomato slices; pour wine or water over; cover.
5. Cook on low (190° to 200°) 8 hours, or on high (290° to 300°) 4 hours, or until chicken is tender.

2 broiler-fryers, quartered (about 2½ pounds each)
¼ cup all-purpose flour
2 teaspoons salt
1 teaspoon leaf basil, crumbled
¼ cup vegetable oil
1 clove garlic, minced
2 cans (1 pound each) cooked dried lima beans
1 can (1 pound) cut green beans, drained
½ cup sliced pitted ripe olives
4 medium-size firm ripe tomatoes, sliced ½-inch thick
½ cup dry white wine or water

81

ROCK CORNISH HENS NÖEL

Cook on 190° to 200° for **7** hours,
or on 290° to 300° for **4** hours.
Makes 4 servings.

For that special holiday dinner, these little birds are just the perfect choice.

1. Thaw hens; remove giblets and reserve. Wash and dry hens well.
2. Crumble sausage and fry until well-done in a large heavy kettle or an electric slow cooker with a browning unit. Remove sausage with a slotted spoon and reserve to use in making WILD RICE PILAF.
3. Add butter or margarine to sausage fat in kettle. Brown hens slowly on all sides in fat; remove from pan and reserve. Sauté onion, celery and carrot in fat until soft. Stir in 1½ cups broth and salt, tarragon and pepper; bring to boiling; lower heat.
4. Combine hens, breast-side up and flavored broth in slow cooker; cover.
5. Cook on low (190° to 200°) 7 hours, or on high (290° to 300°) 4 hours. Remove from slow cooker and keep warm while making gravy.
6. Press pan juices through a sieve and into a large bowl. Skim off fat; measure 3 tablespoons into a medium-size saucepan. Add flour and cook, stirring constantly, until mixture bubbles; pour in pan juices.
7. Cook, stirring constantly, until sauce thickens and bubbles 3 minutes; stir in gravy coloring.
8. Spoon WILD RICE PILAF onto heated serving platter; arrange hens on platter and garnish with lemons and watercress, if you wish.

4 frozen Rock Cornish hens (about 14 ounces each)
½ pound bulk pork sausage
3 tablespoons butter or margarine
1 large onion, chopped (1 cup)
1 cup chopped celery
1 cup finely chopped carrot
Broth (recipe follows)
1 teaspoon salt
1 teaspoon leaf tarragon, crumbled
½ teaspoon pepper
3 tablespoons all-purpose flour
1 teaspoon bottled gravy coloring
Wild Rice Pilaf (recipe follows)

BROTH—   *Makes about 1½ cups.*
Combine giblets, water, parslied garlic salt, instant minced onion and lemon pepper in a medium-size saucepan. Heat to boiling; lower heat; cover saucepan. Simmer 1 hour, or until giblets are tender. Strain and reserve broth. Chop giblets and use in soup.

WILD RICE PILAF—   *Makes 4 servings.*
1. Sauté rices in butter or margarine until white rice turns a light brown in a large skillet; remove; add onion and sauté until soft.
2. Stir in seasoning mix packet, cooked sausage, and boiling water and rice. Bring to boiling; cover.
3. Simmer 30 minutes, or until liquid is absorbed and rice is tender.

Broth
4 packages Rock Cornish hen giblets
2 cups water
1 teaspoon parslied garlic salt
1 teaspoon instant minced onion
¼ teaspoon lemon pepper

Wild Rice Pilaf
1 package (6 ounces) long grain and wild rice mix
2 tablespoons butter or margarine
1 medium-size onion, chopped (½ cup)
Cooked sausage (see Rock Cornish Hens Nöel)
2½ cups boiling water

MEMPHIS BURGOO

Burgoo is another name for stew. This one is filled with chicken, ham hocks, limas and okra.

1. Place chicken and ham hocks in a 5-quart slow cooker; add water, potatoes, carrots, onion, lima beans, cabbage, celery, green pepper, Worcestershire sauce, salt and cayenne; cover.
2. Cook on low (190° to 200°) 8 hours, or on high (290° to 300°) 4 hours, or until chicken is tender. Remove chicken and ham hocks from slow cooker. Cool.
3. Turn heat control to high (290° to 300°). Stir in okra and parsley; cover and cook 15 minutes.
4. While okra cooks, remove skin from chicken and ham hocks; take meat from bones, discarding fat; dice meat; return to slow cooker; cover.
5. Cook 10 minutes; ladle into heated soup bowls. Serve with corn bread or crusty hard rolls, if you wish.

1 broiler-fryer (about 3 pounds)
2 smoked ham hocks (about 1 pound each)
4 cups water
2 large potatoes, pared and diced
2 large carrots, pared and diced
1 large onion, chopped (1 cup)
1 package (10 ounces) frozen Fordhook lima beans
2 cups shredded cabbage
1 cup sliced celery
1 large green pepper, halved, seeded and chopped
1 tablespoon Worcestershire sauce
2 teaspoons salt
½ teaspoon cayenne pepper
1 package (10 ounces) frozen whole okra, thawed
Chopped parsley

CAPE COD CHICKEN

Cranberry and spices are the special flavor secrets of this festive chicken dish.

1. Rub chickens with salt to coat well. Brown, a few quarters at a time, in oil in a large skillet or an electric slow cooker with a browning unit; remove.
2. Sauté onion in pan drippings until soft; stir in orange rind and juice, lemon juice, cranberry sauce, cinnamon and ginger; bring to boiling; stir constantly.
3. Combine chicken quarters and sauce in slow cooker; cover.
4. Cook on low (190° to 200°) 8 hours, or on high (290° to 300°) 4 hours, or until chicken is tender. Serve with fluffy rice and buttered peas, if you wish.

2 broiler-fryers, quartered (about 2½ pounds each)
2 teaspoons salt
¼ cup vegetable oil
1 large onion, chopped (1 cup)
1 tablespoon grated orange rind
½ cup orange juice
3 tablespoons lemon juice
1 can (1 pound) whole-berry cranberry sauce
1½ teaspoons ground cinnamon
1½ teaspoons ground ginger

GLAZED ROCK CORNISH HENS

Cook on 190° to 200° for **7** hours.
Makes 4 servings.

Elegant enough to serve to the most discriminating guest, yet a breeze to prepare. You'll need your 5-quart slow cooker for this one. Pictured on page 63.

1. Dip apple quarters into soy sauce in a 1-cup measure; tuck one piece into the cavity of each hen.
2. Stir wine, marmalade, lemon rind and juice, salt and pepper into remaining soy sauce; brush over hens.
3. Place hens, breast side down, in a 5-quart electric slow cookers; pour remaining glaze over; cover.
4. Cook on low (190° to 200°) for 3 hours. Baste at this point, if possible. Cook 4 hours longer, or until tender.
5. Arrange hens on a heated serving platter and serve with canned pear halves filled with prepared chicken-flavored stuffing mix, if you wish.

1 large red cooking apple, quartered and cored
1 tablespoon soy sauce
4 frozen Rock Cornish game hens, thawed
¼ cup dry white or rosé wine
3 tablespoons orange marmalade Rind and juice of ½ lemon
½ teaspoon salt
⅛ teaspoon pepper

SANTA CLARA CHICKEN

Cook on 190° to 200° for **10** hours,
or on 290° to 300° for **5** hours.
Makes 8 servings.

Springtime vegetables are especially flavorful when you simmer them with chicken in a slow cooker.

1. Combine chicken with potatoes, onion, lettuce, salt, pepper and rosemary in a 5-quart electric slow cooker.
2. Dissolve instant chicken broth in hot water in 4-cup measure; pour over chicken and vegetables; cover.
3. Cook on low (190° to 200°) 10 hours, or on high (290° to 300°) 5 hours. Remove chicken and vegetables with a slotted spoon to the center of a heated serving platter; arrange cooked peas and squash in piles; keep warm while making sauce.
4. Strain juices in slow cooker into a large saucepan; bring to boiling. Combine cornstarch and ¾ cup water in a cup; stir into hot liquid; cook, stirring constantly, until mixture thickens and bubbles 1 minute; spoon over platter.

2 broiler-fryers, cut up (about 3 pounds each)
12 small new potatoes, pared
1 Bermuda onion, sliced thin
4 cups shredded lettuce
1 teaspoon salt
¼ teaspoon pepper
1 teaspoon leaf rosemary, crumbled
3 envelopes instant chicken broth
3 cups hot water
3 cups frozen peas, cooked (from a 1½-pound bag)
4 medium-size yellow squash, tipped, sliced and cooked
⅓ cup cornstarch
¾ cup water

CHICKEN QUEBEC

Serving chicken flavored with bacon is a cooking secret French Canadians brought from France centuries ago.

1. Trim fat from chicken; melt fat in a large skillet or an electric slow cooker with a browning unit. Brown chicken, a few pieces at a time in fat; drain.
2. Fry bacon lightly in same pan; remove and set aside; pour off all fat.
3. Place chicken and bacon in slow cooker; add onion, salt, pepper and water; cover cooker.
4. Cook on low (190° to 200°) 10 hours, or on high (290° to 300°) 5 hours, or until chicken is tender.
5. Turn heat control to high (290° to 300°); add macaroni and parsley flakes. Cook 10 minutes; taste and season with additional salt and pepper, if you wish.

1 stewing chicken, cut up (about 5 pounds)
6 slices bacon
1 medium-size onion, chopped (½ cup)
1 teaspoon salt
½ teaspoon freshly ground pepper
4 cups water
1 package (8 ounces) elbow macaroni, cooked
1 tablespoon parsley flakes, crumbled

DRUMSTICKS DIABLE

Sweet and spicy best describes this chicken treat. A cut-up chicken can be used in place of the drumsticks.

1. Shake drumsticks in a plastic bag with flour, ½ teaspoon of the salt and pepper.
2. Brown in butter or margarine in a large skillet or an electric slow cooker with a browning unit; remove.
3. Stir tomatoes, brown sugar, vinegar, Worcestershire sauce, chili powder, dry mustard, celery seeds, garlic and red-pepper seasoning into pan drippings; bring to boiling; add remaining 1 teaspoon salt.
4. Combine drumsticks and sauce in slow cooker; cover.
5. Cook on low (190° to 200°) 8 hours, or on high (290° to 300°) 4 hours, or until chicken is tender. Serve with spaghetti.

8 drumsticks (about 2 pounds)
¼ cup all-purpose flour
1½ teaspoons salt
Dash pepper
3 tablespoons butter or margarine
1 can (1 pound) tomatoes
2 tablespoons brown sugar
2 tablespoons cider vinegar
2 tablespoons Worcestershire sauce
1 teaspoon chili powder
1 teaspoon dry mustard
½ teaspoon celery seeds
1 clove garlic, minced
Few drops bottled red-pepper seasoning

Cook on 190° to 200° for **8** hours,
or on 290° to 300° for **4** hours.
Makes 8 servings.

BRUNSWICK STEW

Meaty pieces of chicken cook lazily with corn and limas in a peppy tomato sauce. Pictured on pages 60-61.

1. Shake chicken in mixture of flour and salad dressing mix in a plastic bag to coat well; reserve any remaining flour.
2. Brown chicken, a few pieces at a time, in vegetable shortening in a large skillet or an electric slow cooker with browning unit. Remove and reserve.
3. Sauté onion in same pan; blend in reserved seasoned flour; stir in tomatoes and red-pepper seasoning. Bring to boiling, stirring constantly.
4. Place chicken and sauce in slow cooker; cover.
5. Cook on low (190° to 200°) 8 hours, or on high (290° to 300°) 4 hours. Add corn, lima beans and okra; cook 15 minutes longer.

2 broiler-fryers, cut-up (about
    2½ pounds each)
½ cup all-purpose flour
1 envelope (about 1 ounce) herb
    salad dressing mix
¼ cup vegetable shortening
1 large onion, chopped (1 cup)
1 can (1 pound, 12 ounces)
    tomatoes
    Few drops bottled red-pepper
    seasoning
4 ears corn, husked and with silks
    removed, cut into 1-inch
    pieces, cooked
    OR: 1 package (10 ounces)
    frozen whole-kernel corn,
    cooked
1 package (10 ounces) frozen
    Fordhook lima beans, cooked
1 pound okra, washed and
    cooked, (optional)

shopping pointers

To save backtracking, make up your shopping list according to the layout of your market. If the produce counter is right inside the door, list those items first, then move on to the bread or meat sections, or whatever comes next.

Here are rules to follow in deciding how much chicken to buy, although you may want to increase these portions for big eaters in the family:

- Chicken for frying: Allow ¾ to 1 pound per serving.
- Chicken for roasting: Allow ¾ to 1 pound per serving.
- Chicken for broiling or barbecuing: Allow ½ chicken or 1 pound per serving.
- Chicken for stewing: Allow ½ to 1 pound per serving.
- Chicken livers: Allow ¼ pound per serving.

KENTUCKY CHICKEN

Cook on 190° to 200° for **10** hours, or on 290° to 300° for **5** hours. Makes 8 servings.

Even folks who think they don't like lima beans will be sending their plates back for seconds.

1. Shake chicken with flour and salad dressing mix in plastic bag to coat evenly. Brown chicken in oil in a large skillet or an electric slow cooker with a browning unit; remove and reserve.
2. Sauté onion until soft in pan drippings; stir in tomatoes, celery, lima beans and corn; cover. (If using a skillet, place chicken and vegetables in slow cooker; cover.)
3. Cook on low (190° to 200°) 10 hours, or on high (290° to 300°) 5 hours, or until chicken is tender when pierced with a two-tined fork. Stir in okra and pimiento; cover and cook 15 minutes. Sprinkle with parsley just before serving.

1 stewing chicken, cut-up (about 5 pounds)
½ cup all-purpose flour
1 envelope (about 1 ounce) herb salad dressing mix
3 tablespoons peanut oil
1 large onion, chopped (1 cup)
1 can (1 pound) tomatoes
2 cups diced celery
1 can (about 1 pound) lima beans
1 can (12 or 16 ounces) whole-kernel corn
1 package (10 ounces) frozen whole okra, thawed
1 can (4 ounces) pimiento, drained and chopped
¼ cup chopped parsley

GALA FRUITED CHICKEN

Cook on 190° to 200° for **8** hours, or on 290° to 300° for **4** hours. Makes 6 servings.

All the flavor of tropical islands come together to sauce plump chicken parts.

1. Rub chicken pieces with a mixture of paprika, salt, pepper and cayenne. Brown in oil on all sides in a large skillet or an electric slow cooker with a browning unit.
2. Combine chicken pieces with crushed pineapple, raisins, orange juice, wine, cinnamon and allspice in slow cooker; cover cooker.
3. Cook on low (190° to 200°) 8 hours, or on high (290° to 300°) 4 hours, or until chicken is tender.
4. Lay orange sections over chicken and sprinkle with almonds; cook 15 minutes longer, just to heat through. Serve with fluffy rice, if you wish.

1 roasting chicken, cut-up (about 5 pounds)
2 teaspoons paprika
1½ teaspoons salt
¼ teaspoon pepper
   Dash cayenne pepper
3 tablespoons vegetable oil
1 can (8 ounces) crushed pineapple in pineapple juice
½ cup golden raisins
1 cup orange juice
½ cup dry white wine
⅛ teaspoon ground cinnamon
⅛ teaspoon ground allspice
2 California oranges, sectioned
½ cup toasted slivered almonds

87

Cook on 190° to 200° for **10** hours,
or on 290° to 300° for **6** hours.
Makes 4 servings.

AU PORTO CHICKEN

Chicken in wine with a Portuguese touch—white Port is the cooking liquid. If you prefer a less sweet flavor, choose a dry white wine, such as Chablis.

1. Season chicken with ½ teaspoon of the salt and ¼ teaspoon of the pepper. Skewer neck skin to back and tie legs.
2. Sauté onion, garlic and carrots until soft in oil in a large skillet or 3½-quart electric slow cooker with a browning unit. Stir in remaining 1 teaspoon salt, ¼ teaspoon pepper and rosemary. Spoon into the bottom of electric slow cooker.
3. Place chicken on top of vegetables; pour in wine or chicken broth; cover.
4. Cook on low (190° to 200°) 10 hours, or on high (290° to 300°) 6 hours, or until chicken is tender when pierced with a two-tined fork. Remove chicken to a heated platter and keep warm.
5. Turn heat control to high (290° to 300°). Add mushrooms and cook 15 minutes. Combine flour with ¼ cup cold water in a cup; stir into cooker until well-blended. Cover; simmer 15 minutes. Stir in a few drops bottled gravy coloring, if you wish. Slice chicken and pass sauce in heated gravy boat. Serve with a bottle of chilled dry white wine and a crisp salad of tossed greens with marinated artichokes, if you wish.

1 broiler-fryer (about 3 pounds)
1½ teaspoons salt
½ teaspoon pepper
1 large onion, chopped (1 cup)
1 clove garlic, minced
2 large carrots, pared and chopped
2 tablespoons olive oil or vegetable oil
1 teaspoon leaf rosemary, crumbled
1 cup white Port or dry white wine or chicken broth
½ pound fresh mushrooms, quartered
OR: 1 can (6 ounces) whole mushrooms
2 tablespoons all-purpose flour

potato tips

If you are in a hurry boil potatoes 5 minutes before putting them in a hot oven. They'll bake in about half the usual time.

If you are tired of plain old baked potatoes with butter try putting on top:

• Sour cream in big spoonfuls, sprinkled with seasoned salt and pepper, cut chives, crisp bacon bits, dillweed or grated raw carrot.

• Cream Sauce either plain, or mixed with chopped and sautéed mushrooms or cubed cheese.

• Hollandaise Sauce from a jar, or your own; it's glamorous and different.

CAROLINA CHICKEN STEW

Cook on 190° to 200° for **10** hours, or on 290° to 300° for **5** hours.
Makes 8 servings.

In some parts of the south, rabbit, rather than stewing chicken would have gone into the pot, but, either way, the long slow cooking flavor is there.

1. Arrange half the chicken parts in the bottom of an electric slow cooker; sprinkle with onion and green pepper slices and parsley.
2. Layer remaining chicken parts in cooker; season with salt, Worcestershire sauce and red-pepper seasoning; top with thawed corn, beans and tomatoes; cover slow cooker.
3. Cook on low (190° to 200°) 10 hours, or on high (290° to 300°) 5 hours, or until chicken is tender when pierced with a two-tined fork.
4. Turn heat control to high (290° to 300°). Combine cornstarch with ¼ cup cold water in a cup; stir into liquid in slow cooker until well-blended; cover; simmer 15 minutes. Serve with hot cornbread or baking powder biscuits.

Suggested Variations: A tablespoon of chopped fresh oregano or marjoram leaves or a teaspoon of dried oregano or marjoram can be added for a more aromatic flavor.

1 stewing chicken, cut up (about 5 pounds)
2 large onions, peeled and sliced
1 large green pepper, seeded and sliced
¼ cup chopped parsley
1 tablespoon salt
1 tablespoon Worcestershire sauce
Few drops bottled red-pepper seasoning
1 package (10 ounces) frozen whole-kernel corn, thawed
1 package (10 ounces) frozen speckled butter beans or lima beans, thawed
1 can (1 pound) tomatoes, broken up
2 tablespoons cornstarch

CATALAN CHICKEN

Cook on 190° to 200° for **10** hours, or on 290° to 300° for **5** hours.
Makes 4 servings.

Simmer and serve this rich Spanish dish in your ever-helpful slow cooker.

1. Brown chicken pieces in oil with salt in a large kettle or an electric slow cooker with a browning unit. Remove.
2. Add sliced onions to pan and cook until soft.
3. Add pimiento, tomatoes, tomato paste, water, sherry and sugar to pan and bring to boiling.
4. Combine chicken and sauce in slow cooker; cover.
5. Cook on low (190° to 200°) 10 hours, or on high (290° to 300°) 5 hours. Serve with rice and crusty French bread.

1 roasting chicken, cut up (3½ to 4 pounds)
3 tablespoons olive oil
1 teaspoon salt
3 medium-size onions, sliced
1 can (4 ounces) pimiento, sliced
2 medium-size tomatoes, peeled and chopped
2 tablespoons tomato paste
¼ cup water
¼ cup dry sherry
½ teaspoon sugar

SLOW COOKER COQ AU VIN

Use a really good red Burgundy to get a great flavor. Flaming the brandy also does something delicious to the dish.

1. Brown chicken pieces in butter or margarine in a large skillet; warm brandy in a small saucepan; pour over chicken and flame; place in slow cooker.
2. Sauté onions, garlic and mushrooms in pan drippings; remove to slow cooker with a slotted spoon.
3. Stir in Burgundy wine, chicken broth, salt, pepper, parsley, cloves, thyme and bay leaf and bring to boiling, stirring up all the cooked-on bits in the bottom of the skillet; pour over chicken and vegetables; cover.
4. Cook on low (190° to 200°) 8 hours, or on high (290° to 300°) 4 hours, or until chicken is tender when pierced with a two-tined fork. Remove chicken and vegetables to a heated platter and keep warm while making gravy.
5. Turn heat control to high (290° to 300°). Combine cornstarch and cold water in a cup to make a smooth paste; stir into sauce in slow cooker until well-blended. Cover; simmer 15 minutes longer to thicken sauce. Spoon sauce over chicken and serve with a bottle of the same hearty Burgundy used in the cooking and chunks of crusty French bread for soaking up the sauce.

2 chicken breasts, split (about 12 ounces each)
4 chicken legs or thighs
⅓ cup butter or margarine
¼ cup brandy (optional)
12 small white onions, peeled
2 cloves garlic, crushed
½ pound mushrooms, halved
1 cup red Burgundy or dry red wine
1 cup chicken broth
1 teaspoon salt
¼ teaspoon pepper
1 tablespoon chopped parsley
Dash ground cloves
¼ teaspoon leaf thyme, crumbled
1 bay leaf
2 tablespoons cornstarch
¼ cup cold water

time savers

- Break, rather than cut off the woody ends of fresh asparagus spears. The stalks will snap easily where the tender top ends and the tough base begins.

Less cooking time = less energy used = money saved:

- Make mashed potatoes faster? Pare potatoes and cut into small pieces; cook in boiling salted water 15 minutes; drain; add milk and butter to pan with potatoes; heat until butter melts; then remove pan from heat and mash potatoes.
- Brown a batch of meat balls quickly by placing them, in a single layer, in a jelly-roll pan. Bake at 350° for 15 minutes; then add to slow cooker and cook following recipe instructions.

ROSEMARY CHICKEN

Cook on 190° to 200° for **8** hours,
or on 290° to 300° for **4** hours.
Makes 4 servings.

Serve this flavorful chicken on the patio for a summer supper.

1. Place chicken, skin-side down, in an electric slow cooker; top with onion slices.
2. Mix catsup, vinegar, butter or margarine, garlic, rosemary, salt and dry mustard in a small saucepan; bring just to boiling; pour over chicken.
3. Cook on low (190° to 200°) 8 hours, or on high (290° to 300°) 4 hours, or until tender.

2 broiler-fryers, cut-up (2 pounds each)
1 large onion, cut into thick slices
⅔ cup catsup
⅓ cup vinegar
¼ cup (½ stick) butter or margarine
1 clove garlic, minced
1 teaspoon leaf rosemary, crushed
1 teaspoon salt
¼ teaspoon dry mustard

PIMIENTO CHICKEN STEW

Cook on 190° to 200° for **10** hours,
or on 290° to 300° for **5** hours.
Makes 8 servings.

A hearty meal topped with peppy pimiento biscuits.

1. Remove all fat from chicken. Melt fat in large heavy kettle or an electric slow cooker with a browning unit.
2. Shake chicken with flour and herb salad-dressing mix in a plastic bag to coat evenly; brown, a few pieces at a time, in fat in pan. Remove chicken and reserve.
3. Sauté onion until soft in same pan; stir in tomatoes and water; add celery, lima beans, corn and chicken to slow cooker; cover.
4. Cook on low (190° to 200°) 10 hours, or on high (290° to 300°) 5 hours, or until chicken is tender; let stand 5 to 10 minutes; skim excess fat.
5. Save 1 pimiento for PIMIENTO BISCUITS; dice remaining; stir into stew with parsley; serve with PIMIENTO BISCUITS.

1 stewing chicken, cut-up (4 to 5 pounds)
½ cup all-purpose flour
1 envelope (about 1 ounce) herb salad-dressing mix
1 large onion, chopped (1 cup)
1 can (1 pound, 13 ounces) tomatoes
2 cup water
2 cups diced celery
2 cups frozen lima beans
2 cups frozen whole-kernel corn
1 can (4 ounces) pimiento
¼ cup chopped parsley
Pimiento Biscuits (recipe follows)

PIMIENTO BISCUITS—Bake at 400° for 10 minutes.
Makes 12 biscuits.

1. Mix biscuit mix, cornmeal, melted butter or margarine and pimiento with a fork in a medium-size bowl; stir in water just until no dry mix appears; spoon in 12 mounds onto ungreased cooky sheet.
2. Bake in hot oven (400°) 10 minutes, or until golden.

Pimiento Biscuits
1¾ cups biscuit mix
½ cup yellow cornmeal
2 tablespoons melted butter or margarine
1 pimiento, chopped
⅔ cup water

POULET EN CASSEROLE

This chicken dish is a standard on the menus of many gourmet restaurants.

1. Wash and dry chicken; skewer neck skin to back; twist the wing tips flat against skewered neck skin; tie the legs to tail with kitchen string.
2. Heat oil and butter or margarine with the minced garlic in a large skillet or an electric slow cooker with a browning unit. Brown chicken in the hot fat; remove.
3. Sauté onions, potatoes and carrots in drippings; remove and reserve. Stir wine, salt, rosemary and pepper into pan and bring to boiling, scraping up all the cooked-on juices from bottom of pan; stir in chicken broth; place chicken in slow cooker; surround with browned vegetables and sauce; cover.
4. Cook on low (190° to 200°) 10 hours, or on high (290° to 300°) 6 hours, or until chicken is tender. Garnish with a bouquet of parsley and serve with a chilled dry white wine, such as a Chablis, and chunks of crusty French bread, if you wish.

1 broiler-fryer (about 3 pounds)
2 tablespoons vegetable oil
2 tablespoons butter or margarine
2 cloves garlic, minced
12 whole white onions, peeled
12 small white potatoes, pared
4 large carrots, pared and quartered
1 cup dry white wine
2 teaspoons salt
1 teaspoon leaf rosemary, crumbled
½ teaspoon freshly ground pepper
1 can condensed chicken broth

MELBOURNE CHICKEN

This delectable chicken has a light curry-and-fruit-flavored sauce.

1. Pull skin from chicken breasts; halve each.
2. Shake with mixture of flour, curry powder and salt in a plastic bag to coat lightly and evenly.
3. Brown pieces in vegetable oil in a large skillet or an electric slow cooker with browning unit; remove and reserve.
4. Stir sugar, beef broth or bouillon cubes, onion, water, apricots, lemon juice and soy sauce into drippings in pan; heat to boiling, crushing bouillon cubes, if used, with a spoon. Pour over chicken in slow cooker; cover.
5. Cook on low (190° to 200°) 6 hours, or on high (290° to 300°) 3 hours. Serve over hot fluffy rice or noodles.

4 whole chicken breasts (about 12 ounces each)
3 tablespoons all-purpose flour
1 tablespoon curry powder
2 teaspoons salt
¼ cup vegetable oil
1 tablespoon sugar
2 envelopes instant beef broth or 2 beef bouillon cubes
1 large onion, chopped (1 cup)
1 cup water
1 jar (about 5 ounces) baby-pack apricots
2 tablespoons lemon juice
2 teaspoons soy sauce

HALVED CHICKEN ITALIANO

Cook on 190° to 200° for **10** hours, or on 290° to 300° for **5** hours.
Makes 4 servings.

Chicken halves are simmered in an herbed tomato sauce and served over hot spaghetti.

1. Brown chicken in oil in a large skillet or an electric slow cooker with a browning unit. Remove halves as they brown; keep warm.
2. Chop ½ the green pepper; cut other half into strips; reserve strips. Sauté the chopped pepper, onion and garlic until soft in same pan. Stir in tomato sauce, wine, Italian herbs and cloves. Bring to boiling. Combine chicken in slow cooker with sauce; cover.
3. Cook on low (190° to 200°) 10 hours, or on high (290° to 300°) 5 hours.
4. Thirty minutes before serving, cook spaghetti, following label directions; drain. Place on large heated platter.
5. While spaghetti is cooking, sauté pepper strips in butter or margarine in small skillet; add tomato wedges, parsley and salt; cook 2 minutes longer, or just until tomato is soft. Arrange chicken halves on hot spaghetti. Spoon sauce over. Garnish with sautéed pepper-tomato mixture on top of the sauce.

2 broiler-fryers, split (2½ pounds each)
1 tablespoon vegetable oil
1 green pepper, halved and seeded
1 large onion, chopped (1 cup)
1 clove garlic, crushed
1 can (8 ounces) tomato sauce
½ cup dry red wine
1 teaspoon mixed Italian herbs, crumbled
Dash ground cloves
1 package (½ pound) spaghetti
2 tablespoons butter or margarine
1 tomato, cut into wedges
3 tablespoons chopped parsley
½ teaspoon salt

NAPOLI CHICKEN

Cook on 190° to 200° for **8** hours, or on 290° to 300° for **4** hours.
Makes 4 servings.

Italian cooking was never so simple, yet delicious.

1. Arrange chicken quarters in an electric slow cooker. Mix sauce, wine and mushrooms in a medium-size bowl. Spoon over chicken; cover slow cooker.
2. Cook on low (190° to 200°) 8 hours, or on high (290° to 300°) 4 hours.
3. Spread mozzarella cheese over chicken. Combine Parmesan cheese, crumbs and parsley; sprinkle over top. Cook 3 minutes longer, or until cheese melts.

1 broiler-fryer, quartered (about 3 pounds)
1 jar (21 ounces) Italian cooking sauce
¼ cup red cooking wine
1 can (3 or 4 ounces) sliced mushrooms, drained
2 cups diced or shredded mozzarella cheese (8 ounces)
¼ cup grated Parmesan cheese
¼ cup Italian-seasoned dry bread crumbs
2 tablespoons dry parsley flakes

BOUNTIFUL BARBECUED TURKEY

An excellent party dish that needs the 5-quart slow cooker. For something colorful and delicious, serve with herb buttered cauliflower and broccoli.

1. Shake turkey pieces, a few at a time, in a mixture of flour, salt and pepper in a plastic bag to coat evenly.
2. Brown turkey pieces in shortening in a large skillet or a 5-quart electric slow cooker with a browning unit; remove and reserve. Pour off all but 2 tablespoons of the pan drippings. Sauté onion and garlic in drippings until soft. Stir in peppers and lemon slices and cook 2 minutes.
3. Place turkey pieces in slow cooker and coat with onion mixture. Combine chicken broth, tomato sauce, wine and brown sugar in a 4-cup measure; pour over turkey; cover.
4. Cook on low (190° to 200°) 9 hours. Turn heat control to high (290° to 300°); cook 3 hours, or until turkey pieces are tender when pierced with a fork.

COOK'S TIP: To thicken gravy, remove turkey to a heated platter lined with linguini and keep warm. Combine ½ cup all-purpose flour with 1 cup cold water in a 2-cup measure until smooth; stir into liquid; cover; cook 15 minutes.

1 frozen turkey, thawed, and cut up, (about 8 pounds)
¾ cup all-purpose flour
1 tablespoon salt
½ teaspoon pepper
½ cup vegetable shortening
1 Bermuda onion, sliced
1 clove garlic, minced
1 or 2 green chili peppers, seeded and chopped (from a 4-ounce can)
6 slices lemon
1 can condensed chicken broth
1 can (8 ounces) tomato sauce
½ cup dry white wine
1 tablespoon brown sugar
Hot linguini

metric weights and measures

America may soon "go metric" (the House of Representatives is presently reviewing a bill that would require Americans to convert to the metric system of weights and measures). What this would mean, assuming the bill is passed, is that Americans eventually would abandon pounds and ounces, quarts and pints, inches and feet, for grams, liters and meters. (America and Great Britain, by the way, are the only major powers not to have adopted the metric system.)

Metric measures, though they may not seem so at first, are easier to use than our present measures because they are based upon multiples of ten. It is not necessary to print here a complete table of metric weights and measures—you will find them in any good dictionary—but only to include those most commonly used in the kitchen.

*Fortunately, when measures are small, tablespoons (*cuiller à soupe*, in French) and teaspoons (*cuiller a café*)

CHICKEN ORLÉANS

This superb dish is named for the Ile d'Orléans near Quebec City, which is noted for its apple orchards.

1. Rub chicken inside and out with brandy or cognac, then with salt and pepper.
2. Combine bread cubes, celery, chopped apple, raisins, butter or margarine, parsley and thyme in a bowl.
3. Stuff chicken with dressing, packing lightly. Skewer neck skin to back; twist the wing tips flat against skewered neck skin; tie legs to tail with kitchen string.
4. Place bacon in a saucepan; cover with water. Bring to boiling; lower heat and simmer 10 minutes. Dry on paper towels.
5. Fry bacon lightly in an electric slow cooker with a browning unit or a large kettle. Remove bacon and reserve. Brown chicken on all sides in bacon drippings; remove and keep warm.
6. Quarter, core and thickly slice apples; brown lightly in pan drippings. Place chicken on top of apple slices in slow cooker; lay bacon slices over chicken; cover cooker.
7. Cook on low (190° to 200°) 8 hours, or on high (290° to 300°) 4 hours, or until chicken is tender. Pour cream and 2 tablespoons apple brandy or Cognac over, just before serving.

1 broiler-fryer (about 3 pounds)
Apple brandy or cognac
1 teaspoon salt
¼ teaspoon freshly ground pepper
2 cups diced white bread (4 slices)
½ cup chopped celery
½ cup chopped apple
¼ cup raisins
3 tablespoons butter or
*   margarine, melted*
1 tablespoon chopped parsley
½ teaspoon leaf thyme, crumbled
3 slices thickly-sliced bacon
6 medium-size apples
1 cup light cream

Liquid Measures				Weights	
Metric	**U.S.A.**	**U.S.A.**	**Metric**	**Metric**	**U.S.A.**
1 liter	4¼ cups (1 quart + ¼ cup *or* 34 fluid ounces)	1 gallon	3.785 liters	1 kilogram	2.205 pounds
				500 grams	1.103 pounds *or* about 17.5 ounces
1 demiliter (½ liter)	2⅛ cups (1 pint +⅛ cup *or* 17 fluid ounces)	1 quart	0.946 liter	100 grams	3.5 ounces
				10 grams	.35 ounce
1 deciliter (1/10 liter)	A scant ½ cup *or* 3.4 fluid ounces	1 pint	0.473 liter	1 gram	0.035 ounce
				U.S.A.	**Metric**
1 centiliter* (1/100 liter)	Approximately 2 teaspoons *or* .34 fluid ounce	1 cup	0.237 liter *or* 237 milliliters*	1 pound	0.454 kilogram *or* 453.6 grams
				½ pound	0.226 kilogram *or* 226.8 grams
1 milliliter* (1/1000 liter)	Approximately 1/5 teaspoon *or* .034 fluid ounce	1 tbsp.	Approximately 1.5 centiliters *or* 15 milliliters*	¼ pound	0.113 kilogram *or* 113.4 grams
				1 ounce	28.35 grams

are more often used than milliliters.

Cook on 190° to 200° for **10** hours,
or on 290° to 300° for **5** hours.
Makes 8 servings.

CHICKEN MARENGO

This dish originated in the Italian town of Marengo. They say it was invented to serve to Napoleon after his victory over the Austrians there.

1. Fry bacon until almost crisp in large skillet or electric slow cooker with a browning unit. Lift out with slotted spoon; drain on paper towels and reserve. Leave drippings in pan.
2. Shake chicken in mixture of flour, salt and pepper in plastic bag to coat well; reserve remaining flour.
3. Brown chicken, a few pieces at a time, in bacon drippings; reserve.
4. Sauté onion and garlic until soft in same pan; stir in reserved flour mixture. Drain liquid from mushrooms. Stir liquid, tomatoes, parsley and the red-pepper seasoning into pan; bring to boiling, stirring constantly.
5. Spoon over chicken in slow cooker; cover.
6. Cook on low (190° to 200°) 10 hours, or on high (290° to 300°) 5 hours. Uncover; sprinkle with saved bacon pieces and mushrooms. Sprinkle GOLDEN CROUTONS over top; garnish with more chopped parsley.

6 slices bacon, cut in 1-inch pieces
2 broiler-fryers, cut-up (about 3 pounds each)
½ cup all-purpose flour
2 teaspoons salt
¼ teaspoon pepper
1 large onion, chopped (1 cup)
1 clove garlic, minced
1 can (3 or 4 ounces) whole mushrooms
2 cans (1 pound each) tomatoes
¼ cup chopped parsley
Few drops bottled red-pepper seasoning
Golden Croutons (recipe follows)

GOLDEN CROUTONS— Makes 1 cup. Trim crusts from 2 slices of white bread; cut into ½-inch cubes. Spread in single layer in shallow baking pan. Toast in moderate oven (350°) 10 minutes, or until golden.

HOSTESS TIP: This dish is even more delicious when made ahead, removed from slow cooker, cooled and refrigerated until one hour before serving time. Heat in moderate oven (350°) 1 hour, or until bubbly; top with croutons and parsley.

quick tips

- Don't let unused olives or pimientos spoil. Instead, cover with vinegar in a glass jar, screw top on tightly; refrigerate until needed.
- Save those snack food tag-ends. Crush the last of pretzels, potato chips or crackers and use as a slow cooker dish topping.

COUNTRY CAPTAIN

Cook on 190° to 200° for **8** hours, or on 290° to 300° for **4** hours, Makes 8 servings.

A classic Southern dish with a touch of the Orient.

1. Cut chicken into serving-size pieces, following cutting directions on page 74.
2. Combine flour with 1 teaspoon of the salt and ¼ teaspoon of the pepper in a plastic bag. Shake chicken, a few pieces at a time, in flour mixture to coat; tap off excess.
3. Brown chicken, part at a time, in oil in a large skillet or slow cooker with a browning unit. Remove chicken; keep warm.
4. Add onion, green pepper, garlic and curry powder to drippings remaining in kettle; sauté until soft. Add tomatoes, breaking with spoon, raisins and reserved chicken, salt and pepper; cover.
5. Cook on low (190° to 200°) 8 hours, or on high (290° to 300°) 4 hours, or until chicken is tender. Arrange chicken on a bed of hot cooked rice. Spoon sauce over top.

2 broiler-fryers (about 2½ pounds each)
¼ cup all-purpose flour
2 teaspoons salt
½ teaspoon pepper
3 tablespoons vegetable oil
1 large onion, chopped (1 cup)
1 large green pepper, halved, seeded, and chopped
1 large clove garlic, crushed
1 tablespoon curry powder
1 can (1 pound) tomatoes
½ cup raisins or currants
Hot cooked rice

MEXICALI CHICKEN

Cook on 190° to 200° for **10** hours, or on 290° to 300° for **5** hours. Makes 8 servings.

Chicken and peppers are steeped in a tangy tomato sauce.

1. Brown chicken, part at a time, in butter or margarine and oil in a large skillet or an electric slow cooker with a browning unit; remove and reserve.
2. Stir onion and green and red peppers into drippings in pan; sauté until soft. Stir in chili powder; cook 1 minute longer.
3. Sprinkle flour over top, then blend in; stir in tomatoes, salt and pepper. Cook, stirring constantly, until sauce thickens and bubbles 3 minutes.
4. Layer browned chicken, topping each piece with part of the sauce, into slow cooker; cover.
5. Cook on low (190° to 200°) 10 hours, or on high (290° to 300°) 5 hours. Garnish with rings of red and green pepper, if you wish.

2 broiler-fryers, cut up (about 3 pounds each)
2 tablespoons butter or margarine
2 tablespoons olive oil or vegetable oil
1 large onion, chopped (1 cup)
1 large green pepper, halved, seeded, and chopped
1 large sweet red pepper, halved, seeded and chopped
1 tablespoon chili powder
¼ cup all-purpose flour
1 can (about 2 pounds) Italian tomatoes
1 tablespoon salt
¼ teaspoon pepper

CHICKEN CACCIATORE

Cook on 190° to 200° for **8** *hours,*
or on 290° to 300° for **4** *hours.*
Makes 6 servings.

This is the Italian version of Chicken Hunter-style,
with pieces of chicken and green pepper in wine-
tomato sauce.

1. Shake chicken pieces in a mixture of flour, salt and pepper in a plastic bag.
2. Sauté onion and garlic in 2 tablespoons of the oil until soft in a large skillet or an electric slow cooker with a browning unit. Remove with slotted spoon and reserve.
3. Brown chicken, a few pieces at a time, adding remaining oil as needed; remove and reserve. Sauté peppers in drippings until soft; stir in wine; bring to boiling, stirring constantly. Return onion and garlic to pan; stir in tomatoes.
4. Place chicken in slow cooker; spoon sauce over chicken; cover.
5. Cook on low (190° to 200°) 8 hours, or on high (290° to 300°) 4 hours. Sprinkle with chopped parsley, if you wish. Serve with linguini or thin spaghetti.

Suggested Variation: CHICKEN CHASSEUR: This is the French version of Chicken Hunter-style. It is named in honor of the famous Chasseur cavalry regiments who hunted for their food. Follow the recipe for CHICKEN CACCIATORE, except use ½ cup chopped shallots or green onions instead of the yellow onions. Substitute 1 cup brown gravy for the wine and ½ pound sliced fresh mushrooms or 1 can (6 ounces) sliced mushrooms for the green peppers. Sprinkle with chopped parsley and serve with boiled potatoes.

2 broiler-fryers, cut-up (about 2½
pounds each)
⅓ cup all-pupose flour
2 teaspoons salt
¼ teaspoon freshly ground pepper
1 large onion, chopped (1 cup)
2 cloves garlic, minced
¼ cup olive oil or vegetable oil
2 large green peppers, halved,
seeded and cut into chunks
½ cup dry white wine
1 can (1 pound, 1 ounce) Italian
tomatoes
Hot linguini or thin spaghetti

frozen food tips

• Slightly undercook dishes that must be cooked again before being served. Those needing an hour of reheating can be underdone by as much as 30 minutes.
• If foods have been partially thawed but still have some ice crystal in their packages, they can be safely refrozen. To make sure food is only partially thawed (when ice crystals are not discernable), slip a thermometer between the food and its wrapping. If the temperature is below 40°F., the food can be safely refrozen.

GARDEN CHICKEN

Cook on 190° to 200° for **10** hours,
or on 290° to 300° for **5** hours.
Makes 4 servings.

*Fresh asparagus, new potatoes and celery combine
with chicken quarters in this meal-in-one dish.*

1. Sprinkle chicken on both sides with ½ teaspoon of the
   salt and ½ teaspoon tarragon. Heat butter or margarine in large skillet or an electric slow cooker with a
   browning unit; add chicken, skin-side down, and
   brown slowly; turn, and brown other side; remove and
   reserve.
2. Add potatoes to the butter in skillet; cook slowly over
   low heat for about 5 minutes and add to slow cooker
   with chicken. Sprinkle chicken and potatoes with
   chives, parsley and drippings from pan and wine;
   cover slow cooker.
3. Cook on low (190° to 200°) 10 hours, or on high (290°
   to 300°) 5 hours.
4. Ten minutes before serving, add celery pieces and
   asparagus. Sprinkle vegetables with remaining 1
   teaspoon salt and ½ teaspoon tarragon; spoon juices
   in slow cooker over asparagus and celery. Drizzle with
   lemon juice.
5. Cover and cook 5 minutes longer, or until chicken and
   vegetables are tender; baste occasionally with the
   juices in slow cooker.

*1 broiler-fryer, quartered (about 3
   pounds)*
1½ teaspoon salt
*1 teaspoon leaf tarragon,
   crumbled*
2 tablespoons butter or margarine
*1 pound small new potatoes,
   pared*
2 tablespoons chopped chives
2 tablespoons chopped parsley
½ cup dry white wine
*2 cups sliced celery, cooked and
   drained*
*1 pound asparagus (break off ends
   of stems where they snap
   easily), cooked and drained*
1 tablespoon lemon juice

SOY SIMMERED CHICKEN

Cook on 190° to 200° for **10** hours,
or on 290° to 300° for **5** hours.
Makes 4 servings.

*Chicken quarters absorb piquant flavors from the
soy-sherry sauce which glazes the chicken as it
simmers.*

1. Combine water, soy sauce, sherry, corn syrup and
   seasoned salt in an electric slow cooker.
2. Arrange chicken, skin-side down, in a slow cooker.
   Brush generously with part of the sauce; cover cooker.
3. Cook on low (190° to 200°) 10 hours, or on high (290°
   to 300°) 5 hours.

¼ cup water
¼ cup soy sauce
¼ cup dry sherry
¼ cup corn syrup
2 teaspoons seasoned salt
*1 broiler-fryer, cut-up (about 3
   pounds)*

MANDARIN CHICKEN BREASTS

Cook on 190° to 200° for 6 hours, or on 290° to 300° for 3 hours.
Makes 6 servings.

Fruits and chicken make a treat for the eye as well as the palate.

1. Sprinkle inside of chicken breasts lightly with salt.
2. Combine rice, 1 tablespoon of the butter or margarine, ¼ teaspoon salt, parsley, rosemary and basil in a large bowl; toss lightly to mix; spoon into hollows in chicken breasts. Fold edges over stuffing to cover completely; fasten with wooden picks.
3. Mix flour, paprika and ½ teaspoon salt in a pie plate; dip chicken breasts into mixture to coat well. Brown slowly in remaining 2 tablespoons butter or margarine in a large heavy skillet or an electric slow cooker with a browning unit.
4. Stir in chicken broth, water, onion, lemon juice and bay leaf; bring to boiling. Combine stuffed breasts and broth in slow cooker.
5. Cook on low (190° to 200°) 6 hours, or on high (290° to 300°) 3 hours; remove bay leaf. Place chicken on a heated deep serving platter; keep warm.
6. Turn heat control to high (290° to 300°). Smooth cornstarch with a little water to a paste in a cup; stir into liquid in pan. Cook 15 minutes. Stir in mandarin-orange segments and grapes; heat until bubbly. Spoon over chicken. Garnish with additional grapes and mandarin-orange segments and serve with buttered peas, if you wish.

6 whole chicken breasts, boned (about 12 ounces each)
Salt
1½ cups hot cooked rice
3 tablespoons butter or margarine
¾ teaspoon salt
1 tablespoon chopped parsley
¼ teaspoon leaf rosemary, crumbled
¼ teaspoon leaf basil, crumbled
¼ cup all-purpose flour
½ teaspoon paprika
2 envelopes or teaspoons instant chicken broth
1¾ cups water
1 tablespoon instant minced onion
2 tablespoons lemon juice
1 bay leaf
1 tablespoon cornstarch
1 can (about 11 ounces) mandarin-orange segments, drained
1 cup seedless green grapes

tips for frozen food shoppers

• Buy frozen foods last when marketing so they will stay frozen until you get them home.
• Choose clean, firm packages, not those that are misshapen, crystalline inside or broken. The contents have probably thawed and refrozen. Anytime you discover a softened package at the supermarket, by the way, report it to the manager. His freezer cabinet may not be functioning properly. Or his employees may not be handling the frozen foods as carefully as they should.

VERA CRUZ CHICKEN

Cook on 190° to 200° for **6** hours, or on 290° to 300° for **3** hours.
Makes 6 servings.

Serve this dish to guests with adventurous palates. The sauce is a hot one, heady with spices and tart with orange.

1. Heat butter or margarine and the oil in a skillet or an electric slow cooker with a browning unit and sauté chicken breasts until golden. Season with salt and a few dashes of pepper, pour brandy over and carefully set aflame.
2. When flames have died down, add garlic, chili peppers and red-pepper seasoning. Blend in orange juice concentrate. Combine chicken breasts and sauce in slow cooker; cover.
3. Cook on low (190° to 200°) 6 hours, or on high (290° to 300°) 3 hours, remove to a hot platter and pour sauce over. Sprinkle with pine nuts. Garnish with red pepper and orange slices, if you wish. Serve with a pitcher of chilled Sangria.

1 tablespoon peanut oil or vegetable oil
3 whole chickens breasts, split (about 12 ounces each)
3 tablespoons butter or margarine
½ teaspoon salt
Pepper
⅓ cup brandy
2 cloves garlic, thinly sliced
1 can (4 ounces) green chili peppers, seeded and chopped
Few drops bottled red-pepper seasoning
1 can (6 ounces) frozen concentrate for orange juice
½ cup pine nuts (optional)

NORMANDY CHICKEN

Cook on 190° to 200° for **8** hours, or on 290° to 300° for **4** hours.
Makes 4 servings.

This sauced chicken makes a fine company dinner served with hot buttered noodles.

1. Shake chicken pieces, a few at a time, in 4 tablespoons of the flour in a plastic bag to coat well.
2. Brown chicken slowly in oil in a large skillet or an electric slow cooker with a browning unit; remove and reserve.
3. Stir onion and garlic into drippings in pan; sauté just until soft. Blend in saved 2 tablespoons flour, instant broth, salt and pepper; cook, stirring all the time, just until mixture bubbles. Stir in brandy or cider, water, tomato paste and lemon rind; continue cooking and stirring until sauce thickens and bubbles 3 minutes.
4. Combine chicken and sauce in slow cooker; cover.
5. Cook on low (190° to 200°) 8 hours, or on high 290° to 300° 4 hours.

1 broiler-fryer, cut up (about 3 pounds)
6 tablespoons all-purpose flour
¼ cup vegetable oil
1 small onion, sliced and separated into rings
½ clove garlic, minced
1 envelope or teaspoon instant chicken broth
1 teaspoon salt
⅛ teaspoon pepper
½ cup apple brandy or apple cider
½ cup water
2 tablespoons tomato paste
1 teaspoon grated lemon rind

BROWN CHICKEN FRICASSEE

Chicken browned with onions and topped off with cornmeal dumplings should please all.

1. Shake chicken pieces, a few at a time, in mixture of flour, salt, poultry seasoning and pepper in a plastic bag to coat well.
2. Brown chicken slowly in oil in a large skillet or an electric slow cooker with a browning unit; remove and reserve. Add onion rings, sauté until soft, about 3 minutes.
3. Return chicken to slow cooker; add bay leaf and water; cover.
4. Cook on low (190° to 200°) 10 hours, or on high (290° to 300°) 5 hours.
5. Prepare CORNMEAL DUMPLINGS: Turn heat control to high (290° to 300°); drop dough into 12 small mounds on top of fricassee; cover cooker.
6. Cook 30 minutes. (No peeking, or the dumplings won't puff properly.) Serve chicken and dumplings right from cooker.

CORNMEAL DUMPLINGS— Makes 12 dumplings.
Sift 1½ cups sifted all-purpose flour, ¼ cup yellow cornmeal, 1 tablespoon baking powder and 1 teaspoon salt into a medium-size bowl. Cut in 2 tablespoons shortening with a pastry blender until mixture is crumbly. Stir in 1 cup milk just until flour mixture is moistened. (Dough will be soft.)

1 stewing chicken, cut-up (about 5 pounds)
¼ cup all-purpose flour
2 teaspoons salt
1 teaspoon poultry seasoning
¼ teaspoon pepper
3 tablespoons vegetable oil
2 medium-size onions sliced and separated into rings
1 bay leaf
4 cups water
Cornmeal Dumplings (recipe follows)

guide to poultry

- Capon is a fleshy, tender desexed rooster with a high proportion of white meat and a fine flavor. A capon weighs 4 to 7 pounds and is excellent when roasted, steamed or stewed.
- Ducklings: They are usually individually packaged and quick-frozen although some areas sell fresh, ice-chilled ducklings. Weights range from 4 to 6 pounds. Also beginning to appear in supermarkets are duckling parts, quick-frozen and accompanied by full cooking instructions.
  How much to buy: Allow about one-quarter to one-half duckling per person. Each bird cuts neatly into quarters with poultry or kitchen scissors.
- Rock Cornish Game Hen: This is a special breed that was developed originally from a Cornish fowl. It is a very small chicken that weighs 1½ pounds or less; it is

BOMBAY CHICKEN IN A POT

This is a curry with a difference—the roasting chicken is kept whole, but the slow cooker allows the flavor to penetrate into the bird.

1. Stuff chicken with quartered apple and onion and raisins. Skewer neck skin to back; twist the wing tips flat against skewered neck skin; tie the legs to tail with kitchen string.
2. Combine butter or margarine, curry powder, flour and salt in a cup. Rub mixture all over chicken.
3. Sauté carrots, green pepper and onion in oil in a large skillet; spoon into bottom of a 5-quart slow cooker; place coated chicken on vegetables; add sherry and broth; cover cooker.
4. Cook on low (190° to 200°) 12 hours, or on high (290° to 300°) 6 hours.
5. Remove chicken from slow cooker; cut off string and place in the center of a heated platter lined with fluffy rice; keep warm.
6. Strain juices in slow cooker into a large saucepan; bring to boiling. Combine 3 tablespoons cornstarch and ⅓ cup cold water in a cup until smooth; stir into bubbling liquid; cook, stirring constantly, until mixture thickens and bubbles 1 minute; pour into a gravy boat.
7. Serve chicken with gravy and an assortment of curry condiments.

1 roasting chicken (about 5 pounds)
1 large apple, quartered
1 large onion, quartered
¼ cup raisins
3 tablespoons softened butter or margarine
2 to 3 tablespoons curry powder
1 tablespoon all-purpose flour
1 teaspoon salt
6 large carrots, pared and cut into sticks
1 large green pepper, halved, seeded and cut into strips
½ cup frozen chopped onion
2 tablespoons vegetable oil
½ cup cocktail sherry
¼ cup chicken broth
3 tablespoons cornstarch
⅓ cup water

---

available frozen in supermarkets across the country.
How much to buy: Allow 1 game hen per person.
• Turkey—Types Available: (The majority of turkeys are frozen.)
• Fryer-Roaster: A small, meaty turkey weighing from 4 to 9 pounds.
• Roaster: The size range goes from about 10 pounds up to 30 pounds. An advantage of substituting two small birds for one giant is that you double the number of drumsticks, thighs, wings and breasts. A disadvantage: Small birds may not look quite so festive on the table.
• Boneless Turkey Rolls: A plump roast weighing from 2 to 5 pounds.
• Frozen Prestuffed Turkey: Available in a broad range of sizes from 6-pound turkeys to near-20-pounders. The most popular are those in the 8-to-12 pound class.

(continued on next page)

TIJUANA CHICKEN

Cook on 190° to 200° for **8** hours,
or on 290° to 300° for **4** hours.
Makes 4 servings.

A spicy dish with a saucy seasoning of olives, green pepper, tomatoes and herbs.

1. Disjoint wings from chicken. Remove giblets and neck from chicken package and place (except liver) with wings, water, and the ¼ teaspoon salt in a small saucepan; cover. Simmer 45 minutes. Add liver; cover; cook 15 minutes longer. Strain broth into a small bowl; reserve. Chop giblets and the meat from wings and neck.
2. Shake chicken, a few pieces at a time, in a plastic bag with flour to coat; tap off excess. Reserve remaining flour.
3. Sauté chicken in butter or margarine and oil, turning once, about 15 minutes, or until golden brown, in a large skillet or an electric slow cooker with a browning unit; remove and reserve.
4. Add onion and green pepper to drippings in pan; sauté until tender. Stir in basil, the reserved flour, seasoned salt and paprika. Cook 1 minute, stirring constantly. Stir in 1 cup of the reserved broth; cook and stir until sauce thickens and bubbles 1 minute. Stir in chopped chicken and giblets and cheese. Pour over chicken and vegetables in slow cooker; cover.
5. Cook on low (190° to 200°) 8 hours, or on high (290° to 300°) 4 hours. Arrange tomatoes and olives on top and serve.

1 broiler-fryer, cut-up (about 2½ pounds)
2 cups water
¼ teaspoon salt
½ cup all-purpose flour
2 tablespoons butter or margarine
3 tablespoons vegetable oil
1 large onion, chopped (1 cup)
1 large green pepper, halved, seeded and chopped
1 teaspoon leaf basil, crumbled
1 teaspoon seasoned salt
1 teaspoon paprika
⅓ cup grated Parmesan cheese
3 medium-size tomatoes, peeled and quartered
¼ cup pimiento-stuffed olives, sliced

guide to poultry (continued)

- Frozen Self-Basting Turkey: Injected with butter-flavored fat before being frozen, this turkey actually bastes itself as it cooks. Available in a wide range of sizes.
- Frozen Boneless Turkey Pan Roast: It comes raw, or fully cooked or smoked, and also as all-dark or all-white meat or as a combination. Size ranges from 1½ to 3 pounds.
- Frozen Turkey Steaks: These are turkey minute steaks; they are available plain or breaded.
- Turkey Parts: Turkey drumsticks, wings, thighs and breasts are marketed the way chicken parts are. Legs and wings, particularly, offer good eating at relatively low cost.
- Smoked Turkey: A gourmet item, ready to slice and eat.

NEOPOLITAN CHICKEN

Cook on 190° to 200° for **10** hours,
or on 290° to 300° for **5** hours.
Makes 6 servings.

Families that love spaghetti will welcome chicken-and-potatoes with hearty spaghetti-sauce flavor.

1. Shake chicken with flour, salt and pepper in a plastic bag to coat well. Brown, a few pieces at a time, in oil in a large skillet or an electric slow cooker with a browning unit; remove and reserve.
2. Sauté onion and garlic until softened in same pan; stir in water, then spaghetti-sauce mix; bring to boiling. Stir in tomatoes and parsley. Simmer, uncovered, 15 minutes.
3. Pour over chicken in slow cooker; top with potato cubes and pepper strips; cover.
4. Cook on low (190° to 200°) 10 hours, or on high (290° to 300°) 5 hours.

2 broiler-fryers, cut-up (about 3
    pounds each)
¼ cup all-purpose flour
1 teaspoon salt
⅛ teaspoon pepper
2 tablespoons olive or vegetable oil
1 medium-size onion, chopped
    (½ cup)
1 clove garlic, minced
1 cup water
1 envelope (1½ ounces)
    spaghetti-sauce mix
3 medium-size tomatoes, chopped
¼ cup chopped parsley
6 medium-size potatoes, pared
    and cut into 1-inch cubes
1 large green pepper, seeded and
    cut into wide strips

CALIFORNIA CHICKEN

Cook on 190° to 200° for **8** hours,
or on 290° to 300° for **4** hours.
Makes 6 servings.

Crescents of avocado and tomato wedges add color as well as flavor to this chicken dish.

1. Arrange chicken breasts in an electric slow cooker and season with salt and lemon-pepper.
2. Combine onion, celery salt, basil, marjoram, sherry and lemon juice in a small bowl; pour over chicken. Cover slow cooker.
3. Cook on low (190° to 200°) 8 hours, or on high (290° to 300°) 4 hours.
4. Core tomatoes and cut into wedges. Halve, pit and peel avocado and cut into crescents; arrange around chicken breasts with olives; spoon juices in slow cooker over tomatoes; cover.
5. Cook 10 minutes; sprinkle cheese over chicken breasts; cook 5 minutes longer, or until cheese melts. Serve with a tossed salad and a chilled California white wine.

3 whole chicken breasts, split
    (about 12 ounces each)
½ teaspoon salt
¼ teaspoon lemon-pepper
1 medium-size onion, chopped
    (½ cup)
1 teaspoon celery salt
¼ teaspoon leaf basil, crumbled
¼ teaspoon leaf marjoram, crumbled
½ cup dry sherry
1 tablespoon lemon juice
2 medium-size tomatoes
1 medium-size firm ripe avocado
    Pitted ripe olives
½ cup shredded Cheddar cheese

TURKEY CACCIATORE

Here's a great way to feed a crowd inexpensively.

1. Cut sausages into 1-inch lengths. Heat 3 tablespoons of the oil in a heavy, large skillet or an electric slow cooker with a browning unit; brown sausage pieces turning frequently. Remove.

2. Sprinkle turkey pieces with salt and pepper and dredge lightly with flour on wax paper. Brown turkey slowly, a few pieces at a time, in hot sausage fat. Turn pieces frequently until all sides are brown.

3. Pour wine into pan; bring to a boil and scrape in all cooked-on pan juices. Pour over turkey pieces in slow cooker. Add bay leaf, thyme, tomatoes and beef broth.

4. Fry bacon in a skillet; remove with slotted spoon and reserve. Fry garlic and onions in bacon drippings until a deep golden brown. Add to turkey and swirl out pan with a little of the stew liquid, pouring it back into slow cooker; cover.

5. Cook on low (190° to 200°) 12 hours, or on high (290° to 300°) 6 hours. Add sausage pieces and bacon; simmer 20 to 30 minutes longer. Skim off fat and adjust seasonings. Cook polenta or cornmeal, following label directions. Dot with butter or margarine; heap onto dinner plates and top with stew.

1½ pounds Italian sausage, sweet or hot
½ cup olive oil or vegetable oil
1 frozen turkey, thawed and cut up (about 8 pounds)
1 tablespoon salt
1 teaspoon pepper
½ cup all-purpose flour
2 cups dry red wine
1 large bay leaf
1 teaspoon leaf thyme, crumbled
1 can (1 pound, 1 ounce) Italian tomatoes, chopped
1 can (13¾ ounces) beef broth
4 slices bacon, diced
2 to 3 cloves garlic, minced
1 large onion, finely chopped (1 cup)
2 cups Italian polenta or cornmeal
Butter or margarine

cash saver

Give puddings, sauces, gravies, and canned soups the creamy touch by adding evaporated or instant nonfat dry milk. Cup for cup, each supplies the same important nutrients as whole milk—at a big saving. And what perfect keepers!

If you're throwing away the liquids from canned vegetables, you're pouring money down the drain.

Use canned vegetable liquids:
• In soups, sauces and gravies (substitute for part of liquid called for).
• In aspics and jellied vegetable salads (substitute for part of liquid).
• In tomato-juice or vegetable-juice cocktails.

ROMAN FORUM CHICKEN

Flavorful red pimiento, black olives, mushrooms and white wine blend in this tempting Roman chicken-spaghetti dish.

1. Roll chicken pieces in flour, salt and pepper on wax paper; then brown in hot oil in a large heavy skillet or an electric slow cooker with a browning unit.
2. Mix garlic, parsley, poultry seasoning, red-pepper seasoning and wine; pour over browned chicken; simmer a few minutes.
3. Scatter olives, mushrooms, and pimiento pieces over chicken and wine mixture in slow cooker; cover.
4. Cook on low (190° to 200°) 8 hours, or on high (290° to 300°) 4 hours.
5. Serve hot with PARSLEY-BUTTERED SPAGHETTI and pass a bowl of grated Parmesan cheese.

PARSLEY-BUTTERED SPAGHETTI— Cook 1 package (1 pound) thin spaghetti according to package directions. Drain and toss with ¼ cup melted butter or margarine (½ stick) and with 1 cup chopped parsley.

2 broiler-fryers, cut-up (2½ to 3 pounds each)
½ cup all-purpose flour
2 teaspoons salt
¼ teaspoon pepper
¼ cup olive oil
1 clove garlic, crushed
¼ cup chopped parsley
½ teaspoon poultry seasoning
Dash bottled red-pepper seasoning
1 cup dry white wine
¾ cup pitted black olives, sliced
1 can (6 ounces) sliced mushrooms
1 can (4 ounces) pimiento, drained and cut into large pieces
Parsley-Buttered Spaghetti (recipe follows)

TARRAGON CHICKEN CHAMPIGNONS

A French dish of herb-flavored chicken and fresh mushrooms.

1. Sprinkle chicken pieces with blended salt, pepper, and paprika.
2. Cook chicken slowly to a deep golden brown in oil, in a large skillet or an electric slow cooker with a browning unit; remove and keep hot.
3. Sauté onion and mushrooms until tender but not brown.
4. Place chicken in slow cooker; sprinkle with tarragon and cover chicken with the vegetables; add wine; cover slow cooker.
5. Cook on low (190° to 200°) 8 hours, or on high (290° to 300°) 4 hours.

1 broiler-fryer, cut-up (3 pounds)
1 teaspoon seasoned salt
½ teaspoon freshly ground pepper
Dash paprika
¼ cup peanut oil
1 medium-size onion, thinly sliced
½ pound mushrooms, sliced
1 teaspoon leaf tarragon, crumbled
½ cup dry white wine

POULET AUX TOMATES

Cook on 190° to 200° for **10** hours,
or on 290° to 300° for **5** hours.
Makes 8 servings.

A party dish that goes easy on the food budget with fresh tomatoes for flavor.

1. Brown bacon in a large skillet or an electric slow cooker with a browning unit until very crisp; remove bacon with a slotted spoon; reserve.
2. Shake chicken parts in a plastic bag with flour, salt and pepper until all the pieces are evenly coated.
3. Brown chicken, a few pieces at a time, in bacon drippings in pan; remove.
4. Sauté onion and garlic in same pan until soft; stir in chopped tomatoes and tarragon; cook 3 minutes; stir in white wine and bring to boiling. Spoon sauce over chicken in slow cooker and cover.
5. Cook on low (190° to 200°) 10 hours, or on high (290° to 300°) 5 hours or until chicken is tender.
6. One hour before serving, slice mushrooms. Sauté mushrooms in butter or margarine in a large skillet; remove with spoon and reserve.
7. Peel white onions and cut a small cross in the bottom of each one to prevent onions from separating during cooking. Brown onions well in same skillet. Dissolve instant chicken broth in hot water and pour over onions. Cover skillet and simmer 15 minutes, or until onions are tender and liquid has almost evaporated; remove skillet cover and cook onions slowly until they are a rich golden brown.
8. When chicken is cooked, remove cover and add mushrooms and onions; sprinkle crisp bacon over and garnish with chopped parsley, if you wish. Serve with a loaf of French bread and a salad of romaine, thinly sliced raw zucchini and garlic-flavored croutons for a continental touch.

4 slices bacon, diced
2 broiler-fryers, cut-up (about 3 pounds each)
¼ cup all-purpose flour
1 teaspoon salt
¼ teaspoon freshly ground pepper
1 large onion, chopped (1 cup)
1 clove garlic, minced
2 large ripe tomatoes, pared, seeded and chopped
1 teaspoon leaf tarragon, crumbled
1 cup dry white wine
½ pound mushrooms
3 tablespoons butter or margarine
1 pound small white onions
1 envelope or teaspoon instant chicken broth
½ cup hot water

the nose knows

Train your nose to tell you about food:
• Smell vegetables and fruits before you buy them. Fragrant produce will be the most flavorful when cooked.
• Sniff raw fish, meat and poultry. If it has an "off", slightly rancid smell, throw it out. Food is costly, but your health is priceless.

INTERNATIONAL

Variety can spice up your life as a cook if you add dishes from around the world to your basic cuisine. Even the most elaborate continental recipes become a breeze to make in slow cookers that need no tending.

International specialties make great party dishes, too, and some smart women are becoming more relaxed hostesses by putting their company recipes up to cook in the morning and forgetting about them until evening.

Others are learning another carefree cooking trick—they allow their favorite recipes to cook slowly all night while they sleep.

In general, one way to get the rush out of morning is to prepare all your ingredients the night before, then pop them into the slow cooker the next day to cook.

If you cook with leaf or whole herbs and spices, be careful of the amount you use—their flavor tends to get stronger in slow cooking. On the other hand, ground herbs and spices tend to lose some of their flavor and you may want to add them during the last hour of cooking if you're around, or correct your seasoning with them at the very end, before serving.

POLISH HOT POT

Cook on 190° to 200° for **6** hours, or on 290° to 300° for **3** hours.
Makes 4 servings.

Red cabbage and pie-sliced apples turn this dish into a colorful, as well as flavorful family dish. Pictured on page 62.

1. Score kielbasa all around and place in an electric slow cooker.
2. Layer onion, cabbage, and apples in cooker, sprinkling each with part of the salt and pepper; sprinkle with caraway, if used; add bay leaf. Pour beer and chicken broth over; cover cooker.
3. Cook on low (190° to 200°) for 6 hours, or on high (290° to 300°) 3 hours, or until cabbage is very tender. Spoon vegetables into a heated casserole; top with whole cooked sausage.

1 kielbasa or Polish sausage
   (about 1 pound)
1 Bermuda onion, sliced
4 cups shredded red cabbage
1 can (1 pound, 4 ounces) pie-
   sliced apples
1 teaspoon salt
¼ teaspoon pepper
¼ teaspoon caraway seeds
   (optional)
1 bay leaf
½ cup beer
1 can condensed chicken broth

CANNELLINI ALLA CATANIA

Cook on 190° to 200° for **10** hours, or on 290° to 300° for **5** hours.
Makes 6 servings.

This Sicilian-style main dish feeds big appetites on a small budget.

1. Pick over beans and rinse. Cover beans with water in a large kettle; bring to boiling; cover; cook 2 minutes; remove from heat; let stand 1 hour. Pour into an electric slow cooker. (Or cover beans with water in slow cooker and soak overnight at room temperature.)
2. Brown sausages in a small skillet; push to one side; sauté onion and garlic in same pan until soft; stir in tomato, bay leaf, thyme, basil, orange strips, salt, pepper and instant beef broth; bring to boiling; stir into beans; cover.
3. Cook on low (190° to 200°) for 10 hours, or on high (290° to 300°) 5 hours, or until beans are tender. For a classic Italian dessert, serve an assortment of fruits and cheeses.
   Suggested Variations: Dried lima beans can be substituted for the cannellini beans. Sweet Italian sausage, ¼ pound salami or 1 cup sliced pepperoni can be used instead of the hot Italian sausages.

1 package (1 pound) dried
   cannellini beans (white kidney
   beans) or dried Great
   Northern beans
6 cups water
2 hot Italian sausages, sliced
1 large onion, chopped (1 cup)
1 large clove garlic, crushed
2 large ripe tomatoes, peeled and
   coarsely chopped
1 bay leaf, crumbled
½ teaspoon leaf thyme, crumbled
½ teaspoon leaf basil, crumbled
3 one-inch strips orange rind
1 teaspoon salt
¼ teaspoon pepper
1 envelope or teaspoon instant
   beef broth

110

FRENCH POT ROAST

Flavorful beef simmers fork-tender in canned onion soup.

1. Trim excess fat from roast; rub beef well with flour; brown in oil in a large skillet or an electric slow cooker with a browning unit.
2. Place meat in slow cooker; pour onion soup over; cover cooker.
3. Cook on low (190° to 200°) 10 hours, or on high (290° to 300°) 5 hours, or until meat is tender when pierced with a two-tined fork. Place green pepper rings on roast to steam during last 10 minutes of cooking. Remove meat and pepper rings to heated serving platter; keep hot while making gravy.
4. Turn heat control to high (290° to 300°). Combine ¼ cup all-purpose flour and ½ cup cold water in a cup to make a smooth paste. Stir into slow cooker; cover; cook 15 minutes; taste and season with salt and pepper, if you wish.

1 boneless round or chuck roast (about 4 pounds)
2 tablespoons all-purpose flour
2 tablespoons vegetable oil
1 can condensed onion soup
1 green pepper, seeded and cut into rings
¼ cup all-purpose flour
½ cup water

IRISH LAMB STEW

Traditionally, the lamb is not browned in making Irish stew. Peas add color and flavor when cooked just before serving.

1. Layer lamb, onions and carrots in an electric slow cooker; season with salt, pepper, instant chicken broth, basil, thyme and garlic; pour water over; cover slow cooker.
2. Cook on low (190° to 200°) 8 hours, or on high (290° to 300°) 4 hours, or until lamb is tender.
3. Turn heat control to high (290° to 300°). Add peas and lettuce; stir to blend well; cover. Simmer 30 minutes. Serve with slices of brown soda bread.

2 pounds lean boneless lamb shoulder, cubed
18 small white onions, peeled
1 pound carrots, pared and cut into 1-inch pieces
2 teaspoons salt
¼ teaspoon pepper
2 envelopes or teaspoons instant chicken broth
1 teaspoon leaf basil, crumbled
½ teaspoon leaf thyme, crumbled
1 clove garlic, minced
2 cups water
1 package (10 ounces) frozen green peas, thawed
1 cup shredded lettuce

Cook on 190° to 200° for **3** hours,
or on 290° to 300° for **2** hours.

Makes 6 servings.

TERIYAKI CASSEROLE

Not every slow cooker recipe has to take all day. Try this one when you want a deep-down flavor in just 2 hours. Shown on page 129.

1. Cut very cold steak into very thin slices with a sharp knife.
2. Heat oil with garlic until very hot in a large skillet or slow cooker with a browning unit; remove garlic; brown beef quickly, a few pieces at a time; remove.
3. Add onion rings; sauté 2 minutes; add pepper slices, zucchini, yellow squash, mushrooms and carrots; sauté, stirring constantly, until vegetables glisten and have bright color; add soy sauce and saki or sherry. Spoon into slow cooker with steak.
4. Cook on low (190° to 200°) 3 hours, or on high (290° to 300°) 2 hours. Stir in noodles and spoon onto serving platter.

1 boneless sirloin or top round
   steak (about 1½ pounds)
3 tablespoons peanut oil or
   vegetable oil
1 clove garlic, halved
1 large onion, sliced and separated
   into rings
1 large green pepper, halved,
   seeded and sliced
1 large red pepper, halved, seeded
   and sliced
1 large zucchini, tipped and sliced
1 large yellow squash, tipped and
   sliced
½ pound mushrooms, sliced
1 large carrot, pared and cut into
   thin sticks
½ cup soy sauce
¼ cup saki or dry sherry
1 package (1 pound) Chinese
   noodles, cooked and drained
OR: 1 package (1 pound) fine
   noodles, cooked and drained

onion and garlic tips

- Garlic is the most powerful of the onion family and gives character to many international dishes. The whole bulb or bud is made up of individual cloves that fit together like orange sections. It is one or a few of these cloves that are listed as ingredients in our recipes. The following are garlic substitutions:

  1 teaspoon garlic salt = 1 clove
  ⅛ teaspoon garlic powder = 1 clove
  5 drops liquid garlic = 1 clove

- For the subtle flavor of garlic in your cooking, place a few halved cloves of garlic in a cup of olive oil or vegetable oil; allow to stand overnight; remove garlic and store flavored oil in a glass jar with a screw top.
- When the recipe calls for just a little chopped onion, cut deep crisscrosses over cut surface of an onion, then slice. Cover remaining onion with plastic wrap and refrigerate.

DUTCH SPARERIBS

Country-style spareribs are simmered with sauerkraut and topped with caraway flavored dumplings.

1. Trim excess fat from spareribs; place in an electric slow cooker. Wash sauerkraut under running water; drain very well; place over ribs with apple wedges and onion; sprinkle with seasoned salt, seasoned pepper and caraway seeds; cover.
2. Cook on low (190° to 200°) 8 hours, or until ribs are very tender when pierced with a two-tined fork.
3. Make dumplings: Turn heat control to high (290° to 300°). Sift flour, baking powder and salt into a large bowl; stir in caraway seeds. Beat egg in a cup with a fork; beat in milk; pour, all at once, into dry mixture. Stir until blended.
4. Uncover slow cooker. (If there is a level of liquid above the sauerkraut; remove some of the liquid with a bulb baster.) Drop dumplings by spoonfuls on top of sauerkraut; cover. Cook 30 minutes, or until dumplings are fluffy.

3 pounds country-style spareribs, cut up
1 can (1 pound, 13 ounces) sauerkraut
2 tart apples, cored and cut into wedges
1 large onion, chopped (1 cup)
2 teaspoons seasoned salt
½ teaspoon seasoned pepper
¼ teaspoon caraway seeds, crushed

Dumplings
2 cups sifted all-purpose flour
2 teaspoons baking powder
1 teaspoon salt
½ teaspoon caraway seeds
1 egg
¾ cup milk

ZURICH PORK

A German influence is often noted in the cooking of this Swiss city.

1. Trim excess fat from pork; brown pork slowly in remaining fat in a heavy skillet or an electric slow cooker with a browning unit; drain off all fat.
2. Place meat in slow cooker. Sprinkle salt, caraway seeds and pepper over; add onions, garlic and beer or water; cover.
3. Cook on low (190° to 200°) 10 hours, or on high (290° to 300°) 5 hours, or until pork is tender when pierced with a fork.
4. Remove to carving board or heated serving platter; discard garlic. Spoon onions around meat. Serve with refrigerated crescent rolls.

1 fresh pork shoulder butt (about 4 pounds)
2 teaspoons salt
1 teaspoon caraway seeds
¼ teaspoon pepper
2 large onions, peeled and cut into thick slices
1 large clove garlic, peeled
½ cup beer or water

KOENIGSBERGER KLOPS

A classic German meat ball dish garnished with lemon slices and capers.

1. Combine ground beef and pork, chopped onion, crumbs, 1 teaspoon of the salt, pepper and nutmeg in a medium-size bowl until well-blended.
2. Separate eggs, putting whites into a large bowl and yolks into a small bowl; cover and refrigerate. Beat whites until they form soft peaks; fold into meat mixture. Shape into 1-inch balls and place in an electric slow cooker.
3. Combine beef broth, water, onion, vinegar, sugar, mixed pickling spices and remaining ½ teaspoon salt in a small saucepan. Bring to boiling; lower heat and simmer 15 minutes; strain into slow cooker; cover.
4. Cook on low (190° to 200°) 5 hours; remove meat balls to a heated deep serving platter and keep warm.
5. Turn heat control to high (290° to 300°). Combine 1 tablespoon all-purpose flour with 2 tablespoons cold water in a cup; stir into liquid in cooker until smooth; cover. Cook 15 minutes; beat saved egg yolks with a fork; beat in 1 cup of hot sauce; return to cooker; cook 5 minutes; then pour over meat balls. Garnish with lemon slices and capers; serve with boiled parslied potatoes and mugs of dark ale, if you wish.

1 pound ground beef
1 pound ground pork
1 medium-size onion, chopped
 (½ cup)
½ cup packaged dry bread crumbs
1½ teaspoons salt
¼ teaspoon pepper
 Dash ground nutmeg
4 eggs
1 can condensed beef broth
1 cup water
1 large onion, peeled and quartered
¼ cup cider vinegar
1 tablespoon sugar
1 teaspoon mixed pickling spices

quick tips

- Flouring meat balls? Speed up the job by sprinkling the flour from a shaker, or toss the meat balls, a few at a time, in flour in a paper bag to coat well. Place salt, pepper, spices, or herb seasonings in the bag, too—another time-saver step.
- Have extra cheese on hand? Shred and spoon into a plastic container; seal and freeze. Measure out just as much as you need at cooking time.
- To remove foil or wax paper stuck to frozen foods, simply place the package in a 300° oven for 5 minutes.
- Kitchen clean-ups will be easier if you prevent grease from spattering while browning. The easiest way is to invert a colander over the skillet. It will catch the grease, yet allow the steam to escape.

ALDILLA

Try this south-of-the-border steak dish with chili powder and hot chili pepper for a dish with a dash.

1. Score steak and rub with chili powder; coat with a mixture of flour, ½ teaspoon salt and ¼ teaspoon of the seasoned pepper; pound steak on both sides with a wooden mallet or the edge of a plate to tenderize; cut into 6 pieces.
2. Brown steak in hot oil in a large skillet or an electric slow cooker with a browning unit; remove and reserve. Sauté onion, carrot, green pepper and tomato in pan drippings; add remaining 1 teaspoon salt and ¼ teaspoon seasoned pepper; remove from heat.
3. Combine steak and sautéed vegetables in slow cooker; add wine and hot chili pepper; cover.
4. Cook on low (190° to 200°) 8 hours, or on high (290° to 300°) 4 hours, or until meat is tender. Serve with cornbread and an avocado, ripe olive and shredded lettuce salad, if you wish.

1 flank steak (about 1½ pounds)
2 to 4 teaspoons chili powder
½ cup all-purpose flour
1½ teaspoons salt
½ teaspoon seasoned pepper
3 tablespoons vegetable oil
1 large onion, chopped (1 cup)
1 large carrot, pared and
    chopped
1 large green pepper, halved,
    seeded and chopped
2 large ripe tomatoes, peeled and
    chopped
¼ cup dry red wine
1 hot chili pepper, seeded (from a
    4-ounce can)

ENGLISH HOT POT

British cooks have made these one pot specialties for generations.

1. Trim all excess fat from lamb. Shake cubes, part at a time, in flour in a plastic bag to coat well.
2. Mix instant chicken broth, salt, oregano, rosemary and pepper in a cup.
3. Layer meat and vegetables into an electric slow cooker this way: Half of each of lamb, onion and squash, sprinkling each layer with seasoning mixture. Repeat with remaining lamb, vegetables and seasoning mixture.
4. Lay potatoes, rounded side up, on top; pour boiling water over. Brush potatoes with butter; cover.
5. Cook on low (190° to 200°) 8 hours, or on high (290° to 300°) 4 hours, or until meat and vegetables are tender. Serve with hearts of lettuce and cold apple cider, if you wish.

2 pounds boneless lamb shoulder,
    cubed
¼ cup all-purpose flour
2 envelopes or teaspoons instant
    chicken broth
2 teaspoons salt
1 teaspoon leaf oregano, crumbled
½ teaspoon leaf rosemary, crumbled
¼ teaspoon pepper
1 large onion, sliced and separated
    into rings
3 small yellow squash, cut into
    2-inch pieces
12 small potatoes, pared and halved
1 cup boiling water
2 tablespoons butter or
    margarine, melted

"VERY BRITISH" CASSEROLE

Cook on 290° to 300° for **2** hours,
then on 190° to 200° for **4** hours.
Makes 12 servings.

*It's sort of steak and kidney pie in a pot! You could
top it with dumplings, but mashed potatoes are more
British.*

1. Shake beef and veal cubes, part at a time, in a mixture
   of flour, salt and pepper in a plastic bag to coat evenly.
2. Brown meat cubes in a mixture of butter or margarine
   and shortening in a large skillet or an electric slow
   cooker with a browning unit; remove with a slotted
   spoon and reserve.
3. While cubed meats brown, cover veal kidneys with
   water in a medium-size saucepan; add vinegar; bring
   to boiling; lower heat; simmer 4 to 5 minutes; drain on
   paper towels; cut into thin slices.
4. Sauté veal kidneys in pan drippings; remove and
   reserve.
5. Place meats in slow cooker; place onion and tomato
   slices over; combine beef broth, wine, Worcestershire
   sauce, seasoned salt, thyme and seasoned pepper in a
   medium-size bowl; pour into slow cooker; cover.
6. Cook on high (290° to 300°) 2 hours. Turn heat
   control to low (190° to 200°) for 5 hours, or until
   meats are tender. Taste and season with salt and
   pepper, if desired. If you wish to thicken the gravy,
   turn heat control to high (290° to 300°); combine 2
   tablespoons cornstarch and ¼ cup cold water; stir into
   cooker; cover; cook 15 minutes. Serve with mashed
   potatoes.

3 pounds boneless chuck, cubed
*1 pound boneless veal shoulder,
   cubed*
¼ cup all-purpose flour
1 teaspoon salt
¼ teaspoon pepper
*¼ cup (½ stick) butter or
   margarine*
¼ cup vegetable shortening
2 veal kidneys
2 tablespoons white vinegar
2 Bermuda onions, sliced
*3 large tomatoes, peeled, cored
   and sliced*
1 can condensed beef broth
½ cup dry red wine
1 teaspoon Worcestershire sauce
1 teaspoon seasoned salt
½ teaspoon leaf thyme, crumbled
¼ teaspoon seasoned pepper

picking salad greens

• Whatever the green, pick fairly firm, medium-size heads that are springy-crisp.
Larger heads may be overgrown and bitter. If you notice any reddish discolorations
at the base of a head of lettuce, don't be alarmed. This is nature's way of sealing the
cut made when the head was picked and trimmed.
• How many salad greens to buy? As a general rule, you can count on 4 servings
from one medium-size head of iceberg or other lettuce and 4 servings from 1 pound
of loose greens.
• Pick out unpackaged, unprepared greens (extra handling costs extra money).

DUTCH HOT POT

Cook on 190° to 200° for **8** hours,
or on 290° to 300° for **4** hours.
Makes 8 servings.

Coriander seeds and leaf thyme add the distinctive touch to this Amsterdam dish.

1. Trim excess fat from pork. Shake cubes, part at a time, with flour in a plastic bag to coat well.
2. Mix salt, thyme, coriander seeds and pepper in a cup; reserve.
3. Drain liquid from kidney beans into a 2-cup measure; add boiling water to make 1½ cups.
4. Layer vegetables and meat into an electric slow cooker this way: Half each of potatoes, onions, pork, kidney beans and carrots, sprinkling each layer lightly with seasoning mixture. Repeat with remaining vegetables, pork and seasoning mixture for a second layer.
5. Pour liquid over; dot with butter or margarine; cover.
6. Cook on low (190° to 200°) 8 hours, or on high (290° to 300°) 4 hours, or until meat and vegetables are tender. Serve with dark beer, if you wish.

2 pounds boneless pork shoulder, cubed
¼ cup all-purpose flour
1 tablespoon salt
1 teaspoon leaf thyme, crumbled
1 teaspoon coriander seeds, crushed
¼ teaspoon pepper
1 can (1 pound) red kidney beans
  Boiling water
4 medium-size potatoes, pared and cut into ¼-inch thick slices
4 medium-size onions, sliced and separated into rings
8 carrots, pared and cut in 4-inch lengths
2 tablespoons butter or margarine

AUSTRALIAN LAMB "ROASTS"

Cook on 190° to 200° for **8** hours,
or on 290° to 300° for **4** hours.
Makes 4 servings.

Lamb shanks are a meaty treat. Look for them on special, especially in the spring.

1. Trim excess fat from lamb shanks. Brown lamb in its remaining fat in a large skillet or an electric slow cooker with a browning unit; remove and reserve.
2. Add onion and garlic to pan; sauté just until soft. Stir in wine, salt, pepper and bay leaf; remove from heat.
3. Combine lamb shanks and wine mixture in slow cooker; cover.
4. Cook on low (190° to 200°) 8 hours, or on high (290° to 300°) 4 hours, or until lamb shanks are tender. Remove to a heated serving platter and keep warm.
5. Turn heat control to high (290° to 300°). Combine flour and water in a cup. Stir into liquid in slow cooker; cover. Cook 15 minutes. Pass in gravy boat.

4 lamb shanks (about 3 pounds)
1 large onion, chopped (1 cup)
1 clove garlic, minced
1 cup dry white wine
2 teaspoons salt
½ teaspoon pepper
1 bay leaf
2 tablespoons all-purpose flour
¼ cup water

117

MUNICH KRAUT AND KNACKWURST

Cook on 190° to 200° for **6** hours, or on 290° to 300° for **3** hours.
Makes 4 servings.

Try this quick version of Choucroute a l'Alsacienne. Shown on pages 132-133.

1. Sauté onion in 3 tablespoons butter or margarine in a large skillet or slow cooker with a browning unit just until soft; sauté apple 2 minutes. Stir in sauerkraut, brown sugar and caraway seeds; toss lightly with a fork to mix well.
2. Sauté knackwursts in remaining 1 tablespoon butter or margarine in same pan 5 minutes, or until browned; arrange on sauerkraut in slow cooker; drizzle beer or wine over; cover slow cooker.
3. Cook on low (190° to 200°) 6 hours or on high (290° to 300°) 3 hours. Spoon sauerkraut into heated casserole and top with knackwurst. Serve with a zippy mustard, dill pickles and pumpernickel bread, if you wish.

1 large onion, sliced
¼ cup (½ stick) butter or margarine
1 large red apple, quartered, cored and diced
1 can (1 pound, 13 ounces) sauerkraut, washed and drained
3 tablespoons brown sugar
1 teaspoon caraway seeds
1 pound knackwursts, scored
½ cup beer or dry white wine

BERMUDA LAMB STEW

Cook on 190° to 200° for **8** hours, or on 290° to 300° for **4** hours.
Makes 6 servings.

A delightfully mild-seasoned dish with a springtime flavor.

1. Trim all excess fat from lamb. Place lamb in the bottom of an electric slow cooker; add onion rings, lettuce, tomatoes, peas, squash, salt, rosemary and pepper to cover lamb.
2. Dissolve instant broth in hot water in a 2-cup measure; pour over meat and vegetables; stir to mix well; cover.
3. Cook on low (190° to 200°) 8 hours, or on high (290° to 300°) 4 hours, or until lamb is tender.
4. Turn heat control to high (290° to 300°). Combine cornstarch and ⅓ cup cold water in a cup; stir into liquid until well-blended. Cover; simmer 15 minutes longer, until bubbly-hot.

2 pounds boneless lamb shoulder, cubed
1 Bermuda onion, thinly sliced and separated into rings
2 cups shredded lettuce
2 medium-size ripe tomatoes, chopped
2 pounds fresh peas, shelled (2 cups) OR: 2 cups frozen peas (from a 1½-pound bag), thawed
2 medium-size yellow squash, cut into 2-inch pieces
2 teaspoons salt
½ teaspoon leaf rosemary, crumbled
¼ teaspoon freshly ground pepper
1 envelope or teaspoon instant chicken broth
1 cup hot water
3 tablespoons cornstarch

BRAZILIAN FEIJOADA

Cook on 190° to 200° for **8** hours,
or on 290° to 300° for **4** hours.
Makes 12 servings.

Black bean soup is a favorite in all Latin American countries. This is the slow cook method of preparing it.

1. Pick over beans and rinse under running water. Combine beans with water in a large kettle or a 5-quart electric slow cooker; bring to boiling and boil 2 minutes; cover. Remove from heat; let stand 1 hour; add pork butt, pepperoni, onions, wine or beef broth and salt; cover.
2. Cook on low (190° to 200°) 8 hours, stirring after 4 hours, if possible, or on high (290° to 300°) 4 hours, stirring after 2 hours, if possible, or until beans and meat are tender.
3. Remove pork butt; press beans against the side of the slow cooker with a wooden spoon to mash some of them. Serve with orange sections and chopped parsley arranged atop beans.
4. Slice pork butt thinly and pass it around, on a separate plate, with mustard and whole-wheat bread.

2 bags (1 pound each) dried black beans
10 cups water
1 boneless smoked pork butt (about 2 pounds)
½ pound pepperoni, cut into ½-inch pieces
3 large onions, sliced
2 cups dry red wine or beef broth
2 teaspoons salt
3 oranges, peeled and sectioned
¼ cup chopped parsley

HUNGARIAN LAMB

Cook on 190° to 200° for **8** hours,
or on 290° to 300° for **4** hours.
Makes 6 servings.

Eggplant and sour cream give the distinctive flavors to this dish.

1. Shake lamb with flour, salt and pepper in a plastic bag to coat well.
2. Brown quickly in oil in an electric slow cooker with a browning unit, or a large skillet; stir in instant beef broth and water; bring to boiling.
3. Combine lamb mixture, onions and eggplant in slow cooker; cover.
4. Cook on low (190° to 200°) 8 hours, or on high (290° to 300°) 4 hours, or until lamb and onions are tender.
5. Stir 1 cup of hot mixture into sour cream and paprika in a medium-size bowl; return to cooker and stir to blend.

1½ pounds lean lamb shoulder, cubed
¼ cup all-purpose flour
1 teaspoon salt
¼ teaspoon pepper
3 tablespoons vegetable oil
2 envelopes instant beef broth
1½ cups water
12 small white onions, peeled
1 small eggplant, pared and diced
1 cup dairy sour cream
1 teaspoon paprika

PERSIAN STEAK ROLL

Wheat pilaf and spinach are the special ingredients that makes this recipe out of the ordinary.

1. Ask your meatman to split flank steak, butterfly fashion. Or, at home, split it yourself, working slowly with a sharp long-blade knife and cutting with a sawing motion as evenly as possible. Pound steak with a mallet or rolling pin to make it evenly thin.

2. Sauté onion in 2 tablespoons of the oil until soft in a large skillet. Stir in wheat pilaf; cook 2 minutes, or until lightly browned.Stir in curry powder and water; cover skillet.

3. Bring to boiling, then simmer 15 minutes, or until liquid is absorbed. Cool slightly; spread over meat in a thin layer.

4. Drain spinach, then pat as dry as possible between paper towels.

5. Drain kidney beans, saving liquid. Mix beans, spinach, cardamom seeds and ½ teaspoon of the salt in a medium-size bowl; spread over pilaf layer.

6. Starting at one long side, roll up tightly, tucking in any loose stuffing; tie with string every 2 inches. Sprinkle with remaining 1 teaspoon salt and pepper.

7. Brown roll in remaining 2 tablespoons oil in the large skillet or in an electric slow cooker with a browning unit; remove and reserve.

8. Stir tomatoes, lemon juice and saved bean liquid into pan until well-blended.

9. Place the stuffed meat roll and sauce in slow cooker; cover.

10. Cook on low (190° to 200°) 10 hours, turning meat after 5 hours, if possible, or on high (290° to 300°) 5 hours, turning meat after 3 hours, if possible. Place meat on heated serving platter and remove strings. Cut into 1-inch slices and serve with pan sauce.

1 flank steak (about 1½ pounds)
1 small onion, chopped (¼ cup)
4 tablespoons vegetable oil
½ cup wheat pilaf (from a 12-ounce package)
1 teaspoon curry powder
1 cup water
1 package (10 ounces) frozen chopped spinach, thawed
1 can (1 pound) red kidney beans
½ teaspoon cardamom seeds, crushed
1½ teaspoons salt
¼ teaspoon pepper
1 can (1 pound) stewed tomatoes
1 tablespoon lemon juice

bigger buys for stews

Most meat counters carry ready-cubed beef for stewing. But because store labor and meat trimmings cost money, you'll rate a double dividend if you buy beef chuck and cut it up yourself, then simmer the bone and trimmings for broth.

BLACK FOREST BEEF PLATTER

Cook on 190° to 200° for **10** hours, or on 290° to 300° for **5** hours.

Makes 8 servings.

Pot roasts are more flavorful and tender when treated to slow, gentle cooking.

1. Trim excess fat from roast; brown in its remaining fat in a large skillet or an electric slow cooker with a browning unit; remove and reserve.
2. Stir in water, chili sauce, onion soup mix, caraway seeds, paprika and pepper; bring to boiling.
3. Place meat with sauce in slow cooker; mix sauerkraut and brown sugar in a medium-size bowl; stir into liquid around meat; cover.
4. Cook on low (190° to 200°) 10 hours, or on high (290° to 300°) 5 hours, or until meat is very tender. Remove to a carving board; keep hot while finishing sauce for the sauerkraut.
5. Stir about ½ cup of the hot sauerkraut mixture into sour cream in a medium-size bowl; then stir back into remaining sauerkraut mixture in slow cooker. Heat just until hot, about 5 minutes.
6. Spoon sauerkraut into a deep serving platter. Carve meat into ¼-inch thick slices; place on top of sauerkraut. Serve with buttered noodles, if you wish.

1 boneless chuck roast (about 4 pounds)
1 cup water
¼ cup chili sauce
1 envelope (2 to a package) onion soup mix
1 tablespoon caraway seeds, crushed
1 tablespoon paprika
¼ teaspoon pepper
1 can (1 pound, 11 ounces) sauerkraut, drained
¼ cup firmly packed brown sugar
1 container (8 ounces) dairy sour cream

OXTAILS ROMANO

Cook on 290° to 300° for **2** hours, then on 190° to 200° for **8** hours.

Makes 6 servings.

This recipe was inspired by a Roman trattoria specialty. Serve with linguini and a full red wine.

1. Brown oxtails, a few pieces at a time, in oil in an electric slow cooker with a browning unit or a large skillet; remove and keep warm. Sauté onion, garlic, carrots and parsley in drippings until soft.
2. Stir in tomatoes, beef broth, salt and pepper until sauce bubbles. Combine oxtails and vegetables in slow cooker; cover.
3. Cook on high (290° to 300°) 2 hours. Turn heat control to low (190° to 200°) and cook for 8 hours, or until oxtails are so tender that meat falls from bones.
4. Unplug slow cooker and let mixture cool five minutes for fat to rise to the surface; skim off fat. Serve with buttered linguini and a tossed green salad.

3 pounds oxtails, cut up
3 tablespoons olive oil or vegetable oil
1 large onion, chopped (1 cup)
2 cloves garlic, minced
2 large carrots, pared and diced
⅓ cup chopped parsley
1 can (1 pound, 1 ounce) Italian tomatoes
1 cup beef broth
2 teaspoons salt
½ teaspoon freshly ground pepper
2 cups chopped celery

121

SWISS CABBAGE ROLLS

*Cook on 190° to 200° for **8** hours,
or on 290° to 300° for **4** hours.
Makes 6 servings.*

Try serving these delicious rolls with a dollop of sour cream on top.

1. Trim base of cabbage and carefully break off 12 whole leaves. (Save remaining cabbage for another day.)
2. Place leaves in a large saucepan; pour in boiling water and cover; let stand 5 minutes; drain on paper towels; trim off the coarse rib on the back of each leaf with a sharp paring knife.
3. Combine meatloaf mixture, rice, onion, egg, salt, pepper and nutmeg in a medium-size bowl; mix.
4. Lay cabbage leaves flat on a wooden board; spoon meat mixture into the middle of each, dividing evenly. Fold edges of each leaf over filling and roll up; fasten with wooden picks.
5. Coat cabbage rolls with flour on wax paper. Sauté rolls, a few at a time, in shortening in a large skillet or an electric slow cooker with a browning unit.
6. Place cabbage rolls in slow cooker; pour tomato soup, vinegar and Worcestershire sauce over; cover.
7. Cook on low (190° to 200°) 8 hours, or on high (290° to 300°) 4 hours. Serve with a topping of dairy sour cream.

Suggested Variations: Cooked brown rice or kasha can be substituted for the cooked rice. Ground beef or pork can be used in place of the meatloaf mixture.

12 large cabbage leaves
1 pound ground meatloaf mixture
2 cups cooked rice
1 small onion, chopped (¼ cup)
1 egg
1 teaspoon salt
¼ teaspoon pepper
　Dash ground nutmeg
¼ cup all-purpose flour
2 tablespoons vegetable
　shortening
1 can condensed tomato soup
1 teaspoon cider vinegar
1 teaspoon Worcestershire sauce

cooking substitutions

If you're out of some ingredients listed in our recipes you can safely use these substitutes instead:

1 teaspoon dry leaf herb	= 1 tablespoon chopped fresh herb
1 cup dairy sour cream	= 1 tablespoon lemon juice to 1 cup evaporated milk
1 tablespoon finely chopped fresh chives	= 1 teaspoon freeze-dried chives
1 tablespoon cornstarch	= 2 tablespoons all-purpose flour

PICADILLO

This Cuban supper dish is usually served with rice and fried bananas.

1. Sauté onion, green pepper and garlic in oil in a large skillet or an electric slow cooker with a browning unit until soft; stir in tomatoes and sugar; simmer 5 minutes. Stir in diced beef.
2. Combine in slow cooker with beef broth, salt, bay leaf and cloves; cover.
3. Cook on low (190° to 200°) 6 hours, or until ready to serve.

1 large onion, chopped (1 cup)
1 large green pepper, halved, seeded and chopped
1 clove garlic, minced
¼ cup olive oil
4 large ripe tomatoes, peeled and chopped
½ teaspoon sugar
3 cups finely diced cooked beef
1 can condensed beef broth
1 teaspoon salt
1 bay leaf
¼ teaspoon ground cloves

COCIDO

*Cook on 190° to 200° for **10** hours,*
*or on 290° to 300° for **5** hours.*
Makes 6 servings.

Frugal Iberian cooks combine sausage with beef, chick peas and cabbage to satisfy appetites and save pesetas, all at the same time.

1. Combine beef, salt, garlic and water in a slow cooker. Tie bay leaf, peppercorns and coriander seeds in cheesecloth; add to cooker with onion, carrots, potatoes, chick-peas and 2 tablespoons of the parsley.
2. Cook on low (190° to 200°) 10 hours or high (290° to 300°) 5 hours. Stir in cabbage and leek. Cook 20 minutes longer. Remove cheesecloth bag. Thicken, if desired, with a little flour mixed with water.
3. About 15 minutes before serving, brown sausages in a skillet, 10 to 15 minutes; cut them in half and arrange on top of stew. Sprinkle with remaining parsley.
4. Serve in soup plates or shallow bowls with crusty bread, if you wish.

2 pounds lean chuck, cut into 1-inch cubes
1 tablespoon salt
2 cloves garlic, chopped
4 cups water
1 bay leaf coarsely
6 peppercorns
6 whole coriander seeds
1 large onion, sliced
4 carrots, pared and cut into 1-inch pieces
4 potatoes, pared and cut into 1-inch cubes
2 cans (1 pound, 4 ounces each) chick-peas, drained
3 tablespoons chopped parsley
3 cups shredded cabbage
1 large leek, washed and cut into ¼-inch slices (about 1 cup)
6 pork sausages (½ pound)

123

SEVILLE POT ROAST

Cook on 190° to 200° for **10** *hours, or on 290° to 300° for* **6** *hours.*
Makes 8 servings.

Colorful stuffed-olive rings dot each slice of this savory roast.

1. Trim excess fat from beef; make slashes about 1½ inches deep and 2 inches apart all the way around meat with a sharp knife; push an olive deep into each cut.
2. Brown beef in a large skillet or an electric slow cooker with a browning unit; remove and reserve.
3. Sauté onion until soft in same pan; stir in carrots, water, instant coffee, sugar, salt and pepper. Place beef with onion mixture in slow cooker; cover.
4. Cook on low (190° to 200°) 10 hours, or on high (290° to 300°) 6 hours, or until beef is tender when pierced with a two-tined fork. Remove beef to serving platter and keep warm.
5. Turn heat control to high (290° to 300°). Combine cream and flour in a cup. Stir into liquid until well-blended; cover; simmer 15 minutes.
6. Carve meat into ¼-inch thick slices and pass gravy separately. Serve with saffron rice, if you wish.

HOSTESS TIP: To prepare saffron rice, crush about 3 strands of saffron and stir into cooking water for rice. For 8 servings of 1 cup each, you will need 2 cups uncooked rice.

1 round, rump or boneless chuck roast (about 4 pounds)
1 jar (about 5 ounces) stuffed green olives
1 medium-size onion, chopped (½ cup)
1 jar (about 5 ounces) junior strained carrots (baby-pack)
1 cup water
1 tablespoon instant coffee powder
1 tablespoon sugar
1 teaspoon salt
¼ teaspoon pepper
½ cup light cream
2 tablespoons all-purpose flour

COUNTY KERRY PORK ROAST

Cook on 190° to 200° for **10** *hours, or on 290° to 300° for* **5** *hours.*
Makes 8 servings.

Fresh pork shoulder makes an especially delicious gravy to spoon over fluffy, buttered mashed potatoes.

1. Trim excess fat from pork; place in an electric slow cooker; sprinkle with onion and marjoram; pour mixture of barbecue sauce and water over; cover.
2. Cook on low (190° to 200°) 10 hours, or on high (290° to 300°) 5 hours, or until pork is tender when pierced with a fork.
3. Slice hot and serve with mashed potatoes, steamed cabbage and horseradish mustard, if you wish.
   Suggested Variations: Fresh ham, pork loin or lamb shoulder can be substituted for the pork shoulder in this recipe. Also, use leaf savory instead of marjoram.

1 fresh picnic or shoulder butt (about 5 pounds)
1 large onion, chopped (1 cup)
1 teaspoon leaf marjoram, crumbled
¾ cup bottled barbecue sauce
¾ cup water

124

ENSENADA CHILI POT

Cook on 190° to 200° for **8** hours,
or on 290° to 300° for **4** hours.
Makes 8 servings.

There's South-of-the-border flavor in this no-watch special.

1. Trim excess fat from beef; shake beef cubes with flour, chili powder, salt and pepper in a plastic bag to coat well.
2. Brown, a few at a time, in shortening in a large skillet or an electric slow cooker with a browning unit; remove and reserve. Stir in onion; sauté 5 minutes, or until onion is soft. Spoon off any excess drippings; stir any remaining flour-seasoning mixture into pan.
3. Drain liquid from kidney beans and add to pan; stir in tomatoes; bring to boiling; remove from heat.
4. Place beef in slow cooker with tomato mixture; stir in kidney beans and corn; cover cooker.
5. Cook on low (190° to 200°) 8 hours, or on high (290° to 300°) 4 hours; stir in pimiento and green chili peppers.
6. Spoon chili over rice in soup bowls. Top with shredded Cheddar cheese.

2 pounds lean boneless chuck, cubed
¼ cup all-purpose flour
1 to 2 tablespoons chili powder
2 teaspoons salt
¼ teaspoon pepper
¼ cup vegetable shortening
1 large onion, chopped (1 cup)
2 cans (1 pound each) red kidney beans
1 can (1 pound, 13 ounces) tomatoes
1 can (12 or 16 ounces) whole-kernel corn
1 can (4 ounces) pimiento, sliced
1 can (4 ounces) green chili peppers, seeded and chopped
Hot cooked rice
Shredded Cheddar cheese

LAMB CHOPS POLYNESIAN

Cook on 190° to 200° for **8** hours,
or on 290° to 300° for **4** hours.
Makes 6 servings.

Thrifty pork shoulder chops can also be used in this recipe.

1. Trim excess fat from chops. Rub lamb with curry powder. Brown slowly in oil in a large skillet or slow cooker with a browning unit; remove.
2. Sauté onion and garlic until soft in same pan; stir in salt, allspice, water and lemon juice. Bring to boiling; stir in junior fruits.
3. Place lamb chops in slow cooker with fruit sauce; cover.
4. Cook on low (190° to 200°) 8 hours, or on high (290° to 300°) 4 hours, or until tender. Serve with fried rice and sautéed bananas, if you wish.

6 shoulder lamb chops, cut ¾-inch thick
2 teaspoons curry powder
2 tablespoons vegetable oil
1 large onion, chopped (1 cup)
1 clove garlic, minced
1½ teaspoons salt
1 teaspoon ground allspice
1 cup water
¼ cup lemon juice
1 jar (about 8 ounces) junior prunes (baby-pack)
1 jar (about 8 ounces) junior applesauce-and-apricots (baby-pack)

SPAGHETTI TAORMINA

Slow cookers are great for making spaghetti sauce because the longer they cook, the better the flavor. Try this sauce on lasagna, too.

1. Sauté onion, green pepper and garlic lightly in oil in a large skillet or an electric slow cooker with a browning unit. Push to one side; add beef and brown lightly, then add and brown liver.
2. Stir in tomatoes, tomato paste, water, salt, Italian herbs and pepper. Ladle into slow cooker; cover.
3. Cook on low (190° to 200°) 8 hours, or on high (290° to 300°) 4 hours. Remove cover and turn heat control to high (290° to 300°). Simmer while cooking pasta.
4. Cook pasta following label directions; drain; place in a deep heated platter. Spoon sauce over and toss just before serving; sprinkle with freshly grated Parmesan cheese. Pass any extra sauce in a heated gravy boat.

1 medium-size onion, chopped (½ cup)
1 medium-size green pepper, halved, seeded and chopped
½ clove garlic, crushed
3 tablespoons olive or vegetable oil
½ pound lean chuck, cubed
¼ pound beef liver, cut in ½-inch cubes
1 can (2 pounds, 3 ounces) Italian tomatoes
1 can (6 ounces) tomato paste
3 cups water
2 teaspoons salt
2 teaspoons mixed Italian herbs, crumbled
¼ teaspoon pepper
1 package (1 pound) linguini or thin spaghetti
Grated Parmesan cheese

popular pastas

There is an immense variety of pastas in the markets. Here is a guide to using them in cooking:

Pastina—Tiny pasta bits good for use in soups or as baby food.
Spaghetti—The long, round, thin favorite perfect with many kinds of sauces.
Spaghettini— A thinner version of spaghetti most prefered in Italy.
Ziti— Thicker hollow tubes of pasta that can be served in baked dishes.
Elbow Macaroni—Curved hollow tubes most widely used in cold salads, casseroles and macaroni and cheese combinations.
Fettuccine—The Romans call it Tagliatelle. Excellent with clam sauce or just butter and grated cheese.
Linguine—Long flattened macaroni served with cheese, clam or pesto sauces and grated Parmesan.
Alphabets—Letters made of pasta used mainly in soups.
Lasagna—Flat, wide ribbons of pasta that come plain, or with a ruffled edge, in white or spinach-flavored green.
Macaroni Wheels—Pasta shaped like tiny wagon wheels, used in soups and casseroles, and a favorite with children.

HONG KONG PORK STEW

Cook on 190° to 200° for **8** hours, or on 290° to 300° for **4** hours.
Makes 8 servings.

If you like sweet-and-sour pork, you'll rave about this colorful stew.

1. Trim excess fat from pork; place in an electric slow cooker; season with salt, ginger and pepper.
2. Drain syrup from pineapple, adding water to syrup to make 1½ cups; reserve pineapple chunks. Add syrup mixture to pork; stir in sugar, instant broth, molasses and vinegar; cover.
3. Cook on low (190° to 200°) 8 hours, or on high (290° to 300°) 4 hours.
4. Turn heat control to high (290° to 300°). Combine cornstarch and ¼ cup cold water in a cup; stir into pork mixture until well-blended.
5. Add sweet potatoes, tomatoes, pineapple chunks and green pepper; cover; simmer 20 minutes longer.

2 pounds boneless pork shoulder, cubed
1 teaspoon salt
¼ teaspoon ground ginger
⅛ teaspoon pepper
1 can (13¼ ounces) pineapple chunks
¼ cup firmly packed brown sugar
1 envelope or teaspoon instant chicken broth
¼ cup light molasses
¼ cup vinegar
2 tablespoons cornstarch
1 can (1 pound) sweet potatoes
2 firm tomatoes, cut in eighths
1 green pepper, halved, seeded and cut in 1-inch squares

Ravioli—Pillow-shaped pasta filled with either meat or cheese. They are first boiled, then combined with a tomato or cheese sauce.

Farfalle—Pasta shaped like small bows, used in soups, casseroles, or served alone with sauce.

Shells—This pasta comes in small, medium and large sizes. The small ones can be sauced, the larger ones can be stuffed with meat or cheese and baked.

Manicotti—Large pasta tubes, first filled with meat or cheese, then baked in a tomato sauce.

Cannelloni—Fat, ridged tubes of pasta also suitable for stuffing.

Vermicelli—Called 'angel hair' for its fine delicate texture, this spaghetti is best when served with a clam sauce.

Rigati—Tubes of pasta more finely ridged than Cannelloni, usually stuffed and baked in tomato sauce.

Tortellini—These small pasta rings are filled with meat and dished up in clear consomme, or with a creamy cheese sauce, and topped with Parmesan.

Noodles—Flat strands of pasta rich in eggs, and often served as an accompaniment to casserole main dishes such as Beef Stroganoff. Available in plain (white) and spinach (green).

127

OSSOBUCO

Cook on 190° to 200° for **8** hours,
or on 290° to 300° for **4** hours.
Makes 6 servings.

From Milan comes this recipe for veal shanks braised in a rich tomato sauce. Can't find veal shanks? Why not try well-trimmed lamb shanks?

1. Tie veal shanks around the middle with kitchen string to hold the meat in place. Rub with salt and pepper; coat well with flour on wax paper, shaking off excess.
2. Heat oil until almost smoking in a large skillet or an electric slow cooker with a browning unit; brown shanks, a few at a time until golden-brown; remove from cooker and keep warm.
3. Make Soffrito: Add butter or margarine to drippings in pan; sauté onion, leek, carrot, celery and garlic until soft; stir in Italian tomatoes, breaking up with the back of the spoon, add wine, basil and bay leaves, bring to boiling. Lower heat and simmer 5 minutes.
4. Stand veal shanks upright in slow cooker and spoon Soffrito over, if using a skillet. Cover slow cooker.
5. Cook on low (190° to 200°) 8 hours, or on high (290° to 300°) 4 hours, or until meat is very tender and almost falling off bones. Taste sauce and add more salt and pepper, if desired. Sprinkle GREMOLATA on top and serve with Risotto, if you wish.

GREMOLATA— (The traditional topping for OSSO-BUCO)—Combine 1 tablespoon finely chopped Italian parsley, 1 teaspoon grated lemon peel (just the zest, not the white part) and 1 small clove garlic, finely minced. Sprinkle over OSSOBUCO, just as cover is removed from the cooker.

HOSTESS TIP: OSSOBUCO can be made the day ahead and cooked. Cool; cover and refrigerate. One hour before serving, remove from refrigerator; skim any fat on the surface of the sauce; cover casserole. Place in oven; turn oven control to moderate (350°) and bake 55 minutes, or until bubbly-hot. Make GREMOLATA while the casserole bakes, and sprinkle over top just before serving.

4 pounds meaty veal shanks, cut into 3-inch pieces
2 teaspoons salt
½ teaspoon freshly ground pepper
Flour
¼ cup olive oil or vegetable oil

Soffrito
2 tablespoons butter or margarine
1 large onion, finely chopped (1 cup)
1 leek, washed and sliced
1 large carrot, pared and finely chopped
1 stalk celery, finely chopped
1 clove garlic, finely minced
1 can (1 pound, 1 ounce) Italian tomatoes
1 cup dry red wine
1 tablespoon chopped fresh basil OR: 1 teaspoon leaf basil, crumbled
2 bay leaves
Gremolata (recipe follows)

Teriyaki Casserole
is a flavorful variation of a
popular beef, vegetable and noodle
dish that originated in Japan.
Recipe is on page 112.

to store
cooked
poultry:

- Keep for no more than 2 or 3 days in the coldest part of your refrigerator.
- Always refrigerate broth or gravy in separate containers.
- Remove any stuffing from birds; store separately, in an oven-safe casserole, in the refrigerator. Reheat at 350° for 30 minutes.

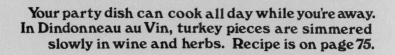

Your party dish can cook all day while you're away.
In Dindonneau au Vin, turkey pieces are simmered
slowly in wine and herbs. Recipe is on page 75.

Plump sausages and
sauerkraut are combined
in Munich Kraut and
Knackwurst, a hearty dish
that is also easy on the
budget. Recipe on page 118.

quick onions for cooking

If you need a lot of onion and want to dice one fast, halve a peeled onion from stem to root end. Place the cut-side down on a board and slice onion about ¼ inch thick, keeping slices together. Give piece a quarter turn and cut again into ¼-inch thick slices.

Turkey combines with
vegetables and chick peas
in exotic Moroccan
Couscous, served on semolina.
Recipe is on page 80.

how many dried beans should you cook?

This depends on the variety, but as a general guide, 1 cup of dried beans will give you 2 to

Meatless Tijuana Bean Pot
is a tasty combination
of dried navy or pea beans,
chunks of green pepper,
tomatoes, cumin. Recipe
is found on page 138.

3 cups of cooked beans. Thus, 1 pound of dried beans will provide 6 very generous servings.

Elegant steamed puddings
can slow cook. Orange-
Lemon Pudding with Mandarin
Orange Sauce, page 178.
Chocolate Nut Pudding with
Orange Liqueur Sauce, page 179.

VEGETABLES

It is no surprise that bean dishes, which have a reputation for needing long cooking, are some of the greatest triumphs of crockery cooking, but vegetables? Yes, vegetables, too, can be delicious and not at all overcooked when they are done the low temperature way. In fact, some vegetables, such as beets, carrots, celery, turnips and parsnips take as long to cook as many meats, and sometimes longer, which is why meats and vegetables combine so successfully in many slow cooker recipes.

Long simmering adds such a special flavor, that even vegetable haters may surprise you by asking for seconds, but if you want to experiment further with flavors try playing with a variety of herbs and spices. Interesting combinations are: a pinch of crumbled leaf rosemary with green peas, ground nutmeg or mace with spinach, a few caraway seeds or a little ground cardamon with cabbage, ground cinnamon or allspice with carrots, a bay leaf or sprig of dill with potatoes, and a pinch of crumbled leaf basil or dried mint flakes with sliced tomatoes.

If you are more inclined to experiment with beans, however, and don't know what variety to use in which kind of dishes, use this as a guide: Large limas go well in French dishes with lamb, pinto beans are used in Mexican and Southwestern dishes. Black beans are wonderful in soups and Caribbean dishes, garbanzos, also known as chick peas, are favorites in Spain and Italy and blackeyed peas are used in many dishes from our own south.

TIJUANA BEAN POT

Cook on 190° to 200° for **10** hours,
or on 290° to 300° for **5** hours.
Makes 8 servings.

Not every bean dish from Mexico needs to be made with chili powder. This flavorful bean pot has oregano and cumin along with chunks of tomato and green peppers. (Shown on pages 134-135.)

1. Pick over beans and rinse under running water. Combine beans and water in a large kettle. Bring to boiling; cover kettle; boil 2 minutes; remove from heat; let stand 1 hour. Return kettle to heat; bring to boiling; add onion; lower heat and simmer 1 hour, or until beans are firm-tender.
2. Heat oil in a slow cooker; sauté green peppers until soft; stir in tomatoes, molasses, salt, oregano, cumin and pepper; heat until bubbling.
3. Drain beans, reserving liquid. Combine beans and green pepper mixture in a slow cooker; add enough reserved liquid to just cover the beans; cover.
4. Cook on low (190° to 200°) 10 hours, or on high (290° to 300°) 5 hours, or until beans are tender.

1 package (1 pound) dried pea beans
4 cups water
1 Spanish onion, chopped (1½ cups)
3 tablespoons olive oil or vegetable oil
2 large green peppers, halved, seeded and cut into 1-inch pieces
1 can (1 pound) tomatoes
½ cup dark molasses
2 teaspoons salt
2 teaspoons leaf oregano, crumbled
½ teaspoon cumin seeds, crushed
½ teaspoon pepper

bean tips

When making bean dishes, you may wish to cut down on cooking time by pre-cooking dried beans in a 4- to 6-quart pressure cooker. To do so, soak 1 package (1 pound) dried beans overnight in a large bowl with ¼ cup vegetable oil, 1 tablespoon salt and enough water to cover beans. In the morning, drain beans; place in pressure cooker with enough water to cover. (Important: Never fill pressure cooker more than half way; the beans will gain bulk as they absorb water.) Cover cooker securely; set pressure regulator on vent pipe; cook, according to the table below:

Black Beans	35 minutes
Blackeyed Peas	20 minutes
Great Northern Beans	30 minutes
Kidney Beans	25 minutes
Lentils	20 minutes
Lima Beans	25 minutes
Navy Beans	30 minutes
Pinto Beans	25 minutes

138

STUFFED GREEN PEPPERS

Cook on 190° to 200° for **8** hours, or on 290° to 300° for **4** hours.
Makes 4 servings.

See how well your slow cooker prepares stuffed vegetables.

1. Cut a thin slice from top of each pepper; scoop out seeds and membrane. Parboil peppers in a small amount of boiling salted water 3 minutes; drain well. Stand peppers in slow cooker.
2. Shape ground beef into a large patty in a skillet; brown 5 minutes on each side, then break up into small chunks.
3. Stir in pork and beans, half of the onion rings and mustard. Spoon into pepper cups, dividing evenly; pour tomato sauce over; cover.
4. Cook on low (190° to 200°) 8 hours, or on high (290° to 300°) 4 hours, or until peppers are tender. Top with remaining French fried onion rings.

4 large green peppers
1 pound ground beef
1 can (1 pound) pork and beans in tomato sauce
1 can (3 ounces) French fried onion rings
1 teaspoon prepared mustard
1 can (8 ounces) tomato sauce

LIMA BEANS IN BROTH

Cook on 190° to 200° for **10** hours. or on 290° to 300° for **5** hours.
Makes 8 servings.

A dish so hearty-rich, no one will suspect that it isn't packed with meat.

1. Pick over beans and rinse under running water. Combine beans and water in a large kettle. Bring to boiling; cover kettle. Boil 2 minutes; remove from heat; let stand 1 hour; pour into an electric slow cooker. (Or soak beans in water in cooker overnight.)
2. Sauté onion and garlic in oil in a medium-size skillet until soft; stir in beef broth, green peppers, salt, mixed Italian herbs and pepper; cook 2 minutes; add to beans in slow cooker. (Add more water, if necessary, to bring liquid level above beans.) Cover.
3. Cook on low (190° to 200°) 10 hours, or on high (290° to 300°) 5 hours, or until beans are tender. Stir cheese into beans.

1 package (1 pound) dried lima beans
8 cups water
1 large onion, chopped (1 cup)
1 clove garlic, minced
2 tablespoons vegetable oil
1 can condensed beef broth
2 large green peppers, halved, seeded and chopped
2 teaspoons salt
1 teaspoon mixed Italian herbs, crumbled
¼ teaspoon pepper
1 package (6 ounces) sliced Provolone cheese, diced

Cook on 190° to 200° for **8** hours,
or on 290° to 300° for **4** hours.

CABBAGE CROWN

Makes 6 servings.

Seasoned ground beef is stuffed into a hollowed-out cabbage, then your slow cooker does the steaming.

1. Combine ground beef, flour, salt, pepper and egg in the large bowl of an electric mixer; beat at medium speed until blended, then gradually beat in milk, a tablespoon at a time, until smooth and paste-like; stir in onion.
2. Trim off outside leaves of cabbage. Cut off a slice about an inch thick from core end; set aside. Cut core from cabbage with a sharp knife, then hollow out cabbage to make a shell about ½-inch thick. (Chop cut-out pieces coarsely and cook as a vegetable another day.)
3. Spoon meat mixture into shell; fit cut slice back into place; tie tightly with soft kitchen string.
4. Place stuffed cabbage, core-end down, in an electric slow cooker; add boiling water to cooker.
5. Cook on low (190° to 200°) 8 hours, or on high (290° to 300°) 4 hours, or until cabbage is tender; remove; keep warm.
6. Turn heat control to high (290° to 300°). Combine 3 tablespoons all-purpose flour and ⅓ cup cold water in a cup; pour into liquid in slow cooker, cover; cook 15 minutes. Season to taste with salt and pepper; darken with a few drops bottled gravy coloring.
7. Place stuffed cabbage on a heated serving platter; remove string. Pour gravy into a separate bowl. Cut cabbage into wedges; spoon gravy over.

1 pound ground beef
⅓ cup all-purpose flour
1½ teaspoons salt
¼ teaspoon pepper
1 egg
1 cup milk
2 tablespoons grated onion
1 large cabbage (about 3 pounds)
1 cup boiling water

rescuing disasters

- If your Hollandaise or Bearnaise sauce has curdled, quickly and vigorously beat in 1 tablespoon of boiling water. If this technique doesn't restore the sauce to smoothness place 1 tablespoon of the curdled sauce and 1 teaspoon of lemon juice in a warmed mixing bowl (bowl quickly rinsed out with hot water). Beat mixture hard until creamy, then beat in the curdled sauce, about 2 teaspoons at a time.
- If you find yourself with a gravy that is lumpy, strain it through a fine sieve.

MACARONI STUFFED PEPPERS

*Cook on 190° to 200° for **8** hours,*
*or on 290° to 300° for **4** hours.*
Makes 4 servings.

An American favorite for luncheon or supper.

1. Cut a slice from top of each pepper; scoop out seeds and membrane. Chop slices and set aside for filling. Parboil peppers in a small amount of boiling water 3 minutes; drain well. Stand peppers in an electric slow cooker.
2. Shape ground beef into a large patty in a skillet; brown with chopped green pepper 5 minutes on each side, then break up into small chunks. Stir in evaporated milk, and cheese; stir in macaroni. Spoon into pepper cups. Add soup to slow cooker; cover.
3. Cook on low (190° to 200°) 8 hours, or on high (290° to 300°) 4 hours, or until peppers are tender.

4 large green peppers
½ pound ground beef
1 small can evaporated milk
½ cup shredded process American cheese
1 cup cooked elbow macaroni
1 can condensed cream of onion soup

LIMA AND TOMATO SCALLOP

*Cook on 190° to 200° for **5** hours,*
*or on 290° to 300° for **3** hours.*
Makes 6 servings.

Canned limas and ready-seasoned stewed tomatoes make this economical dish.

1. Drain liquid from tomatoes and lima beans into a 2-cup measure. (There should be about 1⅓ cups.) Combine vegetables in a 2½-quart electric slow cooker.
2. Melt butter or margarine over low heat in medium-size saucepan. Stir in flour, salt and pepper; cook, stirring all the time, just until mixture bubbles. Stir in vegetable liquids; continue cooking and stirring until mixture thickens and bubbles 1 minute. Pour over vegetables in slow cooker; toss lightly with a fork to mix; cover cooker.
3. Cook on low (190° to 200°) 5 hours, or on high (290° to 300°) 3 hours. Remove to serving platter. Sprinkle buttered bread cubes around edge.

1 can (about 1 pound) stewed tomatoes
1 can (about 1 pound) green lima beans
2 tablespoons butter or margarine
2 tablespoons all-purpose flour
½ teaspoon salt
Dash of pepper
1 cup buttered small bread cubes (2 slices)

141

SOYBEAN STUFFED ZUCCHINI

*Cook on 190° to 200° for **10** hours, or on 290° to 300° for **5** hours.*
Makes 4 servings.

A purée of soybeans, a handful of chopped parsley and green onions blend with brown rice for a hearty main dish.

1. Pick over soybeans and rinse under running water. Cover soybeans with cold water in a glass bowl; cover bowl and let stand at room temperature overnight.
2. Pour soybeans and soaking liquid into a 2½-quart electric slow cooker.
3. Cook on low (190° to 200°) 10 hours, or on high (290° to 300°) 5 hours. (Soybeans will still not be tender.) Drain beans and reserve liquid.
4. While soybeans are cooking, prepare brown rice, following label directions.
5. Halve zucchini, lengthwise, parboil in boiling salted water in a large skillet 5 minutes; drain, cut-side down, on paper towels.
6. Measure ¾ cup soybean liquid into electric blender container; add cooked soybeans; cover container; process at high speed until mixture is very smooth.
7. Combine soybean purée, cooked brown rice, green onions, parsley, salt and pepper in a medium-size bowl.
8. Arrange zucchini, cut-side up, in an 8-cup shallow casserole; fill zucchini shells with soybean mixture. Melt butter or margarine in a small saucepan; stir in wheat germ until well-blended. Sprinkle over zucchini shells.
9. Bake in moderate oven (375°) 15 minutes, or until topping is golden and zucchini shells are heated through.

1 cup dried soybeans
3 cups cold water
½ cup uncooked brown rice
4 medium-size zucchini
½ cup sliced green onions
½ cup chopped parsley
1 teaspoon salt
¼ teaspoon pepper
2 tablespoons butter or margarine
¾ cup plain wheat germ

vegetable tips

- For sand-free fresh vegetables, place trimmed broccoli, cauliflower, asparagus or spinach in a large pan of salted warm water. Soak 5 minutes, then lift the vegetables out. Rinse in cold water, if vegetables are extra sandy.
- If you want to keep the bright color of fresh green vegetables, it's best to cook them in a saucepan at meal time and add to slow cooker, just before serving.

NORTHWEST PEARS AND BEANS

*Cook on 190° to 200° for **8** hours, or on 290° to 300° for **4** hours.*
Makes 4 servings.

West Coast women have been adding fruit to their bean pots for years.

1. Spoon beans into a 2½-quart electric slow cooker; add pear slices, ¼ cup pear syrup, brown sugar, onion and chili sauce; stir gently, just to blend. Arrange sausage links on top; cover.
2. Cook on low (190° to 200°) 8 hours, or on high (290° to 300°) 4 hours, or until you are ready to serve dinner.

COOK'S TIP: The electric slow cooker is a perfect way to add extra flavor to canned beans by slow cooking them with extras such as mustard, brown sugar and chili sauce.

2 cans (1 pound each) lima beans
OR: 2 cans (1 pound, 4 ounces each) white kidney beans (cannellini)
1 can (1 pound) sliced pears
3 tablespoons brown sugar
1 tablespoon minced dried onion
1 tablespoon chili sauce
1 package (8 ounces) heat-and-serve sausage links

COUNTRY BAKED BEANS

*Cook on 190° to 200° for **10** hours, or on 290° to 300° for **5** hours.*
Makes 12 servings.

This is a recipe for the 5-quart slow cookers. If yours is 3½-quart, follow directions for a smaller version below.

1. Pick over beans and rinse under running water. Cover beans with water in a large kettle. Bring to boiling; cover kettle. Boil 2 minutes; remove from heat; let stand 1 hour; pour into a 5-quart electric slow cooker. (Or soak beans in water in slow cooker overnight.)
2. Stud onions with cloves and hide deep in beans. Stir in molasses, sugar, salt and mustard. Cut salt pork into 8 pieces; lay on top. Pour boiling water over just until it shows above beans; cover.
3. Cook on low (190° to 200°) 10 hours, or on high (290° to 300°) 5 hours, or until beans are very tender.

Suggested Variation: For a 6-serving recipe, use 1 pound beans, 1 medium-size onion, ⅓ cup molasses, 1 tablespoon sugar, 1½ teaspoons each salt and dry mustard and ¼ pound salt pork. The cooking times will be the same.

1 package (2 pounds) dried pea beans
Water
2 medium-size onions, peeled
8 whole cloves
¾ cup light molasses
2 tablespoons sugar
1 tablespoon salt
1 tablespoon dry mustard
½ pound lean salt pork

143

BASQUE GARBANZO STEW

Cook on 190° to 200° for **4** hours, or on 290° to 300° for **2** hours.

Makes 8 servings,

A simplified version of Olla Podrida, the popular Spanish soup-stew.

1. Sauté pepperoni in a large skillet or slow cooker with a browning unit for 5 minutes; remove with slotted spoon. Cut chicken breast into 2-inch pieces with poultry or kitchen scissors.
2. Brown chicken pieces in pan drippings; remove with slotted spoon. Sauté leek or onion and garlic in pan drippings; stir in carrots and cook 3 minutes; stir in cabbage and cook 2 minutes. Combine vegetable mixture and chick peas or kidney beans, tomatoes, salt, thyme and pepper; stir to blend well.
3. Place browned chicken and pepperoni in cooker; cover.
4. Cook on low (190° to 200°) 4 hours, or on high (290° to 300°) 2 hours to blend flavors. Serve with shredded lettuce and avocado slices, if you wish.

½ pound piece pepperoni, sliced
1 chicken breast (about 12 ounces)
1 large leek, chopped
   OR: 1 large onion, chopped
   (1 cup)
2 cloves garlic, minced
4 medium-size carrots, sliced
2 cups shredded cabbage (¼ head)
2 cans (1 pound, 4 ounces each)
   chick peas (garbanzos),
   drained
   OR: 2 cans (1 pound each) red
   kidney beans, drained
1 can (1 pound) tomatoes
2 teaspoons salt
1 teaspoon leaf thyme, crumbled
½ teaspoon pepper

to save the most on vegetables

Buy them at the peak of the growing season. Here is a chart to use as a guide to buying:
• Winter—Artichokes, avocados, broccoli, Brussel sprouts, cauliflower, mushrooms, parsnips, potatoes
• Spring—Asparagus, cabbage, carrots, green onions, spinach
• Summer—Green and wax beans, beets, corn, okra, onions, peas, sweet green and red peppers, summer squash, tomatoes, zucchini
• Fall—Broccoli, cauliflower, eggplant, mushrooms, onions, parsnips, potatoes, sweet potatoes, acorn and Hubbard squash.

Be frugal. Don't throw out bits of chopped onion. Store in the refrigerator in a tightly sealed jar. That way the onion stays fresh and the refrigerator remains free of onion odor.

GLAZED ONIONS

Cook on 190° to 200° for **6** *hours,*
or on 290° to 300° for **3** *hours.*
Makes 4 servings.

As easy as can be—these onions are great with a roast.

1. Parboil onions in boiling salted water in large saucepan 15 to 20 minutes.
2. Pour butter or margarine into a 2½-quart electric slow cooker; stir in water, brown sugar, lemon juice, salt and ginger. Roll each onion in mixture; cover cooker.
3. Cook on low (190° to 200°) 6 hours, or on high (290° to 300°) 3 hours; remove cover; cook 20 minutes, or until water evaporates.

1 pound small white onions,
  peeled
Boiling salted water
¼ cup (½ stick) butter or
  margarine, melted
½ cup water
¼ cup brown sugar
1 tablespoon lemon juice
½ teaspoon salt
¼ teaspoon ground ginger

EASY BAKED BEANS

Cook on 190° to 200° for **8** *hours,*
or on 290° to 300° for **4** *hours.*
Makes 6 servings.

Two big favorites—canned beans and franks—star in this stick-to-the-ribs dish.

1. Mix molasses, mustard, and instant coffee in a cup.
2. Place beans in a 2½-quart electric slow cooker; stir in vinegar and all but about 2 tablespoons of the molasses mixture.
3. Arrange halved frankfurters in a chevron design on top; brush with remaining molasses mixture.
4. Cook on low (190° to 200°) 8 hours, or on high (290° to 300°) 4 hours. Just before serving crush onion rings and sprinkle evenly over the top.

⅓ cup molasses
2 tablespoons prepared mustard
1 teaspoon instant coffee powder
3 cans (about 1 pound each) baked
  beans
2 tablespoons cider vinegar
1 pound frankfurters, halved
  crosswise
½ cup French-fried onion rings
  (from an about-4-ounce can)

quick peeling

A fast way to peel a tomato is to hold it on the bowl of a slotted spoon, then dip in simmering water for about 30 seconds. The skin will slip right off. If you are peeling a lot of tomatoes, pile them in a colander or large strainer, then dunk quickly in a pot of hot water. The same treatment works for peaches and onions.

MEXICAN JACK BEANPOT

Cook on 190° to 200° for **5** hours,
or on 290° to 300° for **3** hours.
Makes 6 servings.

The perfect cooked-ahead dish for a picnic.

1. Sauté onion and celery in oil in a large skillet or electric slow cooker with a browning unit just until soft; push to one side. Add meat and brown lightly. Stir in chili powder and oregano; cook 2 minutes. Stir in tomato sauce and beans; bring to boiling.
2. Spoon into an electric slow cooker.
3. Cook on low (190° to 200°) 5 hours, or on high (290° to 300°) 3 hours. Stir in cheese and cook 10 minutes. Garnish with sliced ripe olives, if you wish.

1 cup frozen chopped onion
1 cup chopped celery
2 tablespoons vegetable oil
1 can (12 ounces) pork luncheon meat, cubed
1 to 3 teaspoons chili powder
1 teaspoon leaf oregano, crumbled
1 can (8 ounces) tomato sauce
2 cans (1 pound each) red kidney beans, drained
1 cup shredded Monterey Jack or Cheddar cheese (4 ounces)

RED CABBAGE

Cook on 190° to 200° for **8** hours,
or on 290° to 300° for **4** hours.
Makes 4 servings.

Sparked with red apples and jelly.

1. Combine the cabbage, apple, jelly, water and salt in an electric slow cooker; cover.
2. Cook on low (190° to 200°) 8 hours, or on high (290° to 300°) 4 hours.

1 small red cabbage (about 1½ pounds), finely shredded
1 red apple, quartered, cored and sliced
¼ cup red currant jelly
½ cup water
1 teaspoon salt

the biggest is not always the best

Large oranges and grapefruits, big potatoes and apples are not always your best buys. What counts is how you use them. For example, small citrus fruits, packed dozens in a bag, are perfect for juice, while the large thick-skin ones taste extra-luscious for eating out of hand. Small-size potatoes to boil and serve in their jackets save money, too. Little apples are just right for children because there's no waste; they're also good buys for making applesauce.

BOSTON BAKED BEANS

Every Bostonian has a favorite bean recipe. This is ours.

1. Pick over beans and rinse. Place in a large kettle and add water. Bring to boiling; boil 2 minutes; remove kettle from heat and cover. Allow to stand 1 hour. (Or soak beans in water in an electric slow cooker overnight at room temperature.)
2. Place beans and liquid in slow cooker with onion, brown sugar, molasses, mustard and salt. Stir to blend well; push salt pork slices into mixture; cover.
3. Cook on low (190° to 200°) 10 hours, stirring after 4 hours, if possible, or on high (290° to 300°) 5 hours, stirring after 3 hours, if possible, or until beans are tender. Serve with coleslaw.

1 package (1 pound) dried pea beans
6 cups water
1 large onion, chopped (1 cup)
½ cup firmly-packed dark brown sugar
½ cup light molasses
2 tablespoons prepared mustard
1 teaspoon salt
½ pound lean salt pork, thinly sliced

INDIANA BEANS

Midwest USA contibutes this hearty favorite with its big mealy lima beans.

1. Pick over beans and rinse under running water. Combine beans and water in a large kettle. Bring to boiling; cover kettle; boil 2 minutes; remove from heat; let stand 1 hour; add salt. (Or soak beans in water in an electric slow cooker overnight at room temperature.)
2. Heat oil in a medium-size skillet; sauté onion until soft; stir in molasses, chili sauce and mustard; bring to boiling.
3. Drain beans, reserving liquid. Combine beans and onion mixture in an electric slow cooker; add enough reserved liquid to just cover the beans; cover cooker.
4. Cook on low (190° to 200°) 10 hours, or on high (290° to 300°) 5 hours, or until beans are very tender. Serve with slices of sharp cheese on homemade bread.

1 package (1 pound) dried lima, navy or Great Northern beans
6 cups water
2 teaspoons salt
2 tablespoons vegetable oil
1 large onion, chopped (1 cup)
½ cup light molasses
½ cup chili sauce
¼ cup prepared mustard

Cook on 190°. to 200° for **10** hours,
or on 290° to 300° for **5** hours.
Makes 6 servings.

GARBANZOS CATALAN

*Garbanzo is the Spanish word for chick-pea and this
recipe comes originally from Catalonia.*

1. Place the chick peas in a large heavy kettle, add water
and bring to a boil over moderate heat. Cover, turn off
heat; cool 1 hour. Bring to boiling; reduce the heat;
cover kettle; simmer for 1 hour, 15 minutes, or until
firm-tender.

2. While the chick peas cook, fry bacon in a large, heavy
skillet until crisp; remove from skillet and drain on
paper towels. Brown sausages in same skillet; pour all
but 2 tablespoons drippings from skillet; add onion
and garlic; sauté until lightly browned.

3. When the chick peas are firm and tender, add with
bacon, sausage, onion and garlic, bay leaves, thyme,
mint, parsley, wine, salt and pepper to an electric slow
cooker; cover.

4. Cook on low (190° to 200°) 10 hours, or on high (290°
to 300°) 5 hours.

1 package (1 pound) dried chick
  peas, sorted
8 cups cold water
⅛ pound slab bacon, cut in small
  dice
½ pound chorizos or other
  garlic-flavor, smoked
  sausage, sliced ¼-inch thick
1 large Spanish onion, coarsely
  chopped
1 small clove garlic, crushed
2 bay leaves
¼ teaspoon leaf thyme, crumbled
1 tablespoon minced mint
  OR: 1 teaspoon dried mint
  flakes
2 tablespoons minced parsley
1 cup dry white wine
  OR: ½ cup each wine and water
2 teaspoons salt
¼ teaspoon freshly ground pepper

delicious leftover vegetables

• Leftover string beans or stalks of broccoli are delicious marinated, then mixed
with mayonnaise—particularly if you haven't overcooked or buttered the vegetables. The vegetables can be wrapped in aluminum foil and tucked into a lunch box
along with a plastic fork. Or they can be added to salad greens and tossed with a
French dressing. After all, haven't you ever eaten marinated vegetables served as
part of the hors d'oeuvres in a French restaurant, or as an antipasto in an Italian
restaurant?

• Those few pieces of boiled potato left from dinner can be quickly sliced and fried
for breakfast with some scrambled eggs. Even mashed potatoes can be made into
patties or rolled inside a meat loaf, jelly-roll fashion.

SPICY EGGPLANT AND SAUSAGES

*Cook on 190° to 200° for **8** hours, or on 290° to 300° for **4** hours.*
Makes 6 servings.

Breakfast sausages make an interesting addition to one-pot cooking.

1. Brown sausage links slowly in a large skillet or an electric slow cooker with a browning unit; remove and reserve.
2. Pour off all but 2 tablespoons of the fat; sauté eggplant cubes, one third at a time, in drippings; remove and reserve, using additional fat as needed to sauté eggplant. Then add several tablespoons vegetable oil, if needed.
3. Sauté onion and garlic in pan drippings until soft; stir in parsley, curry powder and oregano; cook 2 minutes. Return sausages to pan and blend well.
4. Layer half the eggplant, sausage mixture and sliced tomatoes in an electric slow cooker; repeat; cover.
5. Cook on low (190° to 200°) 8 hours, or on high (290° to 300°) 4 hours; top with parsley, if you wish.

1 package (1 pound) sausage links
1 medium-size eggplant, pared and cut into 1-inch cubes
1 large onion, chopped (1 cup)
1 clove garlic, minced
¼ cup chopped parsley
1 teaspoon curry powder
1 teaspoon leaf oregano, crumbled
3 large tomatoes, peeled and cut into thick slices

APPLE-YAM DELIGHT

*Cook on 190° to 200° for **6** hours, or on 290° to 300° for **3** hours.*
Makes 6 servings.

A cash saver with lots of style.

1. Mix the apples, potatoes and orange rind in an electric slow cooker.
2. Mix brown sugar, salt and cinnamon in a small bowl. Sprinkle half over apple mixture; toss lightly to mix. Drizzle 3 tablespoons of the melted butter or margarine over top; cover cooker.
3. Cook on low (190° to 200°) 6 hours, or on high (290° to 300°) 3 hours.
4. Toss cereal flakes with remaining brown sugar mixture; lightly stir in remaining melted butter or margarine. Sprinkle over apple mixture and serve.

6 medium-size tart apples, pared, quartered, cored and cut in thick slices (6 cups)
1 can (1 pound) yams or sweet potatoes, halved
1 tablespoon grated orange rind
⅓ cup firmly packed brown sugar
½ teaspoon salt
½ teaspoon ground cinnamon
6 tablespoons (¾ stick) butter or margarine, melted
1½ cups whole-wheat cereal flakes

PINTO BEANS

Cook on 190° to 200° for **10** hours, or on 290° to 300° for **5** hours.
Makes 4 servings.

Hearty budget fare—and nutritious.

1. Pick over beans and rinse. Soak pinto beans overnight in water to cover in large ceramic or glass bowl. Drain.
2. Combine beans, water, onion, garlic, chili powder, salt and pork hocks or salt pork in an electric slow cooker; cover.
3. Cook on low (190° to 200°) 10 hours, or on high (290° to 300°) 5 hours.

1 package (1 pound) dried pinto beans
5 cups water
1 medium-size onion, quartered
1 clove garlic, minced
1 teaspoon chili powder
2 teaspoons salt
½ pound pork hocks or salt pork, cut into cubes

SWEET-SOUR GLAZED BEETS

Cook on 190° to 200° for **10** hours, or on 290° to 300° for **5** hours.
Makes 4 servings.

Not too tart, not too sweet, but just right.

1. Wash the beets. Cut off all but 2 inches of tops; leave root end intact.
2. Place the beets in an electric slow cooker; add ½ cup water; cover cooker.
3. Cook on low (190° to 200°) 10 hours, or on high (290° to 300°) 5 hours; drain.
4. Allow beets to cool slightly; trim root and stem ends; slip skins off with hands. Slice beets (you should have 2 cups).
5. Combine sugar, cornstarch and salt in saucepan; add vinegar. Cook over medium heat, stirring constantly, until the sauce thickens and bubbles 1 minute.
6. Add beets to sauce; heat 3 minutes.

2 bunches beets
¼ cup sugar
1 tablespoon cornstarch
1 teaspoon salt
½ cup cider vinegar

saving on greens

Unless they are badly bruised, save the dark, outer vitamin-rich leaves of salad greens to shred into a salad or slip into sandwiches where appearance isn't as important.

HAM AND LIMA ITALIANO

Cook on 190° to 200° for **10** hours,
or on 290° to 300° for **5** hours.
Makes 8 servings.

Ham and beans bake in one big, cash saving dish.
Vegetables and herbs add interest.

1. Combine beans and cold water in large saucepan; cover. Bring to boiling; cook 2 minutes; remove from heat; let stand, stirring beans once, for 1 hour.
2. Stir in salt and onion; cover again; cook for 30 minutes. Combine beans and liquid with tomatoes, sugar, seasoned salt, basil and thyme in slow cooker.
3. Mix in ham, celery and carrots; cover.
4. Cook on low (190° to 200°) 10 hours, or on high (290° to 300°) 5 hours. Garnish with chopped parsley, if you wish.

1 package (1 pound) dried large lima beans
4 cups cold water
2 teaspoons salt
1 large onion, chopped (1 cup)
1 can (1 pound) tomatoes
1 tablespoon sugar
1 teaspoon seasoned salt
½ teaspoon leaf basil, crumbled
½ teaspoon leaf thyme, crumbled
3 cups diced cooked ham
1 cup sliced celery
1 cup pared shredded carrots

BAVARIAN RED CABBAGE

Cook on 190° to 200° for **8** hours,
or on 290° to 300° for **4** hours.
Makes 8 servings.

This faintly sweet sour cabbage and apple combo
bubbles lazily in a slow cooker.

1. Shred the cabbage; rinse in colander; drain well.
2. Heat bacon drippings or oil in a large kettle or an electric slow cooker with a browning unit. Sauté onion until soft in fat. Add cabbage and cook over low heat, stirring often, 10 minutes, or until cabbage begins to wilt.
3. Combine cabbage mixture with the apple, wine or vinegar, sugar, salt and bay leaf in a slow cooker. Cover.
4. Cook on low (190° to 290°) 8 hours, or on high (290° to 300°) 4 hours. Add jelly; cook 10 minutes.

1 large red cabbage (about 3 pounds)
3 tablespoons bacon drippings or vegetable oil
1 large onion, chopped (1 cup)
2 medium-size apples, peeled, cored and diced
½ cup dry red wine or red wine vinegar
1 tablespoon sugar
1 teaspoon salt
1 bay leaf
½ cup red currant jelly

151

GOLDEN TURNIP SCALLOP

Cook on 190° to 200° for **8** *hours, or on 290° to 300° for* **4** *hours.*
Makes 6 servings.

Peppery turnip, mellowed with apple, simmers buttery-sweet in this easy vegetable dish.

1. Mix turnip, ¾ of the chopped apple, brown sugar, salt, and pepper in an electric slow cooker.
2. Sprinkle remaining chopped apple in a ring on top; dot with butter or margarine; cover.
3. Cook on low (190° to 200°) for 8 hours, or on high (290° to 300°) for 4 hours.

6 cups shredded raw yellow turnip
  (about 1½ pounds)
1 apple, pared, quartered, cored
  and chopped
2 tablespoons brown sugar
1 teaspoon salt
¼ teaspoon pepper
4 tablespoons (½ stick) butter or
  margarine

MICHIGAN LIMA BEAN POT

Cook on 190° to 200° for **10** *hours, or on 290° to 300° for* **5** *hours.*
Makes 8 servings.

Grated Parmesan cheese gives the final touch to this hearty bean dish.

1. Pick over beans and rinse. Place in a large kettle and add water. Bring to boiling; boil 2 minutes; remove from heat and cover kettle. Let stand 1 hour.
2. Return kettle to heat; bring to boiling; lower heat; simmer 1 hour, or until beans are firm-tender. Sauté onion, garlic and carrot in oil in a large skillet or slow cooker with a browning unit until soft.
3. Drain beans and measure liquid. Add enough water to make 4 cups. Stir bean liquid into skillet with instant vegetable broth, salt, rosemary and pepper; bring to boiling; remove from heat.
4. Spoon beans into slow cooker and pour liquid in skillet over beans in slow cooker. Cover.
5. Cook on low (190° to 200°) 10 hours, or on high (290° to 300°) 5 hours. Sprinkle with cheese before serving.

1 package (1 pound) dried lima
  beans
4 cups water
2 large onions, chopped (2 cups)
1 clove garlic, minced
2 medium-size carrots, pared and
  chopped
3 tablespoons vegetable oil
2 envelopes or teaspoons instant
  vegetable broth
2 teaspoons salt
1 teaspoon leaf rosemary,
  crumbled
¼ teaspoon pepper
1 cup grated Parmesan cheese

152

CAROTTES GLACÉES LUTÈCE

*Cook on 190° to 200° for **8** hours, or on 290° to 300° for **4** hours.*
Makes 4 servings.

The secret is cooking the carrots slowly with sugar, salt, butter and water until the water is gone and the carrots are tender and shiny.

1. Pare the carrots; cut into 2-inch lengths. (You should have 3 cups.)
2. Put the carrots in an electric slow cooker with the sugar, salt, butter and water.
3. Cook on low (190° to 200°) 8 hours, or on high (290° to 300°) 4 hours; uncover; cook for 20 minutes, or until water is evaporated and carrots are glazed. Sprinkle with parsley.

1 pound slender young carrots
2 tablespoons sugar
1 teaspoon salt
¼ cup unsalted butter (½ stick)
½ cup water
1 tablespoon minced parsley

SQUASH MOONS WITH CRAB APPLES

*Cook on 190° to 200° for **10** hours, or on 290° to 300° for **5** hours.*
Makes 6 servings.

Acorn squash and rosy crab apples are thrifty plattermates.

1. Cut each squash crosswise into 6 even slices with large heavy-blade knife; scoop out seeds and stringy membrane, but do not pare.
2. Arrange squash slices in an electric slow cooker; brush with melted butter or margarine; sprinkle with salt; add water to cooker; cover.
3. Cook on low (190° to 200°) 10 hours, or on high (290° to 300°) 5 hours or until tender. Uncover; add crab apples; brush squash and apples with liquid in cooker. Cook 10 minutes longer, or until crab apples are heated through.

2 medium-size acorn squashes
¼ cup (½ stick) butter or margarine, melted
1 teaspoon salt
½ cup water
6 spiced crab apples (from a 1-pound jar)

smart ways with onions

Place small white onions in a large bowl; pour boiling water over; wait for 1 minute. Drain and cover with cold water for 3 minutes. Make a cut at the root-end with a paring knife, and the skins will slip off.

ITALIAN BAKED BEANS

Cook on 190° to 200° for **10** *hours,*
or on 290° to 300° for **6** *hours.*
Makes 8 servings.

*You can substitute Great Northern or dried lima beans
for the kidney beans in this recipe.*

1. Pick over beans and rinse. Place in a large kettle and
   add water. Bring to boiling; boil 2 minutes; remove
   from heat and cover. Allow to stand 1 hour.
2. Bring beans in kettle to boiling; reduce heat and
   simmer 1 hour.
3. While beans cook, sauté onion in oil in a large skillet
   or an electric slow cooker with a browning unit; push
   to one side; sauté eggplant until soft in same pan. Stir
   in tomatoes, salt and marjoram; simmer 5 minutes.
4. Drain beans, reserving liquid. Combine beans and
   eggplant mixture in an electric slow cooker. Stir in
   wine or water and 1 cup of reserved bean liquid.
   Cover.
5. Cook on low (190° to 200°) 10 hours, or on high (290°
   to 300°) 6 hours, or until beans are tender.

*1 package (1 pound) dried red
  kidney beans*
4 cups water
1 large onion, chopped (1 cup)
*3 tablespoons olive oil or
  vegetable oil*
*1 small eggplant, sliced, pared and
  cubed*
1 can (1 pound) tomatoes
2 teaspoons salt
*1 teaspoon leaf marjoram,
  crumbled*
½ cup dry red wine or water

VEGETABLES PROVENÇALE

Cook on 190° to 200° for **8** *hours,*
or on 290° to 300° for **4** *hours.*
Makes 8 servings.

*A garden of vegetables go into this Mediterranean
classic. Serve it as a vegetable or an appetizer.*

1. Sauté onion and garlic in oil until soft in a large skillet
   or an electric slow cooker with a browning unit. Trim,
   halve and slice yellow squash and zucchini. Cut eggplant into ½-inch thick slices; pare skin; dice. Add to
   pan and sauté 3 minutes. Stir in tomatoes, salt, thyme,
   basil and pepper until well blended.
2. Place vegetable mixture in slow cooker; cover.
3. Cook on low (190° to 200°) 8 hours, or on high (290°
   to 300°) 4 hours.
4. Serve hot as a vegetable with meats, or chill and serve
   as an appetizer.

1 large onion, chopped (1 cup)
1 clove garlic, minced
*3 tablespoons olive or vegetable
  oil*
1 large yellow squash
1 large zucchini
1 small eggplant
*2 large tomatoes, peeled and
  chopped*
2 tablespoons salt
1 teaspoon leaf thyme, crumbled
1 teaspoon leaf basil, crumbled
¼ teaspoon pepper

154

DIET DISHES

You can treat yourself to a wide variety of tasty foods if you diet with special slow cooker low calorie recipes—and the pleasant surprise is: you won't have to give up rich, mouth-watering gravies. These dishes are good enough to serve to anyone, whether they are trying to lose weight or not.

In general, however, there are some rules you can follow with all your favorite recipes to make sure they don't put on pounds:
• Trim all visible fat from meat before browning or braising.
• Brown meats in a nonstick skillet.
• Substitute cooked shredded cabbage, lettuce or spinach for the bed of pasta or rice on which you like to heap your pot roasts and stews.
• Use skim milk, skim evaporated milk or chicken or beef broth for cream and whole milk in sauces.
• Substitute low-fat cheese, such as low-fat cottage cheese and low-fat mozzarella, for whole-milk cheese.
• Remove every speck of fat from pot roasts and stews by refrigerating or adding a few ice cubes to the liquid. Wait for fat to harden, then skim fat off.

FRENCH CHICKEN IN SHERRY SAUCE

Cook on 190° to 200° for **6** hours,
or on 290° to 300° for **4** hours.
*Makes 6 servings
at 217 calories each.*

Chicken breasts are a dieter's delight! No need to strip the skin if you follow our fat-reducing technique for oven-browning. Add wine sauce for a main course that's quite continental!

1. Place chicken breasts, skin-side up, on rack of broiler pan. Broil 2 inches from heat for 10 minutes, or until skin is brown and crackly. Do not turn.
2. Place browned chicken breasts in an electric slow cooker. Sprinkle with ½ teaspoon salt. Add onion, green pepper and mushrooms.
3. Make sauce. Combine orange juice, sherry, water, brown sugar, 1 teaspoon salt, pepper, orange rind and flour in small saucepan. Blend well. Cook over medium heat, stirring constantly, until sauce thickens and bubbles; add parsley. Pour over chicken breasts; cover.
4. Cook on low (190° to 200°) 6 hours, or on high (290° to 300°) 4 hours. Sprinkle with paprika; garnish with orange slices.

3 whole chicken breasts, split
   (about 10 ounces each)
½ teaspoon salt
1 medium-size onion, sliced
¼ cup chopped green pepper
1 cup sliced mushrooms

Sauce
1 cup orange juice
¼ cup dry sherry
½ cup water
1 tablespoon firmly packed brown
   sugar
1 teaspoon salt
¼ teaspoon pepper
1 teaspoon grated orange rind
1 tablespoon all-purpose flour
2 teaspoons chopped parsley
   Paprika
1 California orange, peeled and
   sliced

saving ways

• Often you can omit the butter, margarine or other fat called for in French recipes. You can add the flavor, without the calories, by using bottled butter flavoring, or butter-flavor salt.
• Crusts cut from sandwiches can be used for stuffing or crumbs. Stale rolls can be used for crumbs, too: Toss in blender or grate them.
The parts of vegetables you usually throw away—for example, the woody ends of asparagus or broccoli—should be saved to simmer in soups.

Cook on 190° to 200° for **8** hours,
or on 290° to 300° for **4** hours.
*Makes 8 servings
at 263 calories each.*

KEY WEST PORK

From Florida comes the inspiration for this sweet-sour combination of tropical fruits that go so well with pork.

1. Brown pork cubes, a few at a time, in oil in a large kettle or electric slow cooker; remove; reserve. Drain on paper towels. Pour off all but 1 tablespoon pan drippings. Sauté onion in pan drippings until soft; add chicken broth, water and salt; bring slowly to boiling; add artichoke hearts and cook 15 minutes longer, or until meat and vegetables are tender; stir in lime rind and juice.
2. Combine pork and sauce in slow cooker with acorn squash slices; cover.
3. Cook on low (190° to 200°) 8 hours, or on high (290° to 300°) 4 hours.
4. Drain liquid from pineapple into a small saucepan; blend in cornstarch; add pineapple chunks to cooker.
5. Stir 1½ cups hot cooking liquid from slow cooker into saucepan. (A bulb baster does a quick job.) Cook, stirring constantly, until sauce thickens and bubbles 1 minute. Taste and sweeten with liquid or granulated sweetener, if you wish. Spoon over pork and vegetables. Garnish with lime slices, if you wish. Serve a low-calorie fruit gelatin as dessert.

2 pounds lean boneless pork shoulder, cubed
2 tablespoons vegetable oil
1 large onion, chopped (1 cup)
2 envelopes or teaspoons instant chicken broth
1¼ cups water
2 teaspoons salt
1 package (9 ounces) frozen artichoke hearts, thawed
1 teaspoon grated lime rind
1 tablespoon lime juice
1 acorn squash, cut into ½-inch slices, pared and seeded
1 can (8 ounces) pineapple chunks in pineapple juice
3 tablespoon cornstarch

Cook on 190° to 200° for **8** hours,
or on 290° to 300° for **4** hours.
*Makes 4 servings
at 221 calories each.*

SEATTLE CHICKEN

This magic chicken cooks golden brown with no fat, no turning.

1. Place chicken in slow cooker; season with salt and pepper; sprinkle with onion slices; pour orange juice over; cover cooker.
2. Cook on low (190° to 200°) 8 hours, or on high (290° to 300°) 4 hours. Serve with a crispy green salad.

1 broiler-fryer, cut-up (about 2 pounds)
1 teaspoon salt
⅛ teaspoon pepper
2 large onions, sliced
½ cup orange juice

157

Cook at 190° to 200° for **10** hours,
or at 290° to 300° for **5** hours.
Makes 4 servings
at 321 calories each.

SLICK CHICK

Each dieter rates a quarter golden-glazed chicken plus spicy apple stuffing in this too-good-to-be-true roast.

1. Sprinkle chicken inside with ½ teaspoon of the salt.
2. Simmer onion in water in a medium-size skillet 5 minutes, or until soft; stir in coriander, curry powder, apples and ½ teaspoon of salt.
3. Cook, stirring often, over medium heat 10 minutes, or until apples are slightly soft. Remove from heat.
4. Stuff neck and body cavity of chicken lightly with apple mixture. Smooth neck skin over stuffing and skewer to back; tie legs to tail with string. Place chicken in an electric slow cooker; pour chicken broth over.
5. Mix remaining ½ teaspoon salt and paprika in a cup; sprinkle over chicken; cover cooker.
6. Cook on low (190° to 200°) 10 hours, or on high (290° to 300°) 5 hours.
7. Remove chicken to a heated serving platter; cut away strings and remove skewers. Garnish platter with parsley and a few thin apple slices, if you wish. Cut chicken in quarters; divide stuffing evenly.

1 broiler-fryer (about 2 pounds)
1½ teaspoons salt
1 large onion, chopped (1 cup)
¼ cup water
¼ teaspoon ground coriander
¼ teaspoon curry powder
3 medium-size apples, pared, quartered, cored and chopped
½ cup chicken broth
1 teaspoon paprika

Cook on 190° to 200° for **8** hours,
or on 290° to 300° for **4** hours.
Makes 8 servings
at 252 calories each.

CHICKEN MARENGO, DIET STYLE

Mushrooms and herbs add the gourmet touch without extra calories.

1. Place chicken pieces, skin-side down, in a nonstick skillet. Brown slowly over moderate heat. (Chicken will brown in its own fat.) Turn; brown other side; drain fat.
2. Add the soup, mushrooms, garlic powder, salt, thyme, and onion liquid. Place in an electric slow cooker; cover.
3. Cook on low (190° to 200°) 8 hours, or on high (290° to 300°) 4 hours; add onions and cook 15 minutes longer.

2 broiler-fryers, cut-up (about 2½ pounds each)
1 can condensed tomato soup
½ pound mushrooms
Instant garlic powder
1 teaspoon salt
½ teaspoon leaf thyme, crumbled
1 can (1 pound) small boiled onions

SMOTHERED CHICKEN

Cook on 190° to 200° for **6** hours,
or on 290° to 300° for **3** hours.
Makes 6 servings
at 267 calories each.

Old-fashioned eating with new-fashioned calorie-paring preparation.

1. Arrange chicken pieces on rack in broiler pan. Sprinkle with salt and paprika. Broil 10 minutes, until brown. Turn; brown other side.
2. Place browned chicken in an electric slow cooker. Stir in soup mix, water and poultry seasoning; cover.
3. Cook on low (190° to 200°) 6 hours, or on high (290° to 300°) 3 hours, or until tender.
4. Remove chicken to heated serving platter; keep warm.
5. Turn heat control to high (290° to 300°). Combine milk and cornstarch in a cup; stir into liquid in slow cooker; cover. Cook 15 minutes or until sauce thickens and bubbles. Pour over chicken.

1 broiler-fryer, cut-up (about 3 pounds)
1 teaspoon salt
½ teaspoon paprika
1 envelope (2 to a package) chicken-vegetable soup mix
1½ cups boiling water
½ teaspoon poultry seasoning
1 cup evaporated skimmed milk
2 tablespoons cornstarch

DIET STYLE POT AU FEU

Cook on 190° to 200° for **10** hours,
or on 290° to 300° for **5** hours.
Makes 4 servings
at 380 calories each.

A low calorie version of a French classic.

1. Trim all fat from beef. Place steak in an electric slow cooker. Add water, broth, onion, garlic and salt. Tie parsley, bay leaf, peppercorns and thyme in a small piece of cheesecloth; add to slow cooker. Add chicken breast.
2. Pare carrots and cut in sticks; trim zucchini, cut in sticks about 4 inches long; add to slow cooker with celery sticks; cover cooker.
3. Cook on low (190° to 200°) 10 hours, or on high (290° to 300°) 5 hours, or until tender. Remove.
4. Strain broth into a large bowl, pressing onion and garlic through sieve into liquid; let stand about a minute, or until fat rises to top, then skim off.
5. Carve meats; combine with broth and vegetables in a heated tureen.

1 pound boneless round steak
3 cups water
1 can condensed beef broth
1 large onion, chopped (1 cup)
1 clove garlic, minced
2 teaspoons salt
4 sprigs parsley
1 bay leaf
6 peppercorns
½ teaspoon leaf thyme
1 whole chicken breast (about 12 ounces)
4 large carrots
2 medium-size zucchini
3 cups celery sticks

Cook on 190° to 200° for **8** hours,
or on 290° to 300° for **4** hours.
*Makes 4 servings
at 306 calories each.*

TERIYAKI CHICKEN

The Oriental way to diet—delicious.

1. Marinate chicken with teriyaki sauce or soy sauce in a bowl for 15 minutes.
2. Heat oil in a wok or large skillet; remove chicken from sauce; brown quickly in hot oil. Place in an electric slow cooker with yellow squash and green beans, add remaining teriyaki sauce or soy sauce, water, lemon juice; cover.
3. Cook on low (190° to 200°) 8 hours, or on high (290° to 300°) 4 hours.
4. Thirty minutes before serving, turn heat control to high; drain liquid from pineapple into small cup; stir in cornstarch to make a smooth paste.
5. Add pineapple and sliced water chestnuts to cooker. Stir cornstarch mixture into liquid in slow cooker; cover; cook 15 minutes, until mixture thickens and bubbles. Stir in your favorite low-calorie sweetener, using the equivalent of 1 tablespoon sugar. Serve with Chinese noodles, if you wish (70 calories per ⅓ cup for noodles).

2 whole chicken breasts (about 12 ounces each)
3 tablespoons teriyaki sauce or soy sauce
1 tablespoon vegetable oil
2 medium-size yellow squash, trimmed and sliced
1 package (9 ounces) frozen cut green beans
2 cups water
2 tablespoons lemon juice
1 can (8 ounces) pineapple chunks in pineapple juice
2 tablespoons cornstarch
1 can (5 ounces) water chestnuts, sliced
Granulated or liquid low calorie sweetener

Cook on 190° to 200° for **8** hours,
or on 290° to 300° for **4** hours.
*Makes 4 servings
at 323 calories each.*

KOREAN CHICKEN

Quarters of chicken are baked in a soy-green onion sauce and served with golden pineapple chunks.

1. Arrange chicken quarters, skin-side up in an electric slow cooker.
2. Drain juice from pineapple chunks into a 2-cup measure; add enough water to make 1 cup; reserve chunks.
3. Add green onions and soy sauce to pineapple liquid; spoon over chicken; cover cooker.
4. Cook on low (190° to 200°) 8 hours, or on high (290° to 300°) 4 hours. Add pineapple chunks and baste with sauce. Cook 15 minutes longer.

1 broiler-fryer, quartered (about 3 pounds)
1 can (8 ounces) pineapple chunks in pineapple juice
Water
¼ cup sliced green onions
OR: 1 small onion, chopped (¼ cup)
¼ cup soy sauce

LOW CALORIE FRICASSEE

Cook on 190° to 200° for **6** hours,
or on 290° to 300° for **3** hours.
Makes 6 servings
at 200 calories each.

A happy combination of rich tasting gravy and sensible calorie count.

1. Combine the chicken with onion, celery, salt, pepper and water in an electric slow cooker; cover.
2. Cook on low (190° to 200°) 6 hours, or on high (290° to 300°) 3 hours or until tender; remove to a heated serving platter and keep warm.
3. Turn heat control up to high (290° to 300°); mix flour and skim milk in a cup; stir into liquid in slow cooker; cover. Cook until gravy thickens and bubbles 15 minutes. Serve in a separate bowl.

3 whole chicken breasts, split (about 12 ounces each)
1 small onion, chopped (¼ cup)
½ cup finely chopped celery
2 teaspoons salt
⅛ teaspoon pepper
1 cup water
2 tablespoons all-purpose flour
½ cup skim milk

CALICO CHICKEN FRICASSEE

Cook on 190° to 200° for **8** hours,
or on 290° to 300° for **4** hours.
Makes 4 servings
at 306 calories each.

Simmered chicken with a creamy gravy.

1. Place chicken pieces, skin-side down, in a large skillet over *very low* heat. (Do not add fat.) Cook until chicken is a rich brown on skin-side, about 10 minutes; turn and brown on other side. Place in an electric slow cooker.
2. Add carrots, onion and celery to skillet; toss to coat with drippings from chicken. Cook and stir 10 minutes.
3. Add hot water, instant chicken broth, salt and sage; mix well; add to slow cooker; cover.
4. Cook on low (190° to 200°) 8 hours, or on high (290° to 300°) 4 hours, or until chicken and vegetables are tender; stir in peas.
5. Turn heat control to high (290° to 300°). Combine flour and skim milk in a cup; stir into liquid in slow cooker; cook 15 minutes or until sauce is thickened.

1 broiler-fryer, cut-up (2 pounds)
1 pound carrots, pared and sliced
1 large onion, chopped (1 cup)
1 cup thinly sliced celery
1 cup hot water
1 envelope or teaspoon instant chicken broth
2 teaspoons salt
1 teaspoon leaf sage, crumbled
1 cup frozen peas (from a plastic bag), thawed
2 tablespoons all-purpose flour
½ cup skim milk
2 tablespoons chopped parsley

RUTH MUMBAUER'S DIET STEW

Cook on 190° to 200° for **10** hours, or on 290° to 300° for **5** hours.
Makes 6 servings at 304 calories each.

Try her method for browning onions and beef, without using a drop of fat.

1. Simmer onion in the ½ cup water in a nonstick large skillet for 10 minutes or just until water evaporates. Continue cooking and stirring constantly over low heat until onion browns lightly; spoon into an electric slow cooker.
2. Brown beef, a few pieces at a time, in same skillet; place into slow cooker; stir beef broth, wine or water, bay leaf, seasoned salt and pepper into skillet; bring to boiling, stirring up the cooked-on juices; pour over beef in slow cooker with potatoes, celery and zucchini; cover.
3. Cook on low (190° to 200°) 10 hours, or on high (290° to 300°) 5 hours; stir in lettuce and cherry tomatoes; cover; cook 15 minutes longer, or until meat and vegetables are tender. Remove bay leaf. Serve in heated soup bowls.

Suggested Variations: Lean lamb or pork can be substituted for the beef in this recipe. Chicken broth, green beans, carrots, broccoli or cauliflower can also be used in place of the beef broth and listed vegetables.

1 small onion, chopped (¼ cup)
½ cup water
1½ pounds lean boneless beef round, cubed
1 can condensed beef broth
1 cup dry red wine or water
1 bay leaf
1 teaspoon seasoned salt
¼ teaspoon seasoned pepper
6 small potatoes, pared
3 cups sliced celery
3 small zucchini, tipped and cut into sticks
3 cups shredded lettuce
12 cherry tomatoes

PEACHY LOW-CALORIE CHICKEN

Cook on 190° to 200° for **8** hours, or on 290° to 300° for **4** hours.
Makes 6 servings at 210 calories each.

Chicken pieces baked with fruit and a seasoned glaze that add almost no calories.

1. Arrange chicken pieces in an electric slow cooker.
2. Drain peach syrup into a cup; place peaches in slow cooker. Add lemon juice and soy sauce to syrup; pour over chicken; cover.
3. Cook on low (190° to 200°) for 8 hours, or on high (290° to 300°) 4 hours.

COOK'S TIP: for golden, glazed chicken pieces, place cooked chicken in a single layer on broiler pan and broil 4 inches from heat, 5 minutes.

3 whole chicken breasts, split (about 10 ounces each)
3 drumsticks
3 thighs
1 can (1 pound) diet-pack cling peach halves
2 tablespoons lemon juice
1 teaspoon soy sauce

FRENCH PROVINCIAL LAMB RAGOÛT

Cook on 190° to 200° for **8** hours,
or on 290° to 300° for **4** hours.
*Makes 8 servings
at 229 calories each.*

Rich brown stews aren't necessarily off limits for dieters.

1. Sprinkle lamb with garlic salt and pepper. Heat oil in a nonstick Dutch oven or an electric slow cooker with a browning unit; brown lamb cubes well on all sides. Drain off oil. Add beef broth, tomato juice, thyme and bay leaf. Bring to boiling.
2. Combine lamb and tomato sauce in a slow cooker with carrots and onions; cover.
3. Cook on low (190° to 200°) 8 hours, or on high (290° to 300°) 4 hours or until vegetables are almost tender. Add green beans and simmer 15 minutes longer.
4. Turn heat control to high (290° to 300°). Combine flour and water in a cup; stir into liquid in slow cooker; cover; cook 15 minutes.

*2 pounds boneless leg of lamb,
    fat-trimmed and cut in cubes*
1 teaspoon garlic salt
¼ teaspoon pepper
1 tablespoon vegetable oil
1 can condensed beef broth
*1 cup tomato juice
    Pinch leaf thyme, crumbled*
1 bay leaf
*1 pound carrots, pared and cut
    into 2-inch pieces*
*¾ pound small white onions,
    peeled*
*1 package (10 ounces) frozen
    French-style green beans,
    thawed*
3 tablespoons all-purpose flour
⅓ cup water

DEVILED CHICKEN

Cook on 190° to 200° for **6** hours,
or on 290° to 300° for **3** hours.
*Makes 4 servings
at 240 calories each.*

Onion and mustard make this a tangy way to pare calories.

1. Place chicken, skin-side up, in an electric cooker; sprinkle with salt and paprika. Place onion slices on top.
2. Blend deviled ham, wine and mustard in a cup; spoon over chicken; cover cooker.
3. Cook on low (190° to 200°) 6 hours, or on high (290° to 300°) 3 hours. Place on a heated serving platter; spoon onion and remaining liquid in cooker over top.

*2 whole chicken breasts, split
    (about 14 ounces each)*
½ teaspoon salt
¼ teaspoon paprika
*1 medium-size onion, peeled and
    sliced*
1 can (2¼ ounces) deviled ham
½ cup dry white wine
½ teaspoon prepared mustard

Cook on 190° to 200° for **8** hours,
or on 290° to 300° for **4** hours.

Makes 6 servings
at 218 calories each.

STUFFED BEEF BUNDLES

Steak rolls stuffed with vegetables and smothered with gravy—all for fewer calories then you'd get from a can of diet formula.

1. Pound steak very thin with a mallet or rolling pin; cut into 6 equal-size pieces. (If using round steak, trim off all fat first.)
2. Drain mushrooms, saving liquid. Mix mushrooms with onion, catsup and salt in small bowl; spread evenly over the steak pieces. Place carrot sticks, dividing evenly, crosswise at end of each; roll up, jelly-roll fashion, and fasten with one or two wooden picks.
3. Brown steak rolls, part at a time, in a large skillet or electric slow cooker. Place beef bundles, mushroom liquid, instant beef broth and water in a slow cooker; cover.
4. Cook on low (190° to 200°) 8 hours, or on high (290° to 300°) 4 hours.
5. Remove to a heated serving platter, take out the wooden picks; keep steak rolls hot while making BROWN GRAVY.

BROWN GRAVY— Makes about 1 cup. Pour juices from slow cooker into a 1-cup measure; skim off any fat, then measure 1 tablespoon and return to a small saucepan. Add water, if necessary, to juices to make 1 cup. Stir 1 tablespoon all-purpose flour into fat in pan; add meat-juice mixture. Cook, stirring constantly, till the gravy thickens and bubbles 3 minutes. Taste and season with salt and pepper.

*1 flank steak (about 1½ pounds) or
    1 lean boneless round steak
    (about 1½ pounds)
1 can (3 or 4 ounces) chopped
    mushrooms
1 medium-size onion, finely
    chopped (½ cup)
2 tablespoons catsup
1 teaspoon salt
2 medium-size carrots, pared and
    cut in 4-inch-long sticks
2 envelopes or teaspoons instant
    beef broth
1 cup water
    Brown Gravy (recipe follows)*

diet pointer

Calorie counters can enjoy artichokes with a free conscience. To cook them, trim all leaves with kitchen shears; scoop out the choke with a sharp spoon (a grapefruit spoon is perfect). Place in a kettle with a bit of lemon juice and a few whole allspice; add a 1-inch depth of water. Cover and bring to boiling; lower heat and simmer 30 minutes, or until tender. Cool in cooking liquid. Serve with thin slices of poached chicken breast and a little low-calorie salad dressing.

Cook on 190° to 200° for **8** hours,
or on 290° to 300° for **4** hours.
Makes 8 servings
at 214 calories each.

LOW CALORIE IRISH STEW

You get the traditional meaty chunks of lamb, and carrots, but low calorie turnips substitute for potatoes.

1. Combine lamb, bay leaf, salt, pepper and beef broth in an electric slow cooker.
2. Add onions, turnips and carrots. Cover slow cooker.
3. Cook on low (190° to 200°) 8 hours, or on high (290° to 300°) 4 hours, or until vegetables are tender.
4. Turn heat control to high (290° to 300°). Combine flour and water in a cup; stir into liquid in slow cooker; cover; cook 15 minutes.

2 pounds boneless leg of lamb, fat-trimmed and cut into cubes
1 bay leaf
1 teaspoon salt
¼ teaspoon pepper
1 can condensed beef broth
2 large onions, sliced
1 pound white turnips, pared and sliced
1 pound carrots, pared and sliced
3 tablespoons all-purpose flour
⅓ cup water

Cook on 190° to 200° for **8** hours,
or on 290° to 300° for **4** hours.
Makes 4 servings
at 347 calories each.

VEAL CHOPS SUPREME

A delicious dish that will make you forget you are on a diet.

1. Drain liquid from mushrooms into a small saucepan. Stir chicken broth and flour into liquid; cook, stirring constantly, until sauce thickens and bubbles 1 minute. Stir in lemon juice.
2. Trim all fat from chops; place in an electric slow cooker with sauce; top with pepper rings and mushroom slices; cover cooker.
3. Cook on low (190° to 200°) 8 hours, or on high (290° to 300°) 4 hours.
4. When ready to serve, place chops and rice, dividing evenly, on heated serving plates; top rice with pepper rings; sprinkle with parsley.

1 can (3 or 4 ounces) chopped mushrooms
1 cup chicken broth
2 tablespoons all-purpose flour
1 teaspoon lemon juice
4 loin or rib veal chops, cut ¾ ¾-inch thick
1 small red pepper, seeded and cut into rings
2 tablespoons chopped parsley
2 cups hot cooked rice (½ cup uncooked)

DIETER'S CURRIED LAMB

Cook on 190° to 200° for **8** hours, or on 290° to 300° for **4** hours.
Makes 8 servings at 253 calories each.

Lean lamb, green beans, and yellow squash make good eating that's low in calories, too.

1. Brown lamb, a few pieces at a time, in oil in a large kettle or an electric slow cooker with a browning unit; remove and reserve; drain on paper towels. Pour off all but 1 tablespoon pan drippings. Sauté onion and garlic in pan drippings. Stir in curry powder and cook 2 minutes; return lamb to pan; stir in salt, pepper, chicken broth and 1¼ cups water.
2. Bring slowly to boiling; lower heat. Combine lamb and sauce in slow cooker with yellow squash and green beans; cover.
3. Cook on low (190° to 200°) 8 hours, or on high (290° to 300°) 4 hours. Place meat and vegetables on heated serving platter.
4. Turn heat control to high (290° to 300°). Combine flour and water in a cup; stir into liquid in slow cooker; cover; cook 15 minutes. Spoon over lamb and vegetables. Top with chopped fresh mint, if you wish. *Suggested Variation:* Chicken breasts, green onions, broccoli flowerets and sliced mushrooms can be substituted for the lamb and vegetables in this recipe.

2 pounds lean boneless lamb shoulder, cubed
2 tablespoons vegetable oil
1 large onion, chopped (1 cup)
2 cloves garlic, minced
1 tablespoon curry powder
1 teaspoon salt
¼ teaspoon pepper
1 can condensed chicken broth
1¼ cups water
3 large yellow squash, tipped and sliced
1 pound green beans, tipped and cut into 1-inch pieces
2 tablespoons all-purpose flour
¼ cup water

DIETER'S HAWAIIAN CHICKEN

Cook on 190° to 200° for **8** hours, or on 290° to 300° for **4** hours.
Makes 6 servings at 287 calories each.

Cooked to a turn in a soy and onion sauce.

1. Arrange split chicken, skin-side up in an electric slow cooker. Mix onion, soy sauce and water in a small bowl; pour over chicken; cover.
2. Cook on low (190° to 200°) 8 hours, or on high (290° to 300°) 4 hours.
3. Drain pineapple slices well on paper towels; roll edge of each in chopped parsley. Serve with chicken.

3 broiler-fryers, split (about 1½ pounds each)
1 small onion, chopped (¼ cup)
¼ cup soy sauce
1½ cups water
6 slices pineapple in pineapple juice (from a 1-pound, 4-ounce can)
2 tablespoons chopped parsley

166

MONTEREY PORK

Cook on 190° to 200° for **8** hours, or on 290° to 300° for **4** hours. Makes 6 servings at 307 calories each.

Cubed pork simmers in a pepper and tomato sauce. Rice is even included in this calorie counter's special.

1. Brown pork, a few pieces at a time, in a large nonstick skillet; remove with a slotted spoon and reserve.
2. Sauté onion and green pepper until soft, then stir in chili powder; cook 2 minutes; return meat with tomatoes, celery, salt and pepper to skillet and mix well. Spoon into slow cooker; cover.
3. Cook on low (190° to 200°) 8 hours, or on high (290° to 300°) for 4 hours. Spoon over ½ cup cooked rice per serving.

1½ pounds lean boneless pork shoulder, cubed
1 large onion, chopped (1 cup)
1 large green pepper, halved, seeded and chopped
1½ teaspoons chili powder
1 can (1 pound) tomatoes
½ cup chopped celery
1 teaspoon salt
⅛ teaspoon pepper
3 cups hot cooked rice

GOURMET CHICKEN WITH WILD RICE

Cook on 190° to 200° for **10** hours, or on 290° to 300° for **5** hours. Makes 4 servings at 281 calories each.

Tender chickens are stuffed with wild rice and mushrooms, then coated with a low calorie orange glaze.

1. Drain mushrooms, reserving liquid. Combine rice mix and onion in a medium-size saucepan; stir in chicken broth, reserved mushroom liquid and water. Cook, following label directions. Stir in mushrooms.
2. Lightly stuff chickens with rice mixture; secure with poultry skewers; tuck wings under or tie across back.
3. Place chickens, breast sides up, in large electric slow cooker.
4. Combine orange peel, juice, maple syrup and ground ginger in small bowl. Brush glaze over chickens; cover.
5. Cook on low (190° to 200°) 10 hours, or on high (290° to 300°) 5 hours.

1 can (3 ounces) mushroom stems and pieces
½ package (6 ounces) long grain and wild rice mix
1 tablespoon instant minced onion
1¼ cups chicken broth
2 broiler-fryers (about 2½ pounds each)
2 tablespoons thinly slivered orange peel
¼ cup orange juice
½ cup diet maple syrup
¼ teaspoon ground ginger

Cook on 190° to 200° for **8** hours,
or on 290° to 300° for **4** hours.
Makes 6 servings
at 280 calories each.

PEPPER BEEF LOAFETTES

These tasty meat loaves are a welcome addition to a calorie-counter's diet.

1. Combine ground beef, bread crumbs, nonfat dry milk, onion, egg, water, salt, and pepper in a medium-size bowl.
2. Set half of the green pepper and 3 water chestnuts aside; chop remaining and add to meat mixture; mix lightly.
3. Shape into 6 even-size loaves. Cut remaining green-pepper half into one-inch-long strips; cut water chestnuts into slices.
4. Line an electric slow cooker with a 12-inch square of aluminum foil; sprinkle green pepper and water chestnuts on top; arrange meat loaves on vegetables; pour wine over; cover cooker.
5. Cook on low (190° to 200°) 8 hours, or on high (290° to 300°) 4 hours.
6. Remove loaf from slow cooker by lifting the foil "ears" as easy-lift handles, tilting fat back into slow cooker. Serve on heated serving platter; spoon juices and vegetables in cooker over.

1½ pounds lean ground beef
½ cup fine dry bread crumbs
⅓ cup instant nonfat dry milk
1 tablespoon chopped onion
1 egg, slightly beaten
¼ cup water
1½ teaspoons salt
⅛ teaspoon pepper
1 small green pepper, halved lengthwise and seeded
8 water chestnuts (from a 5-ounce can)
½ cup dry red wine or beef broth

calorie-saving tips

Cooked pasta itself isn't particularly high in calories—only about 155 per cup. It's the sauces, generally, and the cheese toppings that pile on the calories. So sprinkle the Parmesan with a light touch and, instead of using rich gravies and sauces, flavor pasta with tomatoes, mushrooms or seafood.

A medium-sized potato by itself contains only about 90 calories, so it isn't the potato that is fattening by itself, it is what you do with it. When you are counting calories:

• Try boiling potato in chicken or beef broth for flavor.
• Add dillweed or a bay leaf to the cooking water.
• Drizzle a baked potato with lemon juice instead of melted butter.

BAVARIAN PORK AND KRAUT

Cook on 190° to 200° for **8** hours, or on 290° to 300° for **4** hours.
Makes 6 servings at 319 calories each.

Today's lean pork slips as sensibly into diet meals as any other meat. This time it's chops on caraway-seasoned kraut.

1. Trim all fat from chops. Brown chops slowly in a medium-size non-stick skillet or electric slow cooker with a browning unit; remove and reserve.
2. Empty sauerkraut into a strainer; rinse under cold water; drain well. Combine with caraway seeds in slow cooker. Place apple slices in a layer over sauerkraut; top with browned chops. Pour beer over. Cover cooker.
3. Cook on low (190° to 200°) 8 hours, or on high (290° to 300°) 4 hours.
4. Thirty minutes before serving, cook potatoes in boiling salted water in a medium-size saucepan 20 minutes, or until tender, drain well.
5. Place chops, sauerkraut, and potatoes on heated serving platter. Sprinkle potatoes wtih parsley.

6 loin pork chops, cut 1-inch thick (about 2 pounds)
2 packages (1 pound each) sauerkraut
1 teaspoon caraway seeds
2 medium-size tart apples, quartered, cored and sliced thin
1 can (12 ounces) beer
6 small potatoes, pared
2 tablespoons chopped parsley

ORANGE CHICKEN

Cook on 190° to 200° for **6** hours, or on 290° to 300° for **3** hours.
Makes 4 servings at 216 calories each.

A taste of honey... and much more.

1. Place chicken, skin-side up, in an electric slow cooker; sprinkle with salt and pepper.
2. Blend orange juice, honey, Worcestershire sauce and mustard in a cup; brush over chicken; cover cooker.
3. Cook on low (190° to 200°) 6 hours, or on high (290° to 300°) 3 hours, or until chicken is tender.

4 drumsticks with thighs (about 2 pounds)
1 teaspoon salt
¼ teaspoon pepper
½ cup orange juice
1 tablespoon honey
1 teaspoon Worcestershire sauce
¼ teaspoon dry mustard

Cook on 190° to 200° for **10** hours,
or on 290° to 300° for **5** hours.
Makes 6 servings
at 385 calories each.

BOILED-BEEF DINNER

*It is hard to guess that this classic dish—a favorite of
French chefs—is also good for those who want to lose
weight.*

1. Place meat in an electric slow cooker; add salt,
   peppercorns, bay leaf, and water.
2. Cut off a band of skin around middle of each potato;
   place potatoes, onions, and carrots around meat in
   cooker; cover.
3. Cook on low (190° to 200°) 10 hours, or on high (290°
   to 300°) 5 hours.
4. Turn heat control to high (290° to 300°); cut cabbage
   into 6 wedges; arrange on top of meat and vegetables;
   cover. Cook 30 minutes, or until cabbage is tender.
5. Remove cabbage with a slotted spoon and place at
   one side of a heated large serving platter; place meat in
   center and carrots at other side. Spoon onions and
   potatoes into a serving bowl.
6. Skim any traces of fat from broth; remove bay leaf;
   spoon broth over vegetables. Carve meat into
   ¼-inch thick slices.

*1 bottom round roast (about 3
    pounds)*
1 tablespoon salt
2 peppercorns
1 bay leaf
6 cups water
6 small potatoes, scrubbed
6 small onions, peeled
*6 medium-size carrots, pared and
    quartered*
*1 medium-size cabbage (about 2
    pounds)*

calorie-saving tips for birds

- Choose lean birds (chicken, turkey, game hen) instead of the fattier ones
(duckling, goose).
- Pick young birds (broiler-fryers, for example) over the older; they have less fat
and fewer calories.
- Choose light meat instead of dark (chicken breasts are particularly slimming).

Because of the fat in chicken skin, broiler-fryers can be cooked without additional
fat. Simply sprinkle with salt, pepper, monosodium glutamate, lemon juice and an
herb such as tarragon, thyme or basil. Broiled chicken may also be basted with a
barbecue sauce.

LOW CALORIE CHICKEN ORIENTALE

Cook on 190° to 200° for **8** hours, or on 290° to 300° for **4** hours. *Makes 6 servings at 248 calories each.*

A sweet and sour chicken dish that's off the "forbidden list."

1. Place chicken pieces, skin-side up, in an electric slow cooker and surround with pineapple chunks.
2. Mix juice with vinegar, soy sauce, mustard, salt and pepper and pour over chicken.
3. Cook on low (190° to 200°) 8 hours, or on high (290° to 300°) 4 hours. Add pepper strips.
4. Turn heat control to high (290° to 300°). Combine water and cornstarch in a cup; stir into liquid in slow cooker; cover; cook 15 minutes.

2 broiler-fryers, cut-up (1½ pounds each)
1 can (1 pound) unsweetened pineapple chunks in pineapple juice
3 tablespoons wine vinegar
1 tablespoon soy sauce
½ teaspoon dry mustard
1 teaspoon salt
¼ teaspoon pepper
2 green peppers, seeded and cut in strips
1 tablespoon cornstarch
2 tablespoons water

POT ROAST PROVENÇAL

Cook on 190° to 200° for **10** hours, or on 290° to 300 for **5** hours. *Makes 8 servings at 277 calories each.*

Slow cooking is the ideal way to make this robust French country dish.

1. Season the meat with garlic salt and pepper.
2. Heat oil in a heavy nonstick pan or electric slow cooker with a browning unit; brown meat on all sides. Drain off any remaining fat.
3. Add the wine, water, tomato sauce and bay leaf.
4. Combine sauce and browned meat in a slow cooker with onion and carrot; cover cooker.
5. Cook on low (190° to 200°) 10 hours, or on high (290° to 300°) 5 hours.
6. Remove meat to a serving platter; keep warm. Turn to high (290° to 300°). Simmer sauce, uncovered, to thicken slightly. Serve sauce with meat.

1 well-trimmed round roast (about 3 pounds)
2 teaspoons garlic salt
¼ teaspoon pepper
1 tablespoon vegetable oil
½ cup dry red wine
½ cup water
2 cans (8 ounces each) tomato sauce
1 bay leaf
1 medium-size onion, finely chopped (½ cup)
1 cup shredded carrot

CHICKEN BREASTS ITALIANO

Cook on 190° to 200° for **6** *hours, or on 290° to 300° for* **3** *hours.*
Makes 6 servings at 177 calories each.

Spaghetti sauce mix in an envelope gives a zesty flavor to chicken breasts.

1. Brown chicken breasts in a large nonstick skillet or electric slow cooker with a browning unit; remove and reserve.
2. Blend spaghetti sauce mix into drippings in skillet; stir in tomatoes; bring to boiling, stirring constantly. Arrange chicken breasts in slow cooker, top with onion slices. Spoon sauce around chicken breasts and onions; cover slow cooker.
3. Cook on low (190° to 200°) 6 hours, or on high (290° to 300°) 3 hours or until chicken breasts are tender. Serve with Italian green beans, if you wish.
Suggested Variation: PORK CHOPS CACCIATORE, making 6 servings at 287 calories each, is another version of this recipe. Follow the recipe for CHICKEN BREASTS CACCIATORE, using 6 well-trimmed loin pork chops, cut ¾-inch thick. Add 1 large green pepper seeded and cut into 6 slices to Bermuda onion slices and cook in slow cooker.

3 chicken breasts, split (about 12 ounces each)
1 envelope (1½ ounces) spaghetti sauce mix
1 can (1 pound) tomatoes

ARROZ CON POLLO

Cook on 190° to 200° for **8** *hours, or on high 290° to 300° for* **4** *hours.*
Makes 8 servings at 290 calories each.

A version of Spanish chicken with rice that's high on flavor, not calories.

1. Trim away excess fat from chicken pieces. Arrange, skin-side down, in a cold nonstick skillet. Brown slowly over low heat.
2. Add the onions and garlic. Sauté; pour off any fat.
3. Add tomato juice, water, tomatoes, bay leaf, saffron, salt and pepper. Place in an electric slow cooker with green pepper, pimiento and wine; cover.
4. Cook on low (190° to 200°) 8 hours, or on high (290° to 300°) 4 hours. Stir in cooked rice; cook 15 minutes longer.

2 broiler-fryers, cut-up (about 2½ pounds each)
1 large onion, chopped (1 cup)
2 cloves garlic, minced
1 cup tomato juice
1 cup water
3 tomatoes, peeled and choppped
1 bay leaf
½ teaspoon ground saffron
1½ teaspoons salt
¼ teaspoon pepper
1 medium-size green pepper, halved, seeded and diced
1 pimiento, sliced
¼ cup dry sherry
1 cup cooked rice

LOW CALORIE VEAL MARENGO

Cook on 190° to 200° for **6** hours,
or on 290° to 300° for **3** hours.
*Makes 6 servings
at 271 calories each.*

Even classic dishes are possible on a diet, when you know how to trim the calories.

1. Heat oil in a large nonstick skillet or an electric slow cooker with a browning unit; brown veal, a few pieces at a time in oil; remove and reserve.
2. Sauté onion and garlic in pan drippings until soft; sprinkle flour over and toss to blend well.
3. Add tomatoes, beef broth, wine, salt, pepper, thyme and bay leaf; bring to boiling. Place veal and mushrooms in a slow cooker; spoon sauce over; cover.
4. Cook on low (190° to 200°) 6 hours, or on high (290° to 300°) 3 hours. Remove bay leaf; sprinkle with chopped parsley, if you wish.

1 tablespoon vegetable oil
1½ pounds boneless lean veal, cubed
1 large onion, chopped (1 cup)
1 clove garlic, minced
2 tablespoons all-purpose flour
4 medium-size tomatoes, peeled and chopped
½ cup dry white wine
1 teaspoon salt
¼ teaspoon freshly ground pepper
1 teaspoon leaf thyme, crumbled
1 bay leaf
1 pound mushrooms, sliced

DIETER'S CHICKEN WITH PEPPER

Cook on 190° to 200° for **8** hours,
or on 290° to 300° for **4** hours.
*Makes 6 servings
at 248 calories each.*

Plump chunks of chicken and bright green strips of pepper in a spicy wine and tomato sauce. How could this be diet fare?

1. Put chicken, tomato sauce, wine, onion, green pepper, garlic, oregano, salt and pepper in an electric slow cooker; cover.
2. Cook on low (190° to 200°) 8 hours, or on high (290° to 300°) 4 hours.

2 broiler-fryers (about 1½ pounds each)
2 cans (8 ounces each) tomato sauce
½ cup dry white wine
1 medium-size onion, chopped (½ cup)
1 large green pepper, halved, seeded and sliced
1 clove garlic, minced
1 tablespoon leaf oregano, crumbled
½ teaspoon salt
¼ teaspoon pepper

Cook on 190° to 200° for **10** hours,
or on 290° to 300° for **5** hours,
Makes 6 servings
at 334 calories each.

BEEF-VEGETABLE RAGOÛT

A delicious blend of meat and vegetables that leaves you satisfied.

1. Cook onion in ½ cup of the water in a kettle or an electric slow cooker with a browning unit 10 minutes, or just until liquid evaporates. Lower heat and continue cooking, stirring constantly, 3 to 5 minutes, or until onion browns lightly; remove and set aside.
2. Brown beef cubes, a few at a time, in same pan. (No need to add fat.) Return all beef and onion to slow cooker; stir in bay leaf, seasoned salt and pepper, beef bouillon, and the remaining 1 cup water.
3. Arrange potatoes on top with celery and eggplant; cover cooker.
4. Cook on low (190° to 200°) 10 hours, or on high (290° to 300°) 5 hours. Uncover. Lay escarole and tomatoes on top; cover again; simmer 5 minutes, or just until greens wilt.
5. Spoon a potato into each of 6 heated serving dishes; surround with ragoût.

1 small onion, chopped (¼ cup)
1½ cups water
1½ pounds lean beef round or chuck, cut into 1-inch cubes
1 bay leaf
½ teaspoon seasoned salt
¼ teaspoon seasoned pepper
1 can condensed beef bouillion
6 small potatoes, pared
3 cups sliced celery
1 small eggplant, diced (3 cups)
½ small head escarole, chopped (3 cups)
3 medium-size tomatoes, cut in wedges

calorie saver's delight

• When you are trying to lose a few pounds broil meats brown for stews and pot roasts instead of browning in oil or butter. There is no fat needed for broiling, and so you save a few calories.

• Poultry can have a calorie-saving stuffing. Use a mixture of vegetables and herbs, rather than a bread or rice mixture. Then cook with chicken broth.

• If you are on a diet it's smart to know which kind of chopped meat will be kindest to your figure: A four-ounce portion of chopped sirloin is around 220 calories; chopped round, 223 calories; and chopped chuck, 292 calories. These are average cuts of meat and the assumption is that no extra fat has been added.

Cook on 190° to 200° for **10** hours,
or on 290° to 300° for **5** hours.
Makes 10 servings
at 294 calories each.

FLEMISH POT ROAST

Beer adds flavor to this hearty, satisfying, beef-and-onion dish.

1. Season the meat with garlic salt and pepper.
2. Heat the oil in a heavy nonstick pan or electric slow cooker with a browning unit; brown meat on all sides. Drain off any remaining fat.
3. Combine beef, thyme, bay leaf, beer and brown sugar in slow cooker with onions and parsley; cover cooker.
4. Cook on low (190° to 200°) 10 hours, or on high (290° to 300°) 5 hours. Remove meat to serving platter and keep warm.
5. Turn to high (290° to 300°); simmer sauce, uncovered, to thicken slightly. Serve sauce with meat.

1 well-trimmed round roast (about 3½ pounds)
2 teaspoons garlic salt
¼ teaspoon pepper
1 tablespoon vegetable oil
1 teaspoon leaf thyme, crumbled
1 bay leaf
1 bottle or can (12 ounces) light beer
1 teaspoon brown sugar
2 medium-size onions, sliced
2 tablespoons chopped parsley

Cook on 190° to 200° for **6** hours,
or on 290° to 300° for **3** hours.
Makes 6 servings
at 265 calories each.

VEAL FRICASSEE

This creamy gravy won't put on pounds! It's made by stirring evaporated milk into an herb-seasoned broth.

1. Trim any fat from veal; cut veal into 1-inch cubes.
2. Combine bay leaves, celery salt, rosemary, pepper, instant beef broth and water in slow cooker with meat.
3. Place onions on top of meat; wash mushrooms and trim; add to slow cooker; cover.
4. Cook on low (190° to 200°) 6 hours, or on high (290° to 300°) 3 hours. Stir evaporated milk into meat mixture; cover; simmer 10 minutes longer. Remove bay leaves.
5. Spoon onto heated serving plates; sprinkle with parsley.

2 pounds lean boneless veal shoulder
3 bay leaves
2 teaspoons celery salt
1 teaspoon leaf rosemary, crumbled
½ teaspoon pepper
1 envelope or teaspoon instant beef broth
2 cups water
1½ pounds small white onions, peeled
½ pound fresh mushrooms
¼ cup evaporated skim milk
2 tablespoons chopped parsley

Cook on 190° to 200° for **8** hours,
or on 290° to 300° for **4** hours.
Makes 4 servings
at 339 calories each.

DIET COQ AU VIN

This is Family Circle's method of frying chicken without fat, and using the natural fat from the chicken (calories already counted) to sauté vegetables.

1 broiler-fryer, cut-up (2½ pounds)
1 large onion, chopped (1 cup)
1 clove garlic, minced
1¾ cups water
½ cup dry red wine
1 teaspoon salt
1 teaspoon leaf tarragon, crumbled
1 bay leaf
½ pound small white onions, peeled
1 pound mushrooms
2 envelopes or teaspoons instant beef broth
2 tablespoons all-purpose flour

1. Place chicken pieces, skin-side down, in a large skillet over *very low* heat. (Do not add fat.) Cook slowly until skin side is a rich brown, about 10 minutes; turn; brown other side.

2. Remove chicken from skillet with tongs and place in an electric slow cooker. Remove 2 tablespoons of the chicken drippings from skillet; reserve.

3. Sauté chopped onion and garlic slowly, until soft, in remaining drippings in skillet; stir in 1 cup of the water, red wine, salt, tarragon and bay leaf. Bring to boiling. Pour over chicken in cooker; cover.

4. Cook on low (190° to 200°) 8 hours, or on high (290° to 300°) 4 hours, or until the chicken is tender.

5. Thirty minutes before serving, return reserved chicken drippings to skillet; brown peeled onions slowly. Leave 6 of the mushrooms whole for garnish; halve remainder; add all to skillet. Toss to coat with pan drippings.

6. Add instant beef broth and ½ cup boiling water to skillet; cover. Simmer 5 minutes. Remove mushrooms with a slotted spoon and reserve. Continue cooking onions, 15 minutes, or until tender and broth has evaporated, leaving a rich brown residue (watch carefully lest they scorch).

7. Place cooked chicken, mushrooms and onions in a heated serving dish. Remove bay leaf. Pour liquid from cooker into skillet. Bring to boiling. Blend flour with ¼ cup cold water to make a smooth paste. Stir flour mixture into boiling liquid in skillet. Continue cooking and stirring until mixture thickens and bubbles 3 minutes. Pour over chicken and vegetables. Garnish chicken with whole mushrooms and chopped parsley. Serve with asparagus, if desired.

DESSERTS

You don't have to sacrifice desserts that take time to make if you're very busy. A great variety of luscious desserts can be made in slow cookers, while you're away—enough to keep the sweetest tooths in town happy.

Slow cookers are especially good for old-time favorites like Indian Pudding or Cherry Cobbler, but surprising successes are steamed puddings. They are molded in coffee cans which are placed in your slow cooker and are as fabulous to look at, as to taste. If you want to impress both family and friends, follow these general directions for the steamed pudding recipes that start this section:

To steam and unmold puddings:

1. *To steam*: Tear off a 12-inch square of foil. With your fist make a "pouch" in the center of the foil, like a chef's hat. Center the foil over the filled can; fasten to side of can with a rubber band or string. The space formed between the rim of the can and the foil will allow the pudding to rise fully.

2. Place the can securely on the trivet or ring of foil in an electric slow cooker. Pour about 1 inch of boiling water carefully into cooker. Cover.

3. Cook on low (190° to 200°), following individual recipes for cooking times.

4. *To unmold*: Remove pudding from cooker; remove foil. Let pudding stand for about 5 minutes. Partly open other end of can with can opener and pudding will slide right out. Turn pudding over top side up.

ORANGE-LEMON PUDDING

A citrus dessert, refreshing in warm weather. Pictured on page 136.

1. Butter a one-pound coffee can with the 1 tablespoon butter; sprinkle in the 1 tablespoon sugar. Cover with plastic top; shake can until side and bottom are well coated with sugar.
2. Combine lemon peel and orange liqueur or juice in a small bowl. Let stand while preparing batter.
3. Sift flour with baking powder onto wax paper; stir in bread crumbs.
4. Beat remaining butter, sugar and eggs in a large bowl until mixture is smooth.
5. Add flour mixture alternately with orange juice to butter mixture, blending well after each addition. Stir in lemon peel and any unabsorbed liquid. Pour batter into prepared can.
6. Cover and cook on low (190° to 200°) for 4 hours, following General Directions on page 177.
7. Serve warm with MANDARIN ORANGE SAUCE (*see page 181*).

1 tablespoon butter or margarine
1 tablespoon sugar
½ cup (4 ounces) chopped candied lemon peel
¼ cup orange liqueur (or orange juice)
1 cup sifted all-purpose flour
2 teaspoons baking powder
¼ cup packaged bread crumbs
¼ cup (½ stick) butter or margarine, softened
½ cup sugar
2 eggs
¼ cup orange juice
Mandarin Orange Sauce (recipe on page 181)

more about slow cookers

- Use long-handled wooden spoons when stirring foods in your slow cooker. This will protect the inside surface of the cooker and keep your hands from getting too close to the hot food and cooker.
- If your slow cooker has the new removable stoneware bowl, you can prepare the food to be cooked the night before and refrigerate in the stoneware bowl. Then in the morning, place in cooker and follow manufacturer's directions for heating.
- To shine up the surface of a metal slow cooker, use a stainless steel-aluminum cleaner; rub with a soft cloth and don't use too much water with the powder; wipe with a sudsy cloth, rinse well and dry with a towel.
- Do not use sharp-edged utensils in slow cooker with a nonstick surface, such as knives, sharp-edged metal spoons or food choppers.

CHOCOLATE NUT PUDDING

Cook on 190° to 200° for **3½** *hours.*
Makes 6 servings.

Chocolate lovers will appreciate this slow cooker dessert. Pictured on page 136.

1. Butter a one-pound coffee can with the 1 tablespoon butter; sprinkle in the 1 tablespoon sugar. Cover with plastic top; shake until side and bottom are well coated with sugar.
2. Sift flour, baking powder and cocoa onto wax paper; stir in bread crumbs.
3. Beat the remaining butter with remaining sugar and the egg yolks in a large bowl until smooth.
4. Combine milk and brandy in a cup. Add to butter mixture alternately with flour mixture, beating well after each addition. Stir in walnuts.
5. Beat egg whites in a small bowl until stiff peaks form. Fold gently into batter; pour batter into prepared can.
6. Cover and cook on low (190° to 200°) for 3½ hours, following General Directions on page 177.
7. Serve warm with ORANGE LIQUEUR SAUCE (*see page 181*).

1 tablespoon butter or margarine
1 tablespoon sugar
¾ cup sifted all-purpose flour
2 teaspoons baking powder
¼ cup unsweetened cocoa
2 tablespoons packaged bread crumbs
3 tablespoons butter or margarine, softened
¾ cup sugar
2 eggs, separated
⅓ cup milk
2 tablespoons brandy (or apple cider)
½ cup finely chopped walnuts
Orange Liqueur Sauce (recipe on page 181)

MINCEMEAT PUDDING

Cook on 190° to 200° for **4** *hours.*
Makes 6 servings.

This is especially good with holiday feasts.

1. Butter a one-pound coffee can with the 1 tablespoon butter; sprinkle in the granulated sugar. Cover with plastic top; shake until side and bottom are well coated with sugar.
2. Sift flour and baking powder onto wax paper; stir in bread crumbs.
3. Beat the remaining butter, brown sugar and egg in a large bowl until smooth.
4. Combine mincemeat and milk in a 2-cup measure.
5. Add flour mixture and milk mixture alternately to butter mixture, blending well after each addition. Stir in walnuts. Pour batter into prepared can.
6. Cover and cook on low (190° to 200°) 4 hours, following General Directions on page 177.
7. Serve warm with ORANGE LIQUEUR SAUCE (*see page 181*) or HARD SAUCE (*see page 182*).

1 tablespoon butter or margarine
1 tablespoon granulated sugar
1¼ cups sifted all-purpose flour
2 teaspoons baking powder
2 tablespoons packaged bread crumbs
2 tablespoons butter or margarine, softened
½ cup firmly packed brown sugar
1 egg
1 cup ready-to-use mincemeat
⅓ cup milk
½ cup chopped walnuts
Orange Liqueur or Hard Sauce (recipes on pages 181, 182)

179

BRANDIED APPLE PUDDING

Cook on 190° to 200° for **4** *hours.*
Makes 6 servings.

This makes a satisfying finale to any meal.

1. Butter a one-pound coffee can with the 1 tablespoon butter; sprinkle in the granulated sugar. Cover with plastic top; shake until side and bottom are well coated with sugar.
2. Sift flour, baking powder and baking soda onto wax paper; stir in bread crumbs.
3. Beat remaining butter, brown sugar and the egg in a large bowl until mixture is smooth.
4. Combine milk, brandy and molasses in a cup. Add to butter mixture alternately with flour mixture, blending well after each addition. Stir in the chopped apple and raisins. Pour batter into prepared can.
5. Cover and cook on low (190° to 200°) for 4 hours, following General Directions on page 177.
6. Serve warm with cream or HARD SAUCE (*see page 182*).

1 tablespoon butter or margarine
1 tablespoon granulated sugar
1 cup sifted all-purpose flour
1 teaspoon baking powder
¼ teaspoon baking soda
½ cup packaged bread crumbs
¼ cup (½ stick) butter or
  margarine, softened
½ cup firmly packed brown sugar
1 egg
¼ cup milk
¼ cup brandy (or apple cider)
¼ cup molasses
1 medium-size baking apple,
  pared, cored and chopped (1 cup)
⅓ cup raisins
  Hard Sauce (recipe appears on
  page 182) or cream

RUM RAISIN PUDDING

Cook on 190° to 200° for **4** *hours.*
Makes 6 servings.

An update on an early American favorite.

1. Butter a one-pound coffee can with the 1 tablespoon butter; sprinkle in the granulated sugar. Cover with plastic top; shake until side and bottom are well coated with sugar.
2. Sift flour, baking powder and baking soda onto wax paper; stir in bread crumbs.
3. Beat remaining butter, brown sugar and egg in a large bowl until smooth.
4. Combine molasses, milk and rum in a cup. Add to butter mixture alternately with flour mixture, blending well after each addition. Stir in the chopped pecans and the raisins. Pour batter into prepared can.
5. Cover and cook on low (190° to 200°) 4 hours, following General Directions on page 177.
6. Garnish top with pear halves and serve warm with BUTTERSCOTCH SAUCE (*see page 181*).

1 tablespoon butter or margarine
1 tablespoon granulated sugar
1 cup sifted all-purpose flour
1 teaspoon baking powder
¼ teaspoon baking soda
½ cup package bread crumbs
¼ cup butter or margarine, softened
½ cup firmly packed brown sugar
1 egg
½ cup molasses
¼ cup milk
¼ cup light rum
½ cup chopped pecans
⅓ cup raisins
  Butterscotch Sauce (recipe
  on page 181)

ORANGE LIQUEUR SAUCE

Makes about 1½ cups.

1. Combine sugar and eggs in the top of a double boiler or in a medium-size heat-proof ceramic bowl. Beat just to blend.
2. Place over hot—not boiling—water and stir until sugar dissolves. Beat with a rotary hand or electric beater until mixture thickens and triples in volume.
3. Remove from water; stir in orange liqueur. Beat until mixture has cooled to room temperature. Beat cream until stiff in a small bowl; fold into egg mixture with orange rind; chill until serving time.

½ cup sugar
2 eggs
2 tablespoons orange liqueur
½ cup heavy cream
1 teaspoon grated orange rind

BUTTERSCOTCH SAUCE

Makes about 1¾ cups.

1. Combine sugar, corn syrup, water and salt in a medium-size heavy saucepan.
2. Cook over low heat, stirring constantly until sugar dissolves; stir in butter.
3. Heat to boiling; cook, without stirring, until candy thermometer reads 230° (A fine thread spins from the end of a fork when dipped into hot syrup.) Pour into a bowl and stir in vanilla; cool. Serve warm over pudding.

1½ cups firmly packed brown sugar
½ cup dark corn syrup
½ cup water
½ teaspoon salt
2 tablespoons butter or margarine
1 teaspoon vanilla

MANDARIN ORANGE SAUCE

Makes 2 cups.

1. Combine sugar and cornstarch in a medium-size saucepan.
2. Drain juice from mandarin oranges into a 1-cup measure; add orange juice to make 1 cup.
3. Stir juice mixture gradually into saucepan until smooth. Heat to boiling, stirring constantly until thickened; add oranges. Serve warm over pudding.

⅓ cup sugar
2 tablespoons cornstarch
1 can (11 ounces) mandarin oranges
½ cup orange juice

HARD SAUCE

Makes about 2/3 cup.

Melt butter in a small sauce pan. Remove from heat and stir in sugar and brandy or rum. Beat until smooth.

3 tablespoons butter or margarine
¾ cup sifted 10X (confectioners') sugar
3 tablespoons heated brandy or rum

CHERRY COBBLER

Cook on 190° to 200° for 6 hours, or on 290° to 300° for 3 hours.
Makes 6 servings.

Here's the traditional, deep-dish favorite with plenty of fruit.

1. Place cherries in an electric slow cooker; sprinkle with sugar, tapioca, lemon rind and salt; toss lightly to mix; stir in orange juice and butter or margarine; cover.
2. Cook on low (190° to 200°) 6 hours, or on high (290° to 300°) 3 hours.
3. Combine oatmeal, brown sugar and butter or margarine in a small bowl to make a crumb topping. Spoon cherry mixture into dessert dishes and sprinkle with topping.

6 cups pitted tart red cherries
1¾ cups sugar
⅓ cup quick-cooking tapioca
1 teaspoon grated lemon rind
⅛ teaspoon salt
2 tablespoons butter or margarine
1½ cups quick-cooking oatmeal
½ cup brown sugar
¼ cup (½ stick) butter or margarine

use canned fruit syrups

- To sweeten sliced raw fruit
- To glaze baked ham
- To drink. Fruit syrups are too sweet to drink alone but they can easily be combined with other fruit juices.

INDIAN PUDDING

Cook on 190° to 200° for **10** hours, or on 290° to 300° for **5** hours. Makes 6 servings.

The secret of this old-fashioned New England specialty is long, slow cooking.

1. Combine 2 cups of the milk with the cornmeal, sugar, molasses, butter, salt and pumpkin-pie spice in a large, heavy saucepan. Heat slowly until bubbling, then simmer, stirring often, 5 minutes, or until creamy-thick.
2. Pour into an electric slow cooker; stir in remaining milk; cover cooker.
3. Cook on low (190° to 200°) 10 hours, or on high (290° to 300°) 5 hours. Serve warm with cream or ice cream, if you wish. Serves 6.

5 cups milk
½ cup yellow cornmeal
½ cup sugar
½ cup molasses
¼ cup (½ stick) butter or margarine
1 teaspoon salt
1 teaspoon pumpkin-pie spice

APPLESAUCE

Cook on 190° to 200° for **6** hours, or on 290° to 300° for **3** hours. Makes 6 servings.

It's quick to fix, but it has old-fashioned flavor.

1. Wash apples, pare and core; cut into thin slices. Combine with the sugar, water, cinnamon and nutmeg in an electric slow cooker; cover.
2. Cook on low (190° to 200°) 6 hours, or on high (290° to 300°) 3 hours. Serve hot or cold, plain or with cream.

2 pounds tart cooking apples
⅔ cup sugar (for richer flavor, use brown sugar)
½ cup water
Pinch ground cinnamon
Pinch ground nutmeg

slow cooker tips

If you are in a real hurry at mealtime and want to thicken the cooking liquid in your recipe faster than the time it would take in your slow cooker, pour liquid into a saucepan and bring to boiling; add the thickening called for in the recipe and cook, stirring constantly, until gravy thickens and bubbles 3 minutes.

CHRISTMAS PUDDING

Cook on 190° to 200° for **6** *hours.*
Makes 12 servings.

Make this fruit-nut-rich classic a day ahead, if you wish. Recipe tells how to reheat.

1. Measure flour, baking powder, pumpkin-pie spice, and salt into sifter.
2. Cream shortening with brown sugar until fluffy in a large bowl; beat in eggs and vanilla.
3. Sift in dry ingredients, adding alternately with milk; beat well after each addition. Fold in candied fruits and walnuts.
4. Pour into a well-greased 8-cup mold; cover with heavy-duty aluminum foil; fasten with string to hold tightly.
5. Place on rack or trivet in an electric slow cooker; pour in boiling water to the depth of 2-inches; cover cooker.
6. Cook on low (190° to 200°) 6 hours, or until a metal skewer inserted into center comes out clean.
7. Cool mold 5 minutes; loosen pudding around edge with knife; unmold onto serving plate. Spoon part of ORANGE CRYSTAL SAUCE over. Cut pudding in wedges; serve with additional sauce. (To reheat pudding, wrap in foil; heat in slow oven (325°) 15 to 20 minutes, or until heated through.)

2½ cups all-purpose flour
1 tablespoon baking powder
1 teaspoon pumpkin-pie spice
½ teaspoon salt
½ cup vegetable shortening
¾ cup firmly packed brown sugar
2 eggs
1 teaspoon vanilla
¾ cup milk
1 jar (4 ounces) chopped mixed candied fruits
½ cup chopped walnuts
Orange Crystal Sauce (recipe follows)

ORANGE CRYSTAL SAUCE— Makes 2 cups. Combine 1 cup firmly packed light brown sugar and ½ cup orange juice in a medium-size saucepan. Bring to boiling, stirring until sugar dissolves, then simmer 5 minutes. Stir in 1 cup light corn syrup, 2 tablespoons butter or margarine, 1 tablespoon lemon juice, and ¼ teaspoon salt until well blended. Serve warm. (If made ahead, reheat over simmering water.)

sherbert or ice?

- Some people think of sherbet and ice as the same, but they do differ. Ice is considered a non-dairy food because it's made of water, sugar and fruit or juice. It contains no milk products. It is sometimes called "Italian water ice."
- Sherbet, after a big meal, on a sizzling day, or any time at all really refreshes. Recipes combine dairy ingredients, sweetening, fruit or juice and fruit acid.

GINGER-APPLE DESSERT

*Cook on 190° to 200° for **4** hours.*
Makes 6 servings.

Crushed gingersnaps flavor this old-timer to perfection. Serve warm with a big dip of ice cream melting over the top.

1. Pare apples; halve, core and grate. (There should be 4 cups.) Place in a large bowl; sprinkle with ½ cup of the sugar; toss lightly to mix.
2. Mix zwieback and gingersnap crumbs, remaining ½ cup sugar, and walnuts in a medium-size bowl; blend in melted butter or margarine.
3. Layer apple and crumb mixtures into an electric slow cooker, starting and ending with apple mixture. Sprinkle the 1 tablespoon sugar over top.
4. Cook on low (190° to 200°) 4 hours. Serve warm with ice cream or whipped cream on top.

6 medium-size tart cooking apples
1 cup sugar (for pudding)
1 cup zwieback crumbs
1 cup gingersnap crumbs
½ cup chopped walnuts
*½ cup (1 stick) butter or
    margarine, melted*
1 tablespoon sugar (for topping)

APPLE-RAISIN CRUNCH

*Cook on 190° to 200° for **4** hours.*
Makes 6 servings.

A delicious dessert to have waiting when you arrive home.

1. Toast bread lightly; cut into ½-inch cubes; place in an electric slow cooker.
2. Heat milk slowly with butter or margarine in medium-size saucepan until butter or margarine melts. Pour over bread cubes; let stand ½ hour.
3. Beat eggs until thick in medium-size bowl; stir in granulated sugar, apple, raisins, cinnamon, nutmeg, and salt. Pour over bread mixture, then fold in; sprinkle brown sugar over top.
4. Cook on low (190° to 200°) 4 hours, or until apples are tender. Spoon into dessert dishes; serve warm with cream, whipped cream or ice cream.

6 slices white bread
1 cup milk
3 tablespoons butter or margarine
3 eggs
½ cup granulated sugar
1 cup diced pared apple
⅔ cup seedless raisins
¼ teaspoon ground cinnamon
¼ teaspoon ground nutmeg
¼ teaspoon salt
*⅓ cup firmly packed light brown
    sugar*

APPLE SCALLOP

*Cook on 190° to 200° for **4** hours, or on 290° to 300° for **2** hours.*
Makes 8 servings.

For those who hate to pare apples, a spicy apple treat.

1. Combine apples, cinnamon, nutmeg, lemon juice and raisins in an electric slow cooker; cover.
2. Cook on low (190° to 200°) 4 hours, or on high (290° to 300°) 2 hours.
3. Mix crumbs and brown sugar in a medium-size bowl; cut in butter or margarine with a pastry blender until mixture is crumbly.
4. Spoon half of the hot apple mixture into 8 dessert dishes; sprinkle with half of the crumb mixture; repeat layers. Serve warm and top with sweetened whipped cream, if you wish.

2 cans (1 pound, 4 ounces each) pie-sliced apples
1 teaspoon ground cinnamon
½ teaspoon ground nutmeg
2 teaspoons lemon juice
1 cup golden raisins
1 cup crushed vanilla wafers
½ cup firmly packed brown sugar
¼ cup (½ stick) butter or margarine

STRAWBERRY-RHUBARB PUDDING

*Cook on 190° to 200° for **4** hours, or on 290° to 300° for **2** hours.*
Makes 6 servings.

Strawberries and rhubarb are naturally compatible, especially when served with softened ice cream for the sauce.

1. Wash rhubarb; trim ends and cut into 1-inch pieces. (You should have about 3 cups.) Wash strawberries, hull and halve.
2. Combine rhubarb and strawberries in an electric slow cooker; sprinkle with sugar, flour and nutmeg; toss lightly to mix. Dot with butter or margarine; pour orange juice over; cover cooker.
3. Cook on low (190° to 200°) 4 hours, or on high (290° to 300°) 2 hours.
4. Serve warm with softened vanilla ice cream.

1 pound rhubarb
1 pint (2 cups) strawberries
1¼ cups sugar
⅓ cup all-purpose flour
¼ teaspoon ground nutmeg
2 tablespoons butter or margarine
½ cup orange juice
Softened vanilla ice cream

make your egg money count

Compare sizes of eggs and prices and remember that size and color have nothing to do with quality. As a general rule of thumb, the United States Department of Agriculture gives this tip: If the price difference between sizes is more than 7¢ a dozen, you'll get more for your money by buying the smaller size.

PRESERVES

The benefits of slow crockery cooking will last for months if you make old-fashioned preserves in a modern electric slow cooker. Just be careful in preparing your preserves to follow these important "canning" directions:

1. Place hot-water-bath canner onto surface burner; add water to half fill canner; cover canner; bring water to boiling.

2. Wash jars in hot sudsy water; rinse well; leave in hot water until ready to fill with preserves.

3. Place new domed lids in a bowl and cover with boiling water; keep in water until ready to use.

4. Follow individual recipe directions.

5. Remove jars from water, one at a time; place on paper towels or a clean cloth; pack and/or ladle food into jars, leaving the headroom called for in each recipe.

6. Wipe top and outside rim of jar with a clean cloth; place domed lid on top; screw metal rings on tightly, but do not use force.

7. Place jars in canner rack and lower into rapidly boiling water, adding additional boiling water to kettle if the level of the water is not 2 inches above jars; cover kettle. Return to full boil.

8. Process, following the times given in the individual recipes and calculated from the time the water comes to the second boil.

9. Remove jars from canner and place on wire racks or cloth-lined surface at least 3-inches apart until cool, about 12 hours.

10. Test all jars to be sure they are sealed by tapping with a spoon. (A clear ringing sound means a good seal. If jars are not sealed properly store in refrigerator and plan to use within month or pour contents of jar into a bowl and process again beginning with Step 5.)

11. Remove metal rings; wipe jars with a clean dampened cloth; label, date and store jars in a cool, dark place.

GARDEN MUSTARD PICKLES

Cook on 290° for **3** hours.
Makes 7 pint jars.

When you have just a few of each vegetable, this is the recipe for you.

1. Combine cauliflower, onions, green tomato, cucumbers, green and red peppers in a large glass or ceramic bowl; sprinkle salt over vegetables; stir to blend well.
2. Cover bowl with plastic wrap; let stand 12 to 18 hours at room temperature. Next day, pour off all liquid from vegetables; spoon into a 5-quart electric slow cooker.
3. Add brown sugar, mustard, turmeric, mustard seeds and celery seeds; stir in cider vinegar; cover cooker.
4. Cook on high (290° to 300°) 2 hours; *uncover cooker; cook 1 hour longer.*
5. Combine flour and cold water in a small bowl to make a smooth paste. Stir slowly into bubbling liquid; cover cooker; cook 15 minutes.
6. Ladle into hot pint jars, leaving ½-inch headroom. Seal and process 5 minutes in water-bath, following directions on page 187-188.

1 small cauliflower, separated into flowerets
1 pound small white onions, peeled
6 green tomatoes, cored and cut into wedges
6 pickling cucumbers, cut into 1-inch pieces
2 large green peppers, halved, seeded and cut into 1-inch pieces
⅓ cup kosher salt
1 cup firmly packed brown sugar
3 tablespoons dry mustard
2 teaspoons turmeric
2 teaspoons mustard seeds
2 teaspoons celery seeds
4 cups cider vinegar
½ cup all-purpose flour
1 cup cold water

PLUM CHUTNEY

Cook on 290° to 300° for **2** hours, then on 190° to 200° for **5** hours.
Makes 5 pints.

We used plums, but this recipe will work as well with your bounty of peaches, pears or nectarines.

1. Combine plums, onions, raisins, garlic, brown sugar, chili powder and salt in an electric slow cooker; stir in cider vinegar; cover.
2. Cook on high (290° to 300°) 2 hours, *remove cover;* lower heat to low (190° to 200°); cook stirring occasionally, 5 hours, or until mixture thickens.
3. Ladle into hot pint jars, leaving ¼-inch headroom. Seal and process 5 minutes in water bath, following directions on page 187–188 .

2½ pounds purple plums, halved, pitted and diced (8 cups)
2 large onions, chopped (2 cups)
1 cup raisins
1 clove garlic, minced
2 cups firmly packed brown sugar
1 tablespoon chili powder
1½ teaspoons salt
4 cups cider vinegar

TOMATO-PEAR MARMALADE

Cook on 290° to 300° for **4** hours.
Makes 6 half-pint jars.

It's nice to have on the pantry shelf.

1. Place tomatoes in scalding water for 30 seconds; peel and cut into eighths; place in a medium-size saucepan. Bring to a boil; reduce the heat; simmer 10 minutes. (You should have 2¼ cups.)
2. Pare, halve, core and dice pears and apples. Toss with lemon juice and rind in a small bowl.
3. Combine tomatoes, pears, apples, cinnamon stick and sugar in an electric slow cooker; cover cooker.
4. Cook on high (290° to 300°) 2 hours, *uncover cooker;* cook 2 hours, stirring occasionally, or until mixture thickens.
5. Ladle into hot half-pint jars, leaving ¼-inch headroom. Seal and process 5 minutes in water bath, following directions on page 187–188.

3 large ripe tomatoes (about 1½ pounds)
3 medium-size pears (about 1 pound)
2 large apples
¼ cup lemon juice
2 teaspoons grated lemon rind
1 one-inch piece stick cinnamon
5 cups sugar

TOMATO-PINEAPPLE CHUTNEY

Cook on 290° to 300° for 3 hours.
Makes 4 half-pint jars.

An interesting combination for a "different" taste treat.

1. Cover whole orange with cold water in a small saucepan; heat to boiling, then simmer 30 minutes; drain. Cut into quarters and put through food chopper, using fine blade.
2. Combine with brown sugar, vinegar, Worcestershire sauce and salt in an electric slow cooker. Tie spices in cheesecloth; drop into slow cooker.
3. Stir in tomatoes and pineapple; cover cooker.
4. Cook on high (290° to 300°) 2 hours; *remove cover;* cook, stirring often, 1 hour or until thick enough to slide off a spoon in two drops that run together. Remove spice bag.
5. Ladle into hot half-pint jars, leaving ¼-inch headroom. Seal and process 5 minutes in water bath, following directions on page 187–188.

1 large orange
1 package (1 pound) light brown sugar
1½ cups cider vinegar
2 teaspoons Worcestershire sauce
½ teaspoon salt
15 whole cloves
15 whole allspice
1 one-inch piece stick cinnamon
2 cups diced peeled ripe tomatoes OR: 1 can (about 1 pound) solid-pack tomatoes
1 can (about 9 ounces) crushed pineapple

ROYAL PURPLE GRAPE JAM

Cook on 290° to 300° for 3 hours.
Makes 6 half-pint jars.

Wonderful on toast or hot biscuits! It uses both skins and pulp.

1. Wash, stem, and halve grapes; remove seeds.
2. Place about 2 cups at a time in blender container; cover. Blend at high speed 1 minute, or until finely chopped. Pour into an electric slow cooker. Stir in sugar; cover cooker.
3. Cook on high (290° to 300°) 2 hours; *remove cover;* cook, stirring often, 1 hour, or until thick enough to slide off a spoon in two drops that run together.
4. Ladle into hot half-pint jars, leaving ¼-inch headroom. Seal and process 5 minutes in water bath, following directions on page 187–188.

2 pounds Concord grapes
6 cups sugar

STRAWBERRY - PEACH CONSERVE

Cook on 290° to 300° for **2** hours, then on 190° to 200° for **4** hours.
Makes 6 half-pint jars.

The sort of fruit and nut conserve women made in Colonial days—done the modern way.

1. Dip peaches into boiling water for 30 seconds; dip in cold water; peel, halve, pit and chop.
2. Combine peaches, strawberries, raisins and lemon juice in an electric slow cooker; stir in sugar; cover cooker.
3. Cook on high (290° to 300°) 2 hours; *uncover cooker;* lower heat to low (190° to 200°); cook, stirring several times, 4 hours, or until mixture thickens; stir in walnuts.
4. Ladle into hot half-pint jars, leaving ¼-inch headroom. Seal and process 5 minutes in water bath, following directions on page 187-188.

5 medium-size ripe peaches (about 1½ pounds)
1 pint (2 cups) strawberries
1 cup raisins
2 tablespoons lemon juice
7 cups sugar
½ cup coarsely chopped walnuts

FRUIT CHUTNEY

Cook on 290° to 300° for **2** hours, then on 190° to 200° for **5** hours.
Makes 6 half-pint jars.

Delightfully tangy and rich with spice. Try it as a plattermate for chicken or turkey.

1. Place about 2 cups fruit and onions at a time in blender container; cover. Blend at high speed 1 minute, or until finely chopped. Pour into an electric slow cooker.
2. Stir in sugar, salt, cloves, cinnamon, allspice and vinegar; cover cooker.
3. Cook on high (290° to 300°) 2 hours, *remove cover;* lower heat to low (190° to 200°); cook, stirring occasionally, 5 hours, or until mixture thickens.
4. Ladle into hot half-pint jars, leaving ¼-inch headroom. Seal and process 5 minutes in water bath, following directions on page 187-188.

1 pound purple plums, halved and pitted
1 pound firm peaches, peeled, quartered and pitted
2 medium-size apples, pared, quartered and cored
2 large onions, peeled and quartered
1 cup sugar
2 teaspoons salt
1 teaspoon ground cloves
1 teaspoon cinnamon
1 teaspoon ground allspice
1 cup vinegar

OLD-FASHIONED CHILI SAUCE

Cook on 290° to 300° for **2** hours, then on 190° to 200° for **5** hours.
Makes 12 half-pint jars.

The kind grandma used to make.

1. Place tomatoes in scalding water for 30 seconds; peel and dice. (You should have 12 cups.)
2. Combine tomatoes, onions, peppers, celery, sugars, vinegar and salt in a 5-quart electric slow cooker.
3. Tie the mustard seeds, allspice, cloves and cinnamon in cheesecloth. Add to slow cooker; cover.
4. Cook on high (290° to 300°) 2 hours; lower heat to low (190° to 200°); cook, stirring occasionally, 5 hours, or until mixture thickens.
5. Ladle into hot half-pint jars, leaving ¼ inch headroom. Seal and process 5 minutes in water bath, following directions on page 187–188.

12 large ripe tomatoes (about 6 pounds)
2 large onions, chopped (2 cups)
2 large red peppers, seeded and chopped
1 cup chopped celery
½ cup granulated sugar
½ cup firmly packed brown sugar
3 cups cider vinegar
1 tablespoon salt
1 tablespoon mustard seeds
1 teaspoon whole allspice
1 teaspoon whole cloves
4 three-inch pieces stick cinnamon, broken

GINGER PEARS

Cook on 290° to 300° for **4** hours.
Makes 3 pint jars.

Fruit is easiest to handle if you cook it in small batches.

1. Cut pears in half; pare and core. Combine with ginger, sugar, water, and lemon juice in an electric slow cooker; cover.
2. Cook on high (290° to 300°) 3 hours; *remove cover;* cook 1 hour longer, or until pears are tender but still firm enough to hold their shape. Lift from syrup with a slotted spoon and pack into hot sterilized jars. Cover loosely with foil.
3. Cook syrup 1 hour longer, or until reduced by half.
4. Ladle over pears in hot pint jars leaving ¼-inch headroom. Seal and process 5 minutes in water bath following directions on page 187–188.

12 medium-size firm ripe pears (about 4 pounds)
¼ cup sliced preserved or crystallized ginger
3 cups sugar
½ cup water
½ cup lemon juice

SPICY TOMATO CATSUP

Cook on 290° to 300° for 3 hours, then on 190° to 200° for 6 hours.
Makes 4 half-pint jars.

This recipe will turn a hamburger into a gourmet delight.

1. Wash and core tomatoes; cut into chunks; place in a 5-quart electric slow cooker; cover.
2. Cook on high (290° to 300°) 2 hours, or until tomatoes are mushy. Press mixture through a strainer or food mill, a few cups at a time. Return purée to slow cooker; cover.
3. Cook on high (290° to 300°) 1 hour; *remove cover;* stir in vinegar, brown sugar, salt and mixed pickling spices tied in cheesecloth.
4. Lower heat to low (190° to 200°); cook 6 hours, or until mixture has reduced by half; remove spice bag.
5. Ladle into hot half-pint jars leaving ⅛-inch room at top. Seal; process 10 minutes in water bath, following directions on page 187–188.

16 large ripe tomatoes
1 cup cider vinegar
½ cup firmly packed brown sugar
2 tablespoons salt
1 tablespoon mixed pickling spices

GREEN TOMATO CHOWCHOW

Cook on 290° to 300° for 2 hours, then on 190° to 200° for 3 hours.
Makes 3 pint jars.

Here's a very special way to use last-of-the-season tomatoes.

1. Combine tomatoes, onion, sugar, salt, dry mustard, pepper, allspice, cloves and vinegar in an electric slow cooker; cover.
2. Cook on high (290° to 300°) 2 hours; *uncover cooker;* lower heat to low (190° to 200°); cook 3 hours longer, stirring several times, until tomatoes are translucent.
3. Ladle into hot pint jars, leaving ¼-inch headroom. Seal and process 5 minutes in water bath, following directions on page 187–188.

6 medium-size green tomatoes, cored and chopped (about 8 cups)
4 large onions, chopped (4 cups)
1 cup sugar
1½ teaspoons salt
1 teaspoon dry mustard
½ teaspoon pepper
½ teaspoon ground allspice
½ teaspoon ground cloves
2 cups cider vinegar

CUCUMBER RELISH COMPOTE

Cook on 290° to 300° for 3 hours.
Makes 9 pint jars.

Chunks of cucumber, onion, and oranges make this unusual, so-good combination.

1. Quarter cucumbers lengthwise; cut into 1-inch pieces. (There should be about 16 cups.) Halve onions; combine with cucumbers and salt in a large bowl; let stand 1 hour; drain.
2. Slice oranges ¼-inch thick; quarter each. Place in a small bowl; cover with boiling water; let stand 1 hour; drain.
3. Combine sugar and vinegar in an electric slow cooker. Stir in vegetables and oranges; cover.
4. Cook on high (290° to 300°) 2 hours; *remove cover;* cook 1 hour longer.
5. Ladle into hot pint jars, leaving ¼-inch headroom. Seal and process 5 minutes in water bath, following directions on page 187–188.

9 large cucumbers
30 small white onions, peeled
¼ cup salt
2 large seedless oranges
3 cups sugar
3 cups white vinegar

SPICY CRANBERRY CHUTNEY

Cook on 290° to 300° for 3 hours.
Makes 4 half-pint jars.

It's perfect with poultry and game.

1. Combine berries, raisins, sugar, cinnamon, ginger, cloves and water in an electric slow cooker. Stir in onion, apple and celery; cover cooker.
2. Cook on high (290° to 300°) 2 hours; *remove cover;* cook 1 hour longer.
3. Ladle into hot half-pint jars leaving ¼-inch headroom. Seal and process 5 minutes in water bath, following directions on page 187–188.

4 cups (1 pound) fresh
   cranberries
1 cup seedless raisins
1⅔ cups sugar
1 tablespoon ground cinnamon
1½ teaspoons ground ginger
¼ teaspoon ground cloves
1 cup water
1 medium-size onion, chopped
   (½ cup)
1 medium-size apple, pared,
   quartered, cored and
   chopped
½ cup thinly sliced celery

SPICED PICKLED CANTALOUPE

Cook on 290° to 300° for **2** hours, then on 190° to 200° for **3** hours.
Makes 6 half-pint jars.

It's and ideal way to "save" some of summer's best melon to enjoy when the snow flies.

1. Quarter, seed and pare cantaloupes; cut meat into 1-inch cubes. (There should be about 8 cups.)
2. Combine cantaloupe with sugar, lemon, cloves, allspice, cinnamon, salt, vinegar and water in an electric slow cooker; cover.
3. Cook on high (290° to 300°) 2 hours; *uncover cooker;* lower heat to low (190° to 200°); cook 3 hours longer, stirring several times, until cantaloupe is translucent.
4. Ladle into hot half-pint jars, leaving ¼-inch headroom. Seal and process 5 minutes in water bath, following directions on page 187–188.

2 large cantaloupes
3 cups sugar
1 lemon, sliced thin
1 tablespoon whole cloves
1 tablespoon whole allspice
6 one-inch pieces stick cinnamon
1 teaspoon salt
1½ cups vinegar
1½ cups water

FIESTA CORN RELISH

Cook on 290° for **3** hours.
Makes 12 pint jars.

Limas blend with the corn for this mild sweet-sour mealtime extra.

1. Peel husks and silks from corn. Place ears in a kettle; pour in boiling water to cover. Heat to boiling again; cook 5 minutes; drain. Cool until easy to handle, then cut corn from cobs. (There should be 8 cups.)
2. Combine corn with lima beans, celery, onion, red and green pepper, sugar, mustard seeds, salt, vinegar and water in a 5-quart electric slow cooker.
3. Cook on high (290° to 300°) 2 hours; *remove cover;* cook 1 hour longer.
4. Ladle into hot pint jars, leaving ¼-inch headroom. Seal and process 5 minutes in water bath, following directions on page 187–188.

12 medium-size ears of corn
4 cups shelled fresh lima beans
  (about 4 pounds)
1 cup thinly sliced celery
1 large onion, chopped (1 cup)
½ cup chopped red pepper
½ cup chopped green pepper
1½ cups sugar
2 tablespoons mustard seeds
4 teaspoons salt
3 cups white vinegar
2 cups water

INDEX

BUYER'S GUIDE

Page 2: top left, "Beans & Stuff" 2-qt. Automatic Slow-Cooker by The Westbend Co., R.R. 6, West Bend, Wisc. 53095; top right, "Superpot" #696 by Oster Corp., 5055 North Lydell Ave., Milwaukee, Wisc. 53217. Center left, "Crock-Pot" electric slow cooker by Rival Mfg. Co., 36th and Bennington, Kansas City, Mo.. Center right, Presto Slow Cooker #LC1 by National Presto Industries Inc., Eau Claire, Wisc. 54701. Bottom, "Country Festival" 10" covered skillet and table range by Corning Glasswares, Corning, N.Y. 14830. Page 3: Clockwise, beginning at top right: heat control for Oster "Superpot", shown on page 2; "Crock Watcher" #449 by Hamilton Beach, Inc., 100 Hope Ave., Byesville, Ohio 43703; "Crocker" Frypan #7-153 by Sunbeam Corp., 2001 So. York Rd., Oak Brook, Ill. 60521; "Colonial Cooker" by The Westbend Co., R.R. 6, West Bend, Wisc. 53095; 12" square Automatic Skillet also by West Bend; "Pot Luck" Cooker by Nesco, Div. of the Hoover Co., North Canton, Ohio 44720.

CREDITS

PHOTOGRAPHY: Richard Jeffery: pages 60-61, 62-63, 64, 129, 132-133, 134-135. George Nordhausen: page 134. Gordon Smith: pages 57, 58-59, 130-131, 136.
ILLUSTRATIONS: Adolph Brotman: pages 74, 137, 135. Carol Ceraldi: pages 5, 21, 73, 109, 177, 187